Peter Arshinov
HISTORY OF THE
MAKHNOVIST MOVEMENT
(1918 – 1921)

sept. urban Ⓐ's intelligence to help a new mass movement once underway
20

free communes
army — mil staff
local soviets
+ coord btwn
regional congresses
regional mil. council + exec comm
rural-urban coord unions

Farrer
self-managed workers' school

no alliance w/ any statist forces

city conf
org. of workers' self-management — factories + services (R.R.'s)

Council of the Rev. Insurgents. 7-persons. mid-1920
5 sectors

Peter Arshinov

HISTORY OF THE MAKHNOVIST MOVEMENT (1918 – 1921)

Preface by Voline

Translated by Lorraine and Fredy Perlman

Black & Red
Detroit

Solidarity
Chicago

1974

The present work is the first English translation of Peter Arshinov's *Istoriya Makhnovskogo Dvizheniya,* originally published in 1923 by the "Gruppa Russkikh Anarkhistov v Germanii" (Group of Russian Anarchists in Germany) in Berlin. It was translated into English by Lorraine and Fredy Perlman.

The English translation follows the Russian original very closely, except in instances when the translators could not find suitable English equivalents for Russian words. The words *kulak* (wealthy peasant), *pomeshchiki* (landlords, or gentry), and *Cheka* (Ch K, the initials of "Extraordinary Commission," the Bolshevik secret security police) were in general not translated into English, since they refer to very specific Russian phenomena which would be erroneously identified with very different phenomena by available English terms. The Russian territorial division, *guberniya,* was translated as "government" (and not "province" or "department") for similar reasons. The Russian word *rabochii* refers to workers in the narrower sense (industrial workers or factory workers) and was consistently translated as "workers." However, the Russian word *trudyashchiisya* is more inclusive and refers to all people who work. In the present translation, the term used for "all those who work" is "working people," and in passages where the composite term would have made the sentence awkward, "workers" was used (instead of "toilers," "laborers," or "working masses," which have occasionally been used by translators who attempted to maintain the distinction between the two Russian words).

The transliteration of Russian words into English follows generally accepted conventions, though not with absolute consistency. Common first names are given in English. The names of well-known cities and regions are spelled the way they appear on most maps. In one instance, the generally-applied conventions of transliteration were modified for the sake of pronunciation: Gulyai-Pole (pronounced *gool-yai pol-ye*) is here spelled Gulyai-Polye.

In addition to Voline's *Preface,* the map of the insurgent region and the portait of Makhno, all of which appear in the present edition, the original edition also contained an Appendix with a "Protest" by anarchists and syndicalists against Makhno's arrest and imprisonment in Poland on a false charge. Makhno was released soon after Arshinov's book appeared, and the "Protest" is not included in the present edition. The Appendix to the present edition contains documents of the Makhnovist movement: eleven proclamations issued by the Makhnovist insurgent army. These proclamations were translated from Russian by Ann Allen.

The people who took part in the publication of the present work are neither publishers who invested capital in order to profit from the sale of a commodity on the book market, nor wage workers who produced a commodity in order to be paid for their time. Every phase of the work—from the translation and editing of the manuscript, to the typesetting and printing of the book—was carried out by individuals who were moved by Arshinov's account, and who were willing to do the necessary work in order to share this important and virtually unknown book with a larger number of readers.

Black & Red
Box 9546
Detroit, Michigan 48202

Solidarity
713 Armitage Ave.
Chicago, Illinois 60614

ABOLISH THE WAGE SYSTEM
ABOLISH THE STATE
PRINTING
CO-OP
I.U. 450
DETROIT
ALL POWER TO THE WORKERS

CONTENTS

ILLUSTRATIONS

Voline's Preface.

As the reader approaches this book he will first of all want to know what kind of work this is: is it a serious and conscientious analysis, or a fantastic and irresponsible fabrication? Can the reader have confidence in the author, at least with respect to the events, the facts and the materials? Is the author sufficiently impartial, or does he distort the truth in order to justify his own ideas and refute those of his opponents?

These are not irrelevant questions.

It is important to examine the documents on the Makhnovist movement with great discretion. The reader will understand this if he considers some of the characteristics of the movement.

On the one hand, the Makhnovshchina[1]—an event of extraordinary breadth, grandeur and importance, which unfolded with exceptional force and played a colossal and extremely complicated role in the destiny of the revolution, undergoing a titanic struggle against all types of reaction, more than once saving the revolution from disaster, extremely rich in vivid and colorful episodes—has attracted widespread interest not only in Russia but also abroad. The Makhnovshchina has given rise to the most diverse feelings in reactionary as well as revolutionary circles: from feelings of fierce hatred and hostility, of astonishment, distrust and suspicion, all the way to profound sympathy and admiration. The monopolization of the revolution by the Communist Party and the "Soviet" power forced the Makhnovshchina, after long hesitation, to embark on a struggle—as bitter as its struggle against the reaction—during which it inflicted on the Party and the central power a series of palpable physical and moral blows. And finally, the personality of Makhno himself—as complex, vivid and powerful as the movement itself—

---

[1] [Makhnovist Movement.]

has attracted general attention, arousing simple curiosity or surprise among some, witless indignation or thoughtless fright among others, implacable hatred among still others, and among some, selfless devotion.

Thus it is natural that the Makhnovshchina has tempted more than one "storyteller," motivated by many considerations other than a genuine knowledge of the events or by the urge to share their knowledge by elucidating the subject and by placing accurate materials at the disposal of future historians. Some of them are driven by political considerations—the need to justify and strengthen their positions, degrading and slandering an inimical movement and its leading figures. Others consider it their duty to attack a phenomenon which frightens and disturbs them. Still others, stimulated by the legend which surrounds the movement and by the lively interest of the "general public" in this sensational theme, are tempted by the prospect of earning some money by writing a novel. Yet others, finally, are simply seized by a journalistic mania.

Thus "material" accumulates which can only create boundless confusion, making it impossible for the reader to sort out the truth.[2]

---

[2] In addition to the large quantity of articles which have appeared in various Russian and foreign newspapers, and which demonstrate an extraordinary talent for slander or an unbelievable literary shamelessness on the author's part, there are already fairly extensive works which pretend to have a certain ideological or historical importance, but which in reality are conscious falsifications or inept fables. For example, we can cite the book of Ya. Yakovlev, *Russian Anarchism in the Great Russian Revolution* (published in several Russian as well as foreign editions)—a steady stream of falsifications and outright lies. Or we could cite the long and pretentious article of a certain Gerasimenko in the historical-literary anthology *Istorik i Sovremenik* (published by Olga D'yakov and Co., Book III, Berlin, 1922, p. 151, article on "Makhno"), where such fantasies are reported that one is ashamed for the "author" and the "anthology." We should also mention that the anarchist press, which generally treats the Makhnovist movement seriously, thoughtfully and honestly, analyzing it from other vantage points and with other aims than the above-mentioned "authors," also contains numerous errors and inaccuracies which are caused by the fact that the authors themselves did not personally take part in the movement, were not in close contact with it,

On the other hand, the Makhnovist movement, in spite of its scope, was forced by a series of circumstances to develop in an atmosphere of seclusion and isolation.

Being a movement composed exclusively of the lowest stratum of the population, being a stranger to all ostentation, fame, domination or glory; originating at the outskirts of Russia, far from the major centers; unfolding in a limited region; isolated not only from the rest of the world but even from other parts of Russia, the movement—its fundamental and profound characteristics—was almost unknown outside of its own region. Developing in conditions of incredibly difficult and tense warfare, surrounded by enemies on all sides, and having almost no friends outside the working class, mercilessly attacked by the governing party and smothered by the bloody and deafening din of its statist activity, losing at least 90% of its best and most active participants, having neither the time, nor the possibility, nor even a particular need to write down, collect and preserve for posterity its acts, words and thoughts, the movement left very few tangible traces or monuments. Its real development passed by unrecorded. Its documents were neither widely circulated nor preserved. Consequently it has to an enormous extent remained hidden from the view of the outsider or the gaze of the researcher. It is not easy to grasp its essence. Just as thousands of humble individual heroes of revolutionary epochs remain forever unknown, the heroic epic of the Ukrainian workers of the Makhnovist movement has remained almost completely unknown. Until today the treasure of facts and documents of this epic has been completely ignored. And if some of those who took part in the movement, who are thoroughly familiar with it and are also able to

_____

and wrote about it on the basis of hearsay, on the basis of published materials or second-hand accounts and articles. (See, for example, the pamphlet by P. Rudenko, "In the Ukraine—the Insurrection and the Anarchist Movement," published by the Workers' Publishing House, Argentina, March, 1922, reprinted from the journal *Vol'nyi Trud,* organ of the Petrograd Federation of Anarchist Groups, October, 1919. In the pamphlet as well as in the article, major errors appeared which can be explained by the fact that the author did not personally take part in the movement and did not actually experience its complex problems.)

report the truth about it, had not by chance remained alive, it might have remained unreported. . .

This state of affairs puts the serious reader and the historian in a difficult and delicate situation: they must critically untangle and evaluate extremely different and contradictory facts, works and materials, not only without orientation or original data, but also without the slightest indication where such data might be obtained.

This is why it is necessary, from the very beginning, to help the reader separate the wheat from the chaff. This is why it is important for the reader to establish from the start whether or not to consider this work a pure and healthy source. This is why questions about the author and the character of his work are particularly important in this case.

I have taken it upon myself to write a preface for this book to throw light on these questions since, by chance, I am one of the few surviving participants of the Makhnovist movement, and thus possess sufficient knowledge of the movement, of the author, and finally of the conditions in which this book was conceived.

* * *

First I will allow myself a small digression.

I could be asked (and, in fact, am frequently asked) why I don't write about the Makhnovist movement myself. For many reasons. I can mention several of them.

It is possible to set out on the task of describing and clarifying the events of the Makhnovist movement only on the basis of a thorough and precise knowledge of the facts. The theme requires protracted, intensive and painstaking work. But such work has been impossible for me, for numerous reasons. This is the first reason why I considered it necessary to refrain from dealing with this topic now.

The Makhnovist epic is too serious, lofty and tragic, too heavily drenched with the blood of its participants, too profound, complicated and original, to be described and judged "lightly,"—for example on the basis of the accounts and contradictory interpretations of various individuals. To

10

describe the movement by means of documents is not our project either, since documents by themselves are dead things and can never fully express lived experience. To write on the basis of documents will be the task of future historians, who will have no other materials at their disposal. A contemporary must be much more demanding and severe toward his work and toward himself, since it is precisely on him that history will to a great extent depend. A contemporary must avoid judgments and stories about important events unless he has personally participated in them. Nor is it the task of a contemporary to pounce on the narratives and documents with the aim of "making history," but rather to set down his personal experience. If this is not done, the writer will risk obscuring or, worse yet, corrupting the very essence, the living soul of the events, misleading the reader and the historian. Personal experience, to be sure, is not exempted from errors and inaccuracies. But in the present case this is not important. An authentic and vivid picture of the essence of the events will have been drawn—which is what is most important. Comparing this picture with documents and other data will make it easy to locate minor errors. This is why the account of a participant or a witness is particularly important. The more complete and profound the personal experience, the more important and urgent such a work is. If, in addition, the participant himself has documents as well as accounts of other participants, his narrative acquires a relevance of the first order.

I will write about the Makhnovshchina at a later time, in my own way. But I cannot write a *complete history* of the Makhnovist movement precisely because I do not pretend to have a full, detailed and thorough knowledge of the subject. I took part in the movement for about half a year, from August 1919 to January 1920—in other words, I hardly observed it in its entirety. I met Makhno for the first time in August 1919. I completely lost sight of the movement and of Makhno in January 1920, when I was arrested; I was in contact with both for only two weeks in November of the same year, at the time of Makhno's treaty with the Soviet government. After that I again lost sight of the movement. Therefore, even though I saw, experienced and thought a great deal about this movement, my personal knowledge of it is incomplete.

When I am asked why I don't write about the Makhnovshchina, I answer that there is someone far more capable than I am in this respect.

The person I refer to is the author of the present work.

I knew of his unceasing activity in the movement. In 1919 we worked there together. I also knew that he was carefully collecting material on the movement. I knew that he was arduously writing its complete history. And finally, I knew that the book was finished and that the author was preparing to publish it abroad. And I considered that *it was precisely this work that should appear before any other—a complete history of the Makhnovshchina* written by a man who, having himself participated in the movement, at the same time possessed a large number of documents.

Many people are still sincerely convinced that Makhno was a "common bandit," a *"pogromshchik,"*[3] a leader of a gloomy, war-corrupted, plundering mass of soldier-peasants. Many others consider Makhno an "adventurer," and believe that he "opened the front" to Denikin, "fraternized" with Petliura, and "allied" with Wrangel. . . Imitating the Bolsheviks, many people still persist in slandering Makhno, accusing him of being the "leader of a counter-revolutionary *kulak* movement"; they treat Makhno's "anarchism" as a naive invention of certain anarchists skillfully applied by him for his own purposes. . . But Denikin, Petliura and Wrangel are only vivid military episodes: people latch on to them to accumulate a pile of lies. The Makhnovshchina cannot be reduced to the struggle against the counter-revolutionary generals. The essence of the Makhnovist movement, its inner content, its organic characteristics, are almost completely unknown.

This state of things cannot be remedied by short, isolated articles, fragmented observations, partial works. In relation to such an enormous and complex event as the Makhnovshchina, such articles and works offer very little, fail to shed light on the entire picture, and are lost in the sea of printed words, leaving hardly any traces. To deal a decisive

[3]Instigator of Jewish pogroms.

blow against all these narratives and to give impetus to serious interest and familiarity with the subject, it is necessary, first of all, to make available a more or less exhaustive work; only then will it be fruitful to turn to the individual questions, the specific events and the details.

The present book is precisely such an exhaustive work. Its author is better suited for this task than anyone else. We only regret the fact that, because of a series of unfortunate circumstances, this work appears after considerable delay.[4]

* * *

It is noteworthy that the first historian of the Makhnovist movement should be a worker. This fact is not accidental. Throughout its existence, the movement, both ideologically and organizationally, had access only to those forces which could be provided by the mass of workers and peasants. There were, on the whole, no highly educated theorists. During the entire period, the movement was left to itself. And the first historian who sheds light on the movement and gives it a theoretical foundation comes out of its own ranks.

The author, Peter Andreevich Arshinov, son of an Ekaterinoslav factory worker, himself a metalworker by trade, educated himself through strenuous personal effort. In 1904, when he was 17, he joined the revolutionary movement. In 1905, when he was employed as a metalworker in the railway yards of the town of Kizyl-Arvat (in Central Asia), he became a member of the local organization of the Bolshevik Party. He quickly began to play an active role, and became one of the leaders and editors of the local illegal revolutionary workers' newspaper, *Molot (The Hammer)*. (This newspaper was distributed throughout the railway network of Central Asia and had great importance for the revolutionary movement of the railway workers.) In 1906,

[4]Before the publication of the present work, the author published two articles in foreign journals, "Nestor Makhno" and "The Makhnovshchina and Anti-Semitism," in order to acquaint foreign workers and comrades with certain facts about the Makhnovshchina.

pursued by the local police, Arshinov left Central Asia and moved to Ekaterinoslav in the Ukraine. Here he became an anarchist and as such continued his revolutionary work among workers of Ekaterinoslav (especially at the Shoduar factory). He turned to anarchism because of the minimalism of the Bolsheviks which, in Arshinov's view, did not respond to the real aspirations of the workers and caused, together with the minimalism of the other political parties, the defeat of the 1905-06 revolution. In anarchism Arshinov found, in his own words, a collection of all the libertarian-egalitarian aspirations and hopes of the workers.

In 1906-07, when the Tsarist government covered all of Russia with a network of military tribunals, extensive mass activity became completely impossible. Arshinov, because of personal circumstances as well as his aggressive temperament, carried out several terrorist acts.

On December 23, 1906, he and several comrades blew up a police station in the workers' district of Amur, near Ekaterinoslav. (The explosion killed three Cossack officers, as well as police officers and guards of the punitive detachment.) Due to the painstaking preparation of this act, neither Arshinov nor his comrades were discovered by the police.

On March 7, 1907, Arshinov shot Vasilenko, head of the main railroad yard of Aleksandrovsk. Vasilenko's crime toward the working class consisted of his having turned over to the military tribunal more than 100 working people who were accused of taking part in the armed uprising in Aleksandrovsk in December, 1905; many of them were condemned to death or forced labor because of Vasilenko's testimony. Before and after this event, Vasilenko was always an active and pitiless oppressor of workers. On his own initiative, but with the agreement and general encouragement of masses of workers, Arshinov bluntly settled accounts with this enemy of the workers, shooting him near the yards while many workers watched. After this act Arshinov was caught by the police, cruelly beaten, and two days later the military tribunal sentenced him to hanging. Suddenly, when the sentence was about to be administered, it was established that Arshinov's act should by law not be tried by the military tribunal, but by a higher military court. This postponement gave Arshinov the chance to escape. He escaped from the

14

Aleksandrovsk prison on the night of April 22, 1907, during Easter mass, while the prisoners were being led to the prison church. The prison guards assigned to watch the prisoners at the church were surprised by the audacious attack of several comrades; all the guards were killed. All the prisoners had the chance to escape. Fifteen men escaped together with Arshinov.

After this, Arshinov spent about two years abroad, mainly in France. In 1909 he returned to Russia where, for a period of one and a half years, he devoted himself to clandestine anarchist propaganda and organization among workers.

In 1910, while transporting weapons and anarchist literature from Austria to Russia, he was arrested on the frontier by Austrian authorities and jailed in the prison at Tarnopol. After spending about a year in this prison, he was turned over to Russian authorities in Moscow for having committed terroristic acts and was sentenced to 20 years of hard labor by the Court of Assizes in Moscow.

Arshinov served his sentence in the Butyrki prison in Moscow.

It was here, in 1911, that he first met the young Nestor Makhno, who had in 1910 received a life sentence to hard labor for terrorist acts, and who was already familiar with Arshinov's name and his earlier work in the south. They were close friends during their entire prison term, and both left prison during the first days of the revolution, in March, 1917.

As soon as Makhno was free he left Moscow to take up revolutionary activity in the Ukraine, at his birthplace, Gulyai-Polye. Arshinov remained in Moscow and energetically took part in the work of the Moscow Federation of Anarchist Groups.

When, after the occupation of the Ukraine by the Austro-Germans in the summer of 1918, Makhno spent some time in Moscow in order to acquaint himself and his comrades with the state of affairs, he stayed with Arshinov. Here they got to know each other more intimately, and they ardently discussed the problems of the revolution and of anarchism. When, three or four weeks later, Makhno returned to the Ukraine, he and Arshinov agreed to remain in close contact. Makhno promised not to forget Moscow and to give material assistance to the movement. They spoke of the need to start a journal. . . Makhno kept his word: he sent money to Moscow (but due to circumstances over which he had no control, Arshinov did not receive it) and wrote to Arshinov several times. In his letters he invited Arshinov to work in the Ukraine; he waited and was irked by the fact that Arshinov did not come.

Some time later, newspapers began to speak of Makhno as the leader of a powerful partisan detachment.

In April, 1919, at the very beginning of the development of the Makhnovist movement, Arshinov went to Gulyai-Polye and from that time on hardly left the region of the Makhnovshchina until its defeat in 1921. He concerned himself mainly with cultural and educational matters and with organizational work; for some time he directed the cultural and educational section and was editor of the insurgents' newspaper *Put' k Svobode (The Road to Freedom)*. He left the region only in the summer of 1920 after a defeat of the movement. During this time he lost a manuscript on the history of the movement which was almost ready for publication. After this absence, it was only with great difficulty that he was able to return to this region which was hemmed in on all sides (by Whites and Reds); he remained there until the beginning of 1921.

At the beginning of 1921, after the third disastrous defeat inflicted on the movement by the Soviet power,[5] Arshinov left the region with a formal assignment; to finish work on the history of the Makhnovist movement. This time he carried the work through to completion in extremely difficult personal circumstances, partly in the Ukraine and partly in Moscow.

[5]At the time of this defeat, during an attack by a cavalry division of "Red Cossacks," Arshinov was almost killed (and not for the first time). He saw several close comrades massacred when they were unable to avoid the blows of the Cossack sabres.

* * *

Consequently the author of this book is more competent than anyone else to comment on this subject. He was acquainted with Nestor Makhno long before the events which he describes, and he observed him closely in extremely varied situations during the course of the events. He was also acquainted with all of the remarkable participants of the movement. He was himself an active participant in the events, himself experienced their sublime and tragic development. The profound essence of the Makhnovshchina, its ideological and organizational efforts, aspirations and hopes, were clearer to him than to anyone else. He witnessed its titanic struggle against enemy forces which hemmed it in on all sides. Being a worker himself, he was profoundly imbued with the spirit of the movement: the powerful urge of the working masses, inspired by anarchist ideas, to take their destiny and the construction of a new world into their own hands. As an intelligent and educated worker, he was able to analyze the profound essence of the movement and to contrast it sharply with the ideological essence of other forces, movements and tendencies. Finally, he is thoroughly familiar with all the documents of the movement. He, like no one else, was able to critically examine all accounts and materials, to separate the essential from the inessential, the characteristic from the trivial, the fundamental from the secondary.

All of this allowed him to comprehend and elucidate one of the most original and remarkable episodes of the Russian revolution, in spite of the endless series of unfavorable circumstances and the repeated loss of manuscripts, materials and documents.

* * *

Is it necessary to speak of the individual aspects of this work? It seems to us that the book speaks adequately for itself.

We should emphasize, first of all, that this work was

17

written with exceptional care and exactitude. Not a single doubtful fact was included. On the contrary, a number of interesting and characteristic episodes and details which actually took place were left out by the author with a view to brevity.

Some moments, acts or even entire events were omitted because of the impossibility of verifying them with exact data.

The loss of an entire collection of important documents has certainly been harmful to the work. The last—the fourth—disappearance of the manuscript together with extremely valuable documents crushed the author to such an extent that for a long time he hesitated before setting out again. Only his awareness of the necessity of giving a coherent, even if incomplete, history of the Makhnovshchina drove the author to return to his pen.

It is obvious that later works on the history of the Makhnovist movement will need to be expanded and completed with new data. The movement is so vast, so profound and original, that it cannot yet be fully evaluated. This book is only the first serious contribution toward the analysis of one of the broadest and most instructive revolutionary movements in history.

* * *

Some of the author's statements of principle can be disputed. But these are not the basic elements of the book and are not developed to their logical conclusions. We might mention the author's extremely interesting and original evaluation of Bolshevism as a new ruling caste which replaces the bourgeoisie and intentionally aspires to dominate the working masses economically and politically.

* * *

The essence of the Makhnovshchina is brought out in this work more prominently than anywhere else. The very term "Makhnovshchina" acquires, in the work of this author, a broad and almost symbolic meaning. The author uses this term to describe a unique, completely original and independent revolutionary movement of the working class which gradually becomes conscious of itself and steps out on the broad arena of historical activity. The author considers the Makhnovshchina one of the first and most remarkable manifestations of this new movement and, as such, contrasts it to other forces and movements of the revolution. This underlines the fortuitous character of the term "Makhnovshchina." The movement would have existed without Makhno, since the living forces, the living masses who created and developed the movement, and who brought Makhno forward merely as their talented military leader, would have existed without Makhno. Even if the movement had had another name and its ideological orientation had been different, its essence would have been the same.

The personality and the role of Makhno himself are very sharply drawn in this work.

The relations between the Makhnovist movement and various hostile forces (the counter-revolution, Bolshevism) are masterfully described. The pages devoted to the numerous events of the Makhnovshchina's heroic struggle against these forces are gripping and overwhelming.

* * *

The extremely interesting question of the mutual relations between the Makhnovshchina and anarchism is not adequately treated by the author. He expresses the salient fact that anarchists on the whole—more precisely, the "summit" anarchists—remained outside the movement; in the author's words, they "slept through it." This phenomenon, Arshinov maintains, was caused by the fact that a certain number of anarchists were infected by *"Partiinost"* (the Party spirit), by the unhealthy urge to *lead* the masses, their organizations and their movements. This explains the incapacity of these anarchists to understand *truly independent* mass movements which arise without their knowledge and

19

ask of them only sincere and responsible cultural assistance. This also explains their prejudice and, in essence, their contempt toward such movements. But this statement and explanation are inadequate. The theme should be elaborated and developed. Among anarchists there are three types of views of the Makhnovshchina: decidedly skeptical, neutral, and decidedly favorable. The author, without doubt, belongs to the third group. But his position may be debatable, and he might have to treat the theme more profoundly. It is true that this theme is not related to the essence of the book. Furthermore, the author's point of view is strongly supported by the facts which he presents throughout the book. . . Let us hope that this problem will be taken up by the anarchist press, and that a comprehensive treatment of this problem will lead to conclusions useful to the anarchist movement.

* * *

It is certain that all the fables about the banditism, the anti-Semitism, and other somber traits thought to be inherent in the Makhnovist movement, will be discredited by the publication of this book.

If the Makhnovshchina, like every other human project, had its low points, its errors, its deviations, its negative aspects, they were, in the author's view, so trifling and unimportant in relation to the great positive essence of the movement that it is not worth speaking of them seriously. With the slightest possibility for free and creative development, the movement would have outgrown them without the slightest effort.

* * *

The work shows how lucidly and easily, how straightforwardly the movement transcended various prejudices— national, religious and other. This fact is extremely characteristic: it is yet another example of the level of achievement that the working masses, once aroused by a decisive revolutionary jolt, can reach—and how easily!—*if it is actually they themselves who create their revolution,* if they have true and complete freedom to search and freedom to act. Their roads are limitless, if only these roads are not intentionally barricaded.

* * *

What seems to us especially noteworthy and important in the present work is:

1) As opposed to many who considered, and continue to consider, the Makhnovshchina only a unique *military* episode, a foolhardy act of snipers, of partisans with all the faults and all the creative impotence of a military clique (and the relationship of many to the Makhnovist movement was based precisely on such an analysis), the author shows with incontestable data the falsity of such a view. With the greatest precision, the author unfolds before us the picture of a free, *creative and organized,* though short-lived, movement of the broad working masses, imbued with a profound ideal; a movement which created its own military force in response to its need to defend its revolution and its freedom. A widespread prejudice about the Makhnovshchina is thus destroyed.

It should be noted that, when the author makes a *serious* critique of the Makhnovshchina, he criticizes precisely a certain negligence in *military and strategic* affairs. In the chapter on the mistakes of the Makhnovists, he expresses the conviction that if the Makhnovists had in time been able to organize an adequate defense of the outermost frontiers of the region, the whole revolution in the Ukraine as well as in general could have developed very differently. If the author is right, then in this respect the fate of the Makhnovshchina can be compared to that of other revolutionary movements of the past where military errors also played a fatal role. In any case, we call the reader's attention to this point, which gives rise to very provocative thoughts.

2) The *complete independence* of the movement is

21

strongly emphasized: an independence which was consciously and energetically defended from all intruding forces.

3) The attitude of Bolshevism and the Soviet Government toward the Makhnovshchina are firmly and precisely established. A shattering blow is dealt to all the inventions and justifications of the Bolsheviks. All their criminal machinations, all their lies, their entire counter-revolutionary essence, are thoroughly exposed. An appropriate inscription to this part of the book would be the words which once escaped from the director of the secret-operations section of the V. Ch. K. [Supreme *Cheka*], Samsonov (in prison, when I was called for questioning by this "investigator"). When I remarked to him that I considered the behavior of the Bolsheviks toward Makhno, at the time of their treaty with him, treacherous, Samsonov promptly responded: "You consider this treacherous? This simply proves that we are skillful statesmen: *when we needed Makhno, we knew how to use him; now that we no longer need him, we know how to liquidate him.*"

4) Many sincere revolutionaries consider anarchism an idealistic fantasy and justify Bolshevism as the only possible *reality,* unavoidable and necessary for the development of the world social revolution, of which it represents a given stage. The dismal aspects of Bolshevism then appear less-important and are historically justified.

The present work deals a death blow to this conception. It vividly establishes two cardinal points: a) anarchist aspirations appeared in the Russian revolution *whenever it was a really independent revolution of the working masses themselves,* not as a "harmful utopia of visionaries," but as the *real, concrete revolutionary movement of these masses;* b) *as such* it was deliberately, cruelly and basely suppressed by the Bolsheviks.

The facts enumerated in this book clearly show that the "reality" of Bolshevism is, in essence, the same as the reality of Tsarism. These facts concretely and clearly counterpose this "reality" to the profound truth and *reality of anarchism as the only truly revolutionary workers' ideology,* and remove from Bolshevism any trace of historical justification.

5) The book gives anarchists a wealth of materials in

22

the light of which they can review their positions. It brings up several new questions; it provides a series of facts which can help solve a number of earlier questions; finally, it confirms several completely forgotten truths which can usefully be reexamined and reconsidered.

* * *

One last word.

Although this book is written by an anarchist, its interest and significance extend far beyond the limits of one or another circle of readers.

For many people this book will be an unexpected discovery. It will make others aware of the events going on around them. It will throw new light on these events for yet others.

Not only every literate worker or peasant, not only every revolutionary, but also every thinking person who is interested in what goes on around him, should attentively read this book, reflect about the conclusions which flow from it, and be lucidly aware of what it teaches.

Today, when life is fraught with events and the world is replete with struggle; today, when revolution knocks on every door, ready to sweep every mortal into its storm; today, when an immense struggle spreads out in all its amplitude—a struggle not only between labor and capital, between a dying world and a world being born, but also between the advocates of different ways to fight and build; today, when Bolshevism fills the world with its din, demanding blood for its betrayal of the revolution, recruiting adherents by force, treachery and bribery; when Makhno, languishing in a Warsaw prison,[6] could be consoled only by the knowledge

[6] Since the publication of this book in Russian, Makhno was tried by a Polish tribunal, accused of high treason (for having instigated an uprising in Galicia in collaboration with the Bolsheviks). The accusation was recognized to be false, and Makhno was acquitted. He has since then been at liberty. [Footnote in the French edition, Paris: Librairie Internationale, 1924.]

that the ideas for which he fought have not died but are spreading and growing—today every book which sheds light on the paths of the revolutionary struggle should be a reference book in every home.

Anarchism is not a privilege of the chosen, but a profound and broad doctrine and conception of the world with which everyone today should be familiar.

The reader need not become an anarchist. But the reader should not experience what happened to an old professor who accidentally attended an anarchist lecture. Moved to tears, after the lecture, he told the listeners gathered around him: "Here am I, a professor, with white hair, and until today I never knew anything about this remarkable and beautiful doctrine. . . I am ashamed."

The reader need never become an anarchist; to be an anarchist is not obligatory. But it is necessary to *know* anarchism.

Voline
May, 1923.

Author's Preface.

The Makhnovshchina is a colossal event in contemporary Russia. By the breadth and profundity of its ideas, it transcends all the spontaneous working class movements known to us. The factual material about it is enormous. Unfortunately, in the conditions of present day—Communist—reality, one cannot even dream of collecting all the material which could shed light on the movement. This will be the work of the future.

I began to work on the history of the Makhnovist movement four times. All the material relating to the movement was collected for this purpose. But four times the work was destroyed when it was half finished. Twice it was lost at the front during a battle, and two other times in peaceful lodgings during searches. Exceptionally precious documentation was lost in Khar'kov in January, 1921. This material contained everything one could have wanted to know about the front, the Makhnovist camp and the personal archives of Makhno: it included Makhno's memoirs containing a great quantity of facts, most of the publications and documents of the movement, a complete collection of the newspaper *Put' k Svobode*, detailed biographical notes on the most devoted participants of the movement. It is absolutely impossible to reconstruct the lost documentation even partially. Thus I had to complete the present work lacking many of the necessary materials. Furthermore, the work was at first carried out between battles, and later in the extremely unfavorable repressive conditions of contemporary Russia, where I wrote the same way as convicts in Tsarist prisons wrote each other, namely by hiding in any corner or behind a table, with constant fear of being discovered by the guard.

For these reasons it is natural that the work should appear hasty and should contain several gaps. However, the current state of affairs demands that a work on the history of the movement should be issued, even if it is incomplete. Consequently this work is not definitive. It is only a beginning and should be continued and further elaborated. But for this purpose it will be necessary to collect all the materials that relate to the movement. All comrades who possess any of this material are urged to pass them on to the author.

* * *

In this preface I would like to say a few words to comrades-workers in other countries. Many among them, arriving in Russia to attend some congress, see contemporary Russia in an official framework. They visit the factories of Petrograd, Moscow and other cities and learn about their conditions on the basis of data furnished by the governmental party or political groups related to it. Such an acquaintance with Russian reality has no value. The guests are everywhere shown a life which is very far from reality. For example. In 1912 or 1913 a scientist from Amsterdam (Israel Van Kan, if I'm not mistaken) came to Russia to investigate Russian jails and prisons. The Tsarist government gave him the opportunity to observe prisons in Petrograd, Moscow and other cities. The professor strolled from cell to cell, informing himself about the situation of the convicts, and talking with them. In spite of the fact that he established illegal relations with some political prisoners (Minor and others), in the Russian prisons he saw no more than what the prison administration wanted to show him; that which was specific to Russian prisons escaped him. Foreign comrades and workers who come to Russia hoping to become familiar with Russian life in a short time with the help of data furnished by the governing party or by rival politicians, find themselves in the same situation as Israel Van Kan. They unavoidably commit gross errors.

In order to experience Russian reality, it is indispensable to go to the country as a simple agricultural worker, or to a factory as a laborer, to receive the economic and political *payok* (ration) granted to the people by the Communist government, to demand the sacred rights of workers and struggle to obtain them when they are not granted, and to struggle in a revolutionary manner, since revolution is the supreme right of workers. Only then will the actual and not the staged Russian reality be visible to such a daring observer. And then he will not be surprised by the history recorded in this book. With horror and shock he will see that in Russia today, as everywhere else, the great truth of the working class is persecuted and tortured and the heroism of the Makhnovist movement which defended this truth will be clear to him.

It seems to me that every thinking proletarian concerned with the fate of his class will agree that only in this way can one become familiar with Russian—or any other— life. Everything that has until today been the common practice of foreign delegations who came to study Russian life has consisted of trifles, illusions, picnics abroad, a pure waste of time.

Arshinov
Moscow
April, 1921.

P.S. I consider it a pleasant comradely obligation on my own part and on the part of the other participants of the movement, to express my gratitude to all organizations and comrades who helped or tried to help in the work of publishing this book: the Federation of Anarcho-Communist Groups of North America, as well as Italian and Bulgarian comrades.

May, 1923.

[Title Page of the 1923 Edition]

П. АРШИНОВ

ИСТОРИЯ
МАХНОВСКОГО ДВИЖЕНИЯ
(1918—1921 гг.)

С ПОРТРЕТОМ Н. МАХНО И НАГЛЯДНОЙ КАРТОЙ РАЙОНА И ДВИЖЕНИЯ

Предисловие ВОЛИНА (В. М. ЭЙХЕНБАУМ)

Издание „Группы Русских Анархистов в Германии"
БЕРЛИН — 1923

Chapter 1

Democracy and the Working Masses in the Russian Revolution.

There has not been one revolution in the world's history which was carried out by the working people in their own interests—by urban workers and poor peasants who do not exploit the work of others. Although the main force of all great revolutions consisted of workers and peasants, who made innumerable sacrifices for their success, the leaders, ideologists and organizers of the forms and goals of the revolution were invariably neither workers nor peasants, but elements foreign to the workers and peasants, generally inter- mediaries who hesitated between the ruling class of the dying epoch and the proletariat of the cities and fields.

This element was always born and grew out of the soil of the disintegrating old regime, the old State system, and was nourished by the existence of a movement for freedom among the enslaved masses. Because of their class character- istics and their aspiration to State power, they take a revolu- tionary position in relation to the dying political regime and readily become leaders of enslaved workers, leaders of mass revolutionary movements. But, while organizing the revolu- tion and leading it under the banner of the vital interests of workers and peasants, this element always pursues its own group or caste interest, and aspires to make use of the revolution with the aim of establishing its own dominant position in the country. This is what happened in the English revolution. This is what happened in the great French revolu- tion. This is what happened in the French and German revolutions of 1848. This is what happened in a whole series of other revolutions where the proletariat of the cities and the countryside fought for freedom, and spilled their blood profusely—and the fruits of their efforts and sacrifices were divided up by the leaders, politicians with varied labels,

31

operating behind the backs of the people to exploit the tasks and goals of the revolution in the interest of their groups.

In the great French revolution, the workers made colossal efforts and sacrifices for its triumph. But the politicians of this revolution: were they the sons of the proletariat and did they fight for its aspirations—equality and freedom? In no way. Danton, Robespierre, Camille Desmoulins and a whole series of other "high priests" of the revolution were representatives of the liberal bourgeoisie of the time. They struggled for a specific bourgeois type of social relations, and in fact had nothing in common with the revolutionary ideals of equality and freedom of the French popular masses of the 18th century. Yet they were, and still are, generally considered the leaders of the great revolution. In the 1848 revolution the French working class, which had given up to the revolution three months of heroic efforts, misery, privation and sacrifice—did they obtain the "social republic" which had been promised by the managers of the revolution? The working class harvested from them only slavery and mass killings; 50 thousand workers were shot in Paris, when they attempted to rise up against those treacherous leaders.

The workers and peasants of all past revolutions succeeded only in *sketching* their fundamental aspirations, only in defining their *course,* which was generally perverted and then liquidated by the cleverer, more cunning and better educated "leaders" of the revolution. The most the workers got from these revolutions was an insignificant bone, in the form of the right to vote, to gather, to print—in the form of the right to choose their rulers. And even this bone was given to them for a short time, the time needed by the new regime to consolidate itself. After this the life of the masses returned to its former course of submission, exploitation and fraud.

It is only in mass movements from *below,* like the revolt of Razin, or like the revolutionary peasant and worker insurrections of our time, that the people become the masters of the movement, giving it its form and content. But these movements, which are usually greeted by the abuse and the curses of all "thinking" people, have never yet triumphed, and they differ sharply, in terms of their content as well as their form, from revolutions led by political groups and parties.

Our Russian revolution is, without a doubt, a political revolution which uses the forces of the people to serve interests foreign to the people. The fundamental fact of this revolution, with a background of enormous sacrifices, sufferings and revolutionary efforts of workers and peasants, is the seizure of political power by an intermediary group, the so-called socialist revolutionary intelligentsia, the Social Democrats.

A great deal has been written about the Russian as well as the international intelligentsia. They are generally praised, and called the carriers of the highest human ideals, champions of eternal truth. They are rarely abused. But all that has been written about them, the good and the bad, has one essential shortcoming: namely, they are defined by themselves, praised by themselves and abused by themselves. To the independent mind of workers or peasants this is completely unconvincing and can have no weight in the relations between the intellectuals and the people. In these relations the people are concerned only with facts. The real, indisputable fact of life of the socialist intelligentsia is the fact that they have always enjoyed a privileged social position. Living in privilege, the intelligentsia became privileged not only socially but also psychologically. All their spiritual aspirations, everything they call their "social ideals," inevitably carries within itself the spirit of caste privilege. We come across it thoughout the entire social development of the intelligentsia. If we take the era of the Decembrists as the beginning of the revolutionary movement of the intelligentsia, and pass consecutively through all the stages of this movement—the "Narodnichestvo," the "Narodovol'chestvo," Marxism and socialism in general with all their ramifications—we find this spirit of caste privilege clearly expressed throughout.

No matter how lofty a social ideal may be externally, as soon as it carries within itself privileges for which the people will have to pay with their work and their rights, it is no longer the complete truth. A social ideal which does not offer the people the whole truth is a lie for them. It is precisely *such* a lie that the ideology of the socialist intellectuals, and the intellectuals themselves, represent to the people. This fact determines *everything* about the relations

33

between the people and the intelligentsia. The people will never forget and forgive the fact that, speculating on their forced labor and lack of rights, a certain social group created social privileges for itself and tried to carry them into the new society.

The people—that's one thing; democracy and its socialist ideology—that's something else, which comes to the people prudently and cunningly. Certainly isolated heroic individuals, like Sofya Perovskaya, stood above the vile privileges inherent in socialism, but only because they did not understand reality in terms of a democratic-class doctrine, but psychologically or ethically. These are the flowers of life, the beauty of the human race. Inspired by the passion for truth, they lived entirely to serve the people and by their beautiful example exposed the false character of the socialist ideology. The people will never forget them and will eternally carry a great love for them in their hearts.

The vague political aspirations of the Russian intelligentsia in 1825 took shape during the course of half a century in a perfected socialistic Statist system, and this intelligentsia itself, in a well-defined social-economic group: the socialist democracy. The relations between this intelligentsia and the people were definitively established: the people moved toward civic and economic self-determination; the democrats aspired to power over them. The connection between them could be maintained only by means of cunning, trickery and violence, but in no way as the natural result of a community of interests. They are hostile toward each other.

The doctrine of the State itself, the idea of managing the masses by force, was always an attribute of individuals who lacked the sentiment of equality and in whom the instinct of egoism was dominant; individuals for whom the human masses are a raw material lacking will, initiative and intelligence, incapable of directing themselves.

This idea was always held by dominant privileged groups who stood outside the working population—the aristocracy, military castes, nobility, clergy, industrial and commercial bourgeoisie, etc.

It is not by chance that contemporary socialism shows itself to be the zealous servant of this idea: it is the ideology

34

of the new ruling caste. If we attentively observe the carriers and apostles of state socialism, we will see that every one of them is full of centralist urges, that every one sees himself, above all, as a directing and commanding center around which the masses gravitate. This psychological trait of state socialism and its carriers is a direct outgrowth of the psychology of former groups of rulers which are extinct or in the process of dying.

The second fundamental fact of our revolution is that the workers and the peasant laborers remained within the earlier situation of "working classes"—producers managed by authority from above.

All the present day so-called socialist construction carried out in Russia, the entire State apparatus and management of the country, the creation of new social-political relations—all this is largely nothing other than the construction of a new class domination over the producers, the establishment of a new socialist power over them. The plan for this construction and this domination was elaborated and prepared during several decades by the leaders of the socialist democracy and was known before the Russian revolution by the name of collectivism. Today it calls itself the soviet system.

This system makes its first historical appearance on the soil of the revolutionary movement of Russian workers and peasants. This is the first attempt of socialist democracy to establish its statist domination in a country by the force of a revolution. As a first attempt, undertaken at that by only one part of the democracy—by the most active, most enterprising and most revolutionary part, its communist left wing—it surprised the broad masses of democrats, and its brutal forms at first split the democracy itself into several rival groups. Some of these groups (Mensheviks, Socialist-Revolutionaries, etc.) considered it premature and risky to introduce communism into Russia at the present time. They retained the hope of achieving State domination in the country by the so-called legal and parliamentary route: by winning the majority of seats in parliament by means of votes from workers and peasants. This was the basis of their disagreement with their left-wing colleagues, the Communists. This disagreement is temporary, accidental and not serious. It is provoked by a misunderstanding on the part of the broader and more timid section of democrats, who failed to understand the meaning of the political upheaval carried out by the Bolsheviks. As soon as this group sees that the communist system does not contain anything that threatens them, but on the contrary opens up to them superb posts in the new State, all the disagreements between the rival factions of the democracy will disappear, and the entire democracy will carry on under the guidance of the unified Communist Party.

And already today we observe a certain "enlightenment" of the democracy in this direction. A whole series of groups and parties, in Russia and abroad, are rallying to the "soviet platform." Enormous political parties from different countries, until recently animators of the Second International, who fought Bolshevism from that standpoint, are today preparing to join the Communist International and present themselves to the working class with the Communist flag, with "Dictatorship of the Proletariat" on their lips.

But, as in earlier great revolutions in which workers and peasants fought, our revolution was also accompanied by a series of original and independent struggles of working people for freedom and equality, profound currents which marked the revolution. One of these currents, the most powerful and the most vivid, is the *Makhnovshchina.* For a period of three years the Makhnovshchina heroically cleared a path in the revolution by which the working people of Russia could realize their age-old aspirations—freedom and independence. In spite of the savage policy of the Communist government to smother this current, to distort and befoul it, it continued to grow, live and develop, struggling on several fronts in the civil war, frequently dealing serious blows to its enemies, arousing and supporting the revolutionary expectations of the workers and peasants of Great Russia, Siberia and the Caucasus. The continued development of the Makhnovshchina is explained by the fact that many of the Russian workers and peasants were to some extent familiar with the histories of revolutions of other peoples as well as the revolutionary movements of their ancestors, and were able to lean on this experience. In addition, workers came out of the ranks who were able to find, formulate, and attract the attention of the masses, to the most fundamental and basic aspects of their revolutionary movement, to contrast these aspects with the political goals of the democracy, and to defend the workers' aspirations with dignity, perseverance and talent.

Before going on to the history of the Makhnovist movement, it is necessary to note that, when the Russian revolution is called the "October Revolution," two distinct phenomena are confused: the slogans under which the masses carried out the revolution, and its results.

The slogans of the October 1917 mass movement were: "The Factories to the Workers! The Land to the Peasants!" The entire social and revolutionary program of the masses is communicated by this brief but profoundly significant slogan: the destruction of capitalism, wage labor, enslavement to the State, and the organization of a new life based on the self-direction of the producers. But in reality this October program was not realized in any way. Capitalism has not been destroyed but reformed. Wage labor and the exploitation of the producers remains in force. And the new State apparatus oppresses the workers no less than the State apparatus of landowners and private capitalists. Thus the Russian revolution can be called the "October revolution" only in a specific and narrow sense: as a realization of the goals and tasks of the Communist Party.

The October upheaval, as well as the one of February-March 1917, was only a stage in the general advance of the Russian revolution. The revolutionary forces of the October movement were used by the Communist Party for its own plans and goals. But this act does not represent our entire revolution. The general course of the revolution includes a whole series of other currents which do not stop in October but go further, toward the implementation of the historic tasks of the workers and peasants: the egalitarian, stateless community of workers. The currently protracted and already hardened October must, without a doubt, give way to the next popular stage of the revolution. If this does not happen, the Russian revolution, like all its predecessors, will have been nothing but a change of government.

38

Chapter 2

The October Upheaval
in Great Russia and in the Ukraine.

To clarify the development of the Russian revolution, it is necessary to examine the propaganda and the development of revolutionary ideas among the workers and the peasants throughout the period from 1900 to 1917, and the significance of the October upheaval in Great Russia and in the Ukraine.

Beginning with the years 1900-1905, revolutionary propaganda among workers and peasants was carried out by spokesmen of two basic doctrines: state socialism and anarchism. The state socialist propaganda was carried out by a number of wonderfully organized democratic parties: Bolsheviks, Mensheviks, Socialist-Revolutionaries and a number of related currents. Anarchism was put forward by a few numerically small groups who did not have a sufficiently clear understanding of their tasks in the revolution. The field of propaganda and political education was almost completely occupied by the democracy which educated the masses in the spirit of its political program and ideals. The establishment of a democratic republic was its basic goal; political revolution, its means to realize this goal.

Anarchism, on the contrary, rejected democracy as one form of statism, and also rejected political revolution as a method of action. Anarchism considered the basic task of workers and peasants to be social revolution, and it is for this that it called the masses. This was the sole doctrine which called for complete destruction of capitalism in the name of a free, stateless society of working people. But, having only a small number of militants and at the same time lacking a concrete program for the immediate future, anarchism could not spread widely and establish roots among the masses as their specific social and political theory. Nevertheless, because anarchism dealt with the most important aspects of the life of the enslaved masses, because it was never hypocritical toward them, and taught them to struggle directly for their own cause and to die for it—it created a gallery of fighters and martyrs for the social revolution at the very heart of the working class. Anarchist ideas held out through the long ordeal of Tsarist reaction and remained in the hearts of individual workers of cities and countryside as their social and political ideal.

Socialism, being a natural offspring of democracy, always had at its disposal enormous intellectual forces. Students, professors, doctors, lawyers, journalists, etc., were either patented Marxists or to a great extent sympathized with Marxism. Thanks to its extensive forces experienced in politics, socialism always succeeded in attracting a significant number of workers, even though it called them to a struggle for the incomprehensible and suspect ideals of the democracy.

In spite of this, at the time of the 1917 revolution, class interests and instincts led the workers and peasants toward their own direct goals: the appropriation of land and factories.

When this orientation appeared among the masses—and it appeared long before the 1917 revolution—one section of the Marxists, namely their left wing, the Bolsheviks, quickly abandoned their overtly bourgeois-democratic positions, proclaimed slogans which were adapted to the needs of the working class, and in the days of the revolution marched with the rebellious mass, seeking to make themselves masters of the mass movement. They succeeded in this thanks to the extensive intellectual forces in the ranks of Bolshevism as well as the socialist slogans with which they seduced the masses.

We have already mentioned above that the October upheaval was carried out under two powerful slogans: "Factories to the Workers; Land to the Peasants!" The working people gave these slogans a plain meaning, without reservations; i.e., the revolution would place the entire industrial economy directly under the control of the workers, the land and agriculture under that of the peasants. The spirit of justice and self-activity contained in these slogans inspired the masses to such an extent that a significant and very active

40

part of them was ready the day after the revolution to start organizing life on the basis of these slogans. In numerous cities the trade unions and factory committees took over the management of the factories and their goods, getting rid of the proprietors, and themselves determined prices, etc. But all these attempts met the iron resistance of the Communist Party which had already become the State.

The Communist Party, which marched shoulder to shoulder with the revolutionary masses and took up their extremist, frequently anarchist, slogans, abruptly transformed its activity as soon as the coalition government was discarded and the Party came to power. The revolution as a mass movement of working people with the slogans of October, was from that point on finished for the party. The basic enemy of the working class, the industrial and agricultural bourgeoisie, was defeated. The period of destruction, of struggle against the capitalist regime, was over; what began was the period of communist construction, the period of proletarian building. From this point on, the revolution could only be carried out by the organs of the State. The continuation of the earlier condition of the country, when the workers were masters of the streets, factories and workshops, when the peasants, not seeing the new power, tried to arrange their lives independently, could have dangerous consequences and could disorganize the Party's role in the State apparatus. All this had to be stopped by all possible means, up to and including State violence.

Such was the about-face in the activity of the Communist Party as soon as it seized power.

From this moment on, the Party obstinately reacted against all socialist activity on the part of the masses of workers and peasants. Obviously, this about-face of the revolution and this bureaucratic plan for its further development was a cowardly and impudent step on the part of a party that owed its position only to the working people. This was pure imposture and usurpation. But the logic of the position taken by the Communist Party in the revolution was such that it could not have acted otherwise. Any other political party seeking dictatorship and supremacy over the country from the revolution would have acted the same way. Before October it was the right wing of the democracy which sought to

41

command the revolution—Mensheviks and Socialist-Revolutionaries. Their difference with the Bolsheviks was that they were not able to organize their power and catch the masses in their nets.

* * *

Let us now examine how the dictatorship of the Communist Party and its ban on the further development of the revolution outside the organs of the State were received by the working people of Great Russia and the Ukraine. For the workers of Great Russia and the Ukraine, the revolution was the same, but the Bolshevik statist domination of the revolution was not received the same way: in the Ukraine it met more resistance than in Great Russia. Let us begin with Great Russia.

Before and during the revolution, the Communist Party carried on enormous activity among the workers of the cities of Great Russia. During the Tsarist period it tried, being the left wing of social-democracy, to organize them for the struggle for a democratic republic, recruiting a reliable and solid army from among them to struggle for its ideals.

After the overthrow of Tsarism in February-March 1917, a tense period began, when the workers and peasants could not afford to lose any time. The working people saw the provisional government as their avowed enemy. Thus they did not wait to set out to realize their rights by revolutionary means: first of all their right to the eight-hour day, then their rights to the instruments of production and consumption as well as the land. In all this the Communist Party presented itself to them as a superbly organized ally. It is true that through this alliance the Party followed its own aims, but the masses did not know this, and only saw the fact that the Communist Party struggled with them against the capitalist regime. This party directed all the power of its organizations, all its political and organizational experience, its best militants, into the heart of the working class and into the army. The party used all its forces to assemble the masses around its slogans, playing demagogically with the burning questions of the oppressed laborers, snatching the slogans of the peasants

42

about the land, of the workers about voluntary labor, and pushed the working people toward a decisive clash with the coalition government. Day after day, the Communist Party was in the ranks of the working class, carrying on with the workers an untiring struggle against the bourgeoisie, a struggle which it continued until the days of October. Thus it is natural that the workers of Great Russia were accustomed to see in the Party their energetic comrades-in-arms in the revolutionary struggle. This circumstance, as well as the fact that the Russian working class had almost no revolutionary organizations of its own—it was scattered, from an organizational standpoint—allowed the party to easily take the management of affairs into its hands. And when the coalition government was overturned by the working class of Petrograd and Moscow, power simply passed to the Bolsheviks as the leaders of the upheaval.

After this the Communist Party directed all of its energy toward the organization of a firm power and to the liquidation of mass movements of workers and peasants which continued, in various parts of the country, to try to achieve the basic goals of the revolution by means of direct action. The party succeeded in this task without great difficulty due to the enormous influence which it had acquired in the period which preceded October. It is true that immediately after its seizure of power, the Communist Party was obliged, more than once, to stifle the first steps of workers' organizations trying to start production in their enterprises on the basis of workers' equality. It is true that numerous villages were pillaged and thousands of peasants were assassinated by the Communist power for their disobedience and their attempts to do without state power. It is true that in Moscow and in several other cities, in order to liquidate anarchist organizations in April 1918, and later, organizations of the left Socialist-Revolutionaries, the Communist Party was forced to use machine guns and cannons, thus provoking a civil war on the left. But in general, due to a certain confidence of Great Russian workers in Bolshevism after October, a confidence which was short-lived, the Bolsheviks succeeded easily and quickly in taking the masses in hand and in stopping the further development of the workers' and peasants' revolution, replacing it with the governmental decrees of the Party. That ended the revolution in Great Russia.

The period before and during October was very different in the Ukraine. Here the Communist Party did not have a tenth of the organized party forces which it possessed in Great Russia. Here its influence on the peasants and workers had always been insignificant. Here the October upheaval took place much later, not until November, December, and January of the following year. Up to this point the Ukraine had been ruled by the local national bourgeoisie—the *Petliurovtsi* (followers of Petliura). In their relations to the Ukraine, the Bolsheviks did not act in a revolutionary manner, but mainly in a military manner. In Great Russia the passage of power to the soviets meant its passage to the Communist Party. However in the Ukraine, thanks to the powerlessness and unpopularity of the Communist Party, the passage of power to the soviets meant something completely different. The soviets were meetings of delegated workers without any real power to subordinate the masses. The workers in the factories and the peasants in the villages felt themselves to be the real force. But this force was scattered, disorganized, and constantly in danger of falling under the dictatorship of a well-knit party.

During the entire revolutionary struggle, the working class and the peasants of the Ukraine were not accustomed to being surrounded by an ever-present and inflexible tutor like the Communist Party in Great Russia. As a result, the working population experienced a much greater degree of freedom, which inevitably manifested itself during the days of mass revolutionary activity.

Another, still more important aspect of the life of (indigenous) Ukrainian peasants and workers were the *traditions of the Vol'nitsa* which were preserved from ancient times. Whatever efforts the Tsars made, from Catherine II on, to wipe out all traces of the *Vol'nitsa* from the minds of the Ukrainian people, this heritage from the heroic epoch of Zaporozh'e Cossacks of the 14th to the 16th century is nevertheless preserved to the present day, and Ukrainian peasants have retained a particular love for independence. Among present-day Ukrainian peasants this takes the form of stubborn resistance to all powers which try to subjugate

44

them.

The revolutionary movement in the Ukraine was thus accompanied by two conditions which did not exist in Great Russia, and which greatly influenced the character of the Ukrainian revolution: the absence of a powerful and organized political party, and the spirit of the *Vol'nitsa,* a living heritage of the Ukrainian worker. And in fact, when the revolution in Great Russia fell under the domination of the State without much resistance, this domination met great resistance in the Ukraine. The Soviet apparatus installed itself mechanically, and mainly by armed force. At the same time an autonomous mass movement consisting mainly of peasants continued to develop. It had appeared already under the government of the Democratic Republic of Petliura and progressed slowly, still seeking its path. Furthermore, the roots of this movement lay at the very basis of the Russian revolution. It was noteworthy already from the first days of the February upheaval. It was a movement of the lowest strata of the working people, who sought to destroy the economic slave system and create a new system, based on the socialization of means and instruments of labor and the cultivation of the land by the workers themselves.

We have already mentioned that, in the name of these principles, workers got rid of the owners of factories and transferred the management of production to their class organs: trade unions, factory committees or workers' commissions specially created for this purpose. The peasants took over the land of the *pomeshchiks* (gentry) and of the *kulaks* (wealthy peasants) and reserved the produce strictly for the workers themselves, thus sketching a new type of agrarian economy.

This practice of direct revolutionary action by the workers and peasants developed in the Ukraine almost unobstructed during the whole first year of the revolution and created a healthy and clear *line of revolutionary conduct for the masses.*

And every time one or another political group, having taken power, tried to break the workers' line of revolutionary conduct, the workers launched a revolutionary opposition and struggled in various ways against these attempts.

Thus the revolutionary movement of the working

people toward social independence, which had begun in the first days of the revolution, did not weaken no matter what power was established in the Ukraine. It was not even extinguished by the Bolsheviks who, after the October upheaval, tried to introduce their autocratic state system into the country.

What was characteristic about this movement?

Its desire to attain the real goals of the working class in the revolution; its will to win labor's independence; its defiance of all non-laboring social groups.

Despite all the sophisms of the Communist Party seeking to prove that the Party was the brain of the working class, and that its power was that of the workers and peasants—every worker and peasant who had retained his class spirit or instinct was aware that in fact the Party was driving the workers of the cities and the countryside away from their own revolutionary tasks, that the Party had them under its control, and that the very existence of a statist organization was a usurpation of their right to independence and to any form of self-management.

The aspiration to full self-direction became the basis of the movement born in the depths of the masses. In all kinds of ways their thoughts were constantly rooted in this idea. The statist activity of the Communist Party pitilessly stifled these aspirations. But it was precisely this action of the presumptuous party, intolerant of any objection, that enlightened the workers and drove them to resist.

In the beginning, the movement confined itself to ignoring the new power and performing spontaneous acts in which the peasants took possession of the land and goods of the landlords. They found their own ways and means. The unexpected occupation of the Ukraine by the Austro-Germans placed the workers in a completely new situation and precipitated the development of their movement.

Chapter 3

The Revolutionary Insurrection
in the Ukraine.
Makhno.

The Brest-Litovsk treaty concluded by the Bolsheviks with the Imperial German government opened the doors of the Ukraine to the Austro-Germans. They entered as masters. They did not confine themselves to military action, but became involved in the economic and political life of the country. Their purpose was to appropriate its products. To accomplish this easily and completely they reestablished the power of the nobles and the landed gentry, who had been overthrown by the people, and installed the autocratic government of the Hetman Skoropadsky. Their troops were systematically misled by their officers about the Russian revolution. The situation in Russia and the Ukraine was represented to them as an orgy of blind, savage forces, destroying order in the country and terrorizing the honest working people. This way they provoked in the soldiers a hostility towards the rebel peasants and workers, thus creating the basis for the absolutely heartless and plundering entry of the Austro-German armies into the revolutionary country.

The economic pillage of the Ukraine by the Austro-Germans, with the connivance and help of the Skoropadsky government, was colossal and horrifying. They carried off everything—wheat, livestock, poultry, eggs, raw materials, etc.—all in such quantities that the means of transportation were not sufficient. As it was brought to the immense depots which were given over to the loot, the Austrians and the Germans hastened to take away as much as possible, loading one train after another. Hundreds, even thousands of trains, carried everything off. When the peasants resisted this pillage and tried to retain the fruits of their labor, floggings, reprisals and shootings resulted.

The occupation of the Ukraine by the Austro-Germans

constitutes one of the most tragic pages in the history of its revolution. In addition to the violence of the invaders and their cynical military brigandage, the occupation was accompanied by a fierce reaction on the part of the landed gentry. The Hetman's regime meant the annihilation of all the revolutionary conquests of the workers, a complete return to the past. It was therefore natural that this new condition strongly accelerated the march of the movements previously begun, under Petliura and the Bolsheviks. Everywhere, primarily in the villages, insurrectionary acts began against the landowners and the Austro-Germans. It was thus that the new revolutionary movement of the Ukrainian peasants began, a movement which was later given the name of the *Revolutionary Insurrection.* The origin of this revolutionary insurrection is often seen as merely the result of the Austro-German occupation and the regime of the Hetman. This explanation is insufficient and therefore not true. The insurrection had its roots in the depths of the Russian revolution and was an attempt by the workers to lead the revolution to its natural conclusion: the true and complete emancipation and supremacy of labor. The Austro-German invasion and the *pomeshchiks'* (landowners') reaction only accelerated the process.

The movement rapidly took on vast proportions. Everywhere the peasants took a stand against the *pomeshchiks,* assassinated or drove them away, took over their lands and their goods, and paid no attention to the invading Austro-Germans. The Hetman and the German authorities responded by implacable reprisals. The peasants in the rebellious villages were flogged and shot in mass, while all their goods were burned. In a short space of time hundreds of villages suffered a terrible punishment from the military and landed castes. This occurred in June, July and August, 1918.

Then the peasants, persevering in their revolt, started guerrilla warfare. As if by order of invisible organizations, they formed a multitude of partisan detachments almost simultaneously in various places, acting militarily and always by surprise against the nobles, their guards and the representatives of power. As a rule these guerrilla detachments, consisting of 20, 50 or 100 well-armed horsemen, would appear suddenly where they were least expected, attack a nobleman or a State guard, massacre all the enemies of the peasants, and disappear as quickly as they had come. Every landlord who persecuted the peasants, and all of his faithful servants, were noted by the partisans and were in continual danger of being killed. Every guard, every German officer was condemned to almost certain death. These exploits, occurring daily in all parts of the country, cut the heart out of the landowners' counter-revolution, undermined it, and prepared the way for the triumph of the peasants.

It must be noted that, like vast and spontaneous peasant insurrections which rise without any preparation, these organized guerrilla actions were always performed by the peasants themselves, with no help or direction from any political organization. Their methods of action made it necessary for them to look after the needs of the movement themselves, and to direct it and lead it to victory. During their whole fight against the Hetman and the *pomeshchiks,* even at its most difficult moments, the peasants remained alone in the face of their vicious, well-armed and organized enemy. This fact had great influence on the very character of the whole revolutionary insurrection (as we will see later). Wherever it remained to the end a class action, without falling under the influence of political parties or nationalist elements, it retained not only the imprint of its origin in the very depths of the peasant mass, but also a second fundamental trait—the perfect consciousness which all these peasants possessed of being their own guides and the animators of their own movement. The partisan detachments were proud of this special quality of their movement and felt themselves capable of fulfilling their mission.

The savage reprisals of the counter-revolution did not stop the movement; on the contrary, they enlarged and broadened it. The peasants became increasingly united among themselves, driven by the very force of events to a general plan of revolutionary action. To be sure, the peasants of the whole Ukraine were never organized into a single force acting under a single leadership. From the point of view of revolutionary spirit, they were all united; but in practice they were mainly organized locally, by regions; small detachments of partisans, isolated from one another, united to form larger and more powerful units. In so far as the insurrections became more frequent and the reprisals more ferocious and organized, these unions became an urgent necessity. In the south of the Ukraine, it was the region of Gulyai-Polye which took the initiative in unification. There it took place not only for reasons of defense, but also and primarily for the purpose of the complete destruction of the landowners' counter-revolution. This unification had yet another purpose, namely to make of the revolutionary peasants a real and organized force capable of combatting all counter-revolution and of defending the freedom and the territory of the revolutionary people.

The most important role in this effort at unification and in the general development of the revolutionary insurrection in the south of the Ukraine was played by the insurrectionary detachment guided by a peasant native to the region, Nestor Makhno. From the first days of the movement up to its culminating point, when the peasants vanquished the landowners, Makhno played a preponderant and central role to such an extent that the whole insurgent region and the most heroic moments of the struggle are linked to his name. Later, when the insurrection had triumphed completely over the Skoropadsky counter-revolution and the region was threatened by Denikin, Makhno became the rallying point for millions of peasants in several regions. This was the moment in the history of the Ukrainian insurrection when it acquired its form and clarified its historical tasks. For it was not everywhere that the insurrection retained its consciousness, its revolutionary essence, and its loyalty to the interests of its class. While in the southern Ukraine the insurgents raised the black flag of anarchism and set forth on the anti-authoritarian road of the free organization of the workers, in the western and north-western regions of the Ukraine they gradually slipped, after the overthrow of the Hetman, under the influence of foreign elements, enemies of their class, notably the nationalist democrats *(Petliurovtsi)*. For more than two years a part of the insurgents in the western Ukraine supported Petliura, who under the nationalist banner pursued the interests of the local liberal bourgeoisie. Thus, the insurgent peasants of the governments of Kiev, Volyn, Podol'sk and a part of Poltava, while having common origins with the rest of the insurgents, were subsequently unable to discover among themselves either the consciousness of their historic mission or the ability to organize their forces, and they fell under the rod of the enemies of labor, becoming blind instruments in their hands.

The insurrection in the southern Ukraine had an entirely different significance and took on a different aspect. It separated itself strictly from the non-laboring elements of contemporary society, it strictly and resolutely got rid of the national, religious, political and other prejudices of the regime of oppression and slavery; it based itself on the real aspirations of the proletarian class of the city and the country, and it carried out a bitter warfare in the name of these aspirations, against the many enemies of labor.

Makhno.

We have already mentioned that an outstanding role was played by Nestor Makhno in the extensive region of the peasant insurrection in the southern Ukraine. Let us follow him in his activity during the first period, namely until the overthrow of the Hetman, and give some brief biographical notes.

The peasant Nestor Ivanovich Makhno was born on October 27, 1889, and was brought up by his mother in the village of Gulyai Polye in the district of Aleksandrovsk, government[1] of Ekaterinoslav. He was the son of a poor peasant family. He was only ten months old when his father died, leaving him and his four brothers in the care of their mother. Because of the extreme poverty of the family, he worked at the age of seven as a shepherd, tending the cows and sheep of the peasants of his village. At 8 he entered the local school, which he attended in winter, working as shepherd in summer. At 12 he left school and his family to take a job. He worked as a farmhand on the estates of nobles and on

[1] [A territorial subdivision comparable to a "province," a "state," or a "department." (In Russian: *guberniya,* here translated as "government.")]

51

farms of German *kulaks.* Already at this time, when he was 14 or 15, he felt a strong hatred toward the exploiters and dreamed of the way he would some day get even with them, both for himself and for others, if he ever had the power to do so. Later he worked in a foundry in his village.

Until the age of 16 he had no contact with the political world. His social and revolutionary concepts developed spontaneously in a very narrow circle of peasants, proletarians like himself. The revolution of 1905 made him break out of his small circle, and threw him into the great torrent of revolutionary events and actions. He was 17, full of revolutionary enthusiasm and ready to do anything in the struggle for the liberation of the workers. After having made several contacts with political organizations, he decided to enter the ranks of the anarcho-communists and from that moment became an untiring fighter for social revolution.

Russian anarchism at this time faced two concrete tasks: 1) to unmask the political fraud which the socialist parties led by Marxists were preparing against the workers; 2) to point out to workers and peasants the path toward social revolution. In these tasks Makhno discovered an extensive field of activity, and took part in many of the most dangerous acts of the anarchist struggle.

In 1908 he fell into the hands of the Tsarist authorities, who condemned him to be hanged for anarchist associations and for taking part in terrorist acts. Because of his youth, the death penalty was commuted to life imprisonment at hard labor. Makhno served his sentence in the Butyrki central prison of Moscow. Although prison life was without hope and very difficult for him to bear, Makhno used it to educate himself. He showed great perseverance and learned Russian grammar, mathematics, Russian literature, the history of culture, and political economy. In fact, prison was the only school in which Makhno acquired that historical and political knowledge which was a great help to him in his subsequent revolutionary activity. Life, action, deeds were the other schools in which he learned to know and understand men and social events.

It was in prison, while he was still young, that Makhno endangered his health. Stubborn and unable to accept that complete extinction of personality that those condemned to forced labor underwent, he was always insubordinate to the prison authorities and was continually in solitary confinement, where, because of the cold and damp, he contracted pulmonary tuberculosis. During the nine years of his detention, he was frequently in irons for "bad behavior"; he was finally released with all the other political prisoners by the proletarian insurrection in Moscow on March 2, 1917.

On leaving prison, Makhno returned to Gulyai-Polye, where the peasant masses showed profound sympathy for him. In the whole village he was the only political prisoner who was returned to his family by the revolution, and for that reason he became the object of spontaneous respect and confidence for the peasants. He was no longer an inexperienced young man, but a tested fighter with a powerful will and definite ideas about the social conflict.

At Gulyai-Polye he immediately devoted himself to revolutionary work, first seeking to organize the peasants of his village and its surroundings. He founded a farm-workers' union, organized a workers' commune and a local peasants' soviet (council). The problem that concerned him most was that of uniting and organizing the peasants into a powerful and firm alliance so that they would be able once and for all to drive out the landed gentry and the political rulers and to manage their own lives. It was to this end that he guided the organizational work of the peasants, both as a propagandist and as a man of action. He sought to unite them in the face of the flagrant deception, injustice and oppression of which they were victims. During the period of the Kerensky government and in the October days of 1917, he was president of the regional peasants' union, of the agricultural commission, the union of metal and carpentry workers, and, finally, president of the Peasants' and Workers' Soviet of Gulyai-Polye.

It was in this last capacity that in August, 1917, he assembled all the *pomeshchiks* (landed gentry) of the region and made them give him all the documents relating to lands and buildings. He proceeded to take an exact inventory of all this property, and then made a report on it, first at a session of the local soviet, then at the district congress of soviets, and finally at the regional congress of soviets. He proceeded to equalize the rights of the *pomeshchiks* and the *kulaks* with those of the poor peasant laborers in regard to the use of the land. Following his proposal, the congress decided to let the *pomeshchiks* and *kulaks* have a share of the land, as well as tools and livestock, equal to that of the laborers. Several peasant congresses in the governments of Ekaterinoslav, Tauride, Poltava, Khar'kov and elsewhere followed the example of the Gulyai-Polye region and adopted the same measure.

During this time Makhno became, in this region, the soul of the peasants' movement, which was taking over the lands and goods of the *pomeshchiks* and even, if necessary, executing them. He thus made himself the mortal enemy of the rich and of local bourgeois groups.

At the time of the Austro-German occupation of the Ukraine, Makhno was charged by the Gulyai-Polye revolutionary committee with the task of forming batallions of insurgent peasants and workers for the struggle against the invaders and against the Central *Rada* (Supreme governing body of the Ukraine). He was forced to retreat with his partisans from the cities of Taganrog, Rostov and Tsaritsyn, fighting every step of the way. The local bourgeoisie, who had been strengthened by the military support of the Austro-Germans, put a price on his head, and he had to go into hiding. The Ukrainian and German military authorities took revenge by burning his mother's house and shooting his elder brother Emel'yan, who was a war invalid.

In June, 1918, Makhno went to Moscow to consult several old anarchists on methods and directions to follow and on the nature of his work among the Ukrainian peasants. But the anarchists in this period of the Russian revolution were very indecisive and weak, and, receiving no satisfactory suggestions or advice, he returned to the Ukraine with his own ideas.

For a long time he had considered the idea of organizing the vast peasant masses in order to release the revolutionary energy that had been accumulating in them for centuries, and to hurl this formidable power against the existing regime of oppression. Now he judged that this moment had arrived. While in Moscow he read in the newspapers about the numerous insurrectionary acts of the Ukrainian peasants, and he grew agitated and impatient; every day of his stay in

Moscow caused him great moral suffering. In haste, and with the aid of an old friend who was a comrade and former fellow prisoner, he equipped himself and finally left for the Ukraine and his region of Gulyai-Polye. This happened in July, 1918. He accomplished the trip with great difficulty and very secretly, so as not to fall into the hands of the Hetman's agents. On one occasion Makhno was almost killed, being arrested by an Austro-German detachment while carrying a suitcase of anarchist literature. A rich Jew from Gulyai-Polye who had known Makhno personally for a long time, succeeded in saving him by paying a considerable sum of money for his release. On route to the Ukraine, the Bolsheviks proposed to Makhno that he should select a certain region of the Ukraine and carry out secret revolutionary work there in their name. Naturally he refused even to discuss this offer; the tasks he had set himself had nothing in common with those of the Bolsheviks.

Back in Gulyai-Polye, Makhno decided that he would either die or obtain victory for the peasants, and in no event would he leave the region. The news of his return spread rapidly from village to village. Without delay he stated his mission openly among the great masses of peasants, speaking at improvised meetings, writing and distributing letters and leaflets. By pen and mouth he called on the peasants for a decisive struggle against the power of the Hetman and the landlords, emphatically declaring that the workers should now take their fate into their own hands and not let their freedom to act be taken from them. His stirring appeal was heard, in a few weeks, by many villages and whole districts, preparing the masses for the great events of the future.

Makhno proceeded immediately to direct action. His first concern was to form a revolutionary-military unit sufficiently strong to guarantee freedom of propaganda and action in the villages and towns and at the same time to begin guerrilla operations. This unit was quickly organized. In the villages there were marvelously combative elements, ready for action. They only lacked a good organizer. Makhno was the man. His first unit undertook two urgent tasks, namely, a) to pursue energetically the work of propaganda and organization among the peasants, and b) to carry on a stubborn armed struggle against all their enemies. The guiding principle of this merciless struggle was that no lord who had persecuted the peasants, no policeman of the Hetman, no Russian or German officer who was an implacable enemy of the peasants, deserved any pity; he must be destroyed. All who participated in the oppression of the poor peasants and workers, all who sought to suppress their rights or exploit their labor, should be executed.

Within two or three weeks, the unit had already become the terror, not only of the local bourgeoisie, but also of the Austro-German authorities. Makhno's field of revolutionary-military action was immense: it extended from Lozovaya to Berdyansk, Mariupol' and Taganrog, and from Lugansk and Grishino to Ekaterinoslav, Aleksandrovsk and Melitopol'. Rapidity of movement was his special tactic. Thanks to it, and also to the size of the region, he could always appear suddenly where he was least expected. In a short time he enveloped within a circle of iron and fire the whole region in which the local bourgeoisie were reestablishing their power. All those who, during the past two or three months, had succeeded in settling back into their old estates, all those who enslaved the peasants, stole their labor and land, all those who ruled over them as masters, found themselves suddenly under the merciless hand of Makhno and his partisans. Swift as the wind, intrepid, pitiless toward their enemies, they fell thunderously on some estates, massacred all the sworn enemies of the peasants, and disappeared as rapidly as they had come. The next day Makhno would be more than a hundred miles away, would appear in some town, massacre the *Varta* (security police), officers and noblemen, and vanish before the German troops had time to realize what had happened, despite the fact that they were all prepared for him. The next day he would again be a hundred miles away, taking action against a detachment of Hungarians who were taking reprisals, or hanging some guards of the *Varta.*

Both the *Varta* and the Austro-German authorities were alarmed. Several units were sent to capture Makhno. It was in vain. Excellent horsemen since childhood, his partisans could not be caught, for in a day they could cover distances that were impossible for regular cavalry. Often, as though to mock his enemies, Makhno would suddenly appear in the very center of Gulyai-Polye, or in Pologi, where many Austro-German troops were always stationed, or in some other place where troops were concentrated, killing the officers who fell into his hands and escaping, safe and sound, without leaving the slightest indication of the route he was taking. Or else, when it seemed to his pursuers that they had at last found a fresh trail, when they were expecting to overtake and capture him in a town that had been pointed out to them by some peasant, he himself, with a small number of his partisans, in the uniform of the *Varta,* would penetrate into the very midst of the enemy, learning their plans and preparations. Then he would set out with a detachment of the *Varta* in pursuit of Makhno, and would exterminate them on the way.

The partisans held to the following general rule in regard to the Austro-German and Hungarian troops they encountered: they would kill the officers and set the captured soldiers free; they would suggest that the soldiers should return to their own countries, tell what the Ukrainian peasants were doing, and work for the social revolution. Literature, and sometimes even money, were distributed among them. Only soldiers known to have been guilty of acts of violence against the peasants were executed. This way of treating the captured Austro-German and Hungarian soldiers had a certain revolutionary influence on them.

During this first period of insurrectionary activity, Makhno was not only the organizer and guide of the peasants, but also a harsh avenger of the oppressed people. During the short period of his first insurrectionary activity, hundreds of nests of the nobility were destroyed, thousands of oppressors and active enemies of the people were mercilessly wiped out. His bold and resolute method of acting, the rapidity of his appearances and disappearances, the precision of his blows, and the manifest impossibility of capturing him, dead or alive, soon made him a figure that struck terror and hatred in the bourgeoisie, but gave rise to feelings of deep satisfaction, pride and hope among the working people. To the peasants Makhno became a legendary figure. In Makhno's character and his actions, there were in fact qualities worthy of legend: his extraordinary boldness, his stubborn will, his resourcefulness in all circumstances, and finally the delightful humor that frequently accompanied his action.

But these were not all the important qualities in Makhno's personality.

The warlike spirit that was shown in his insurrectionary undertakings of this early period of his activity was only the first manifestation of his enormous talent as a warrior and organizer. We will see later what a remarkable military force and what a magnificent organizer came from the ranks of the peasants in the person of Makhno.

Not merely a remarkable military guide and organizer, but also a good agitator, Makhno constantly increased the number of meetings that took place in numerous villages of the region where he operated. He made reports on the tasks of the moment, on the social revolution, on the free and independent communal life of the peasant-workers that was the final goal of the insurrection. He also published pamphlets on these topics, as well as appeals to the peasants and workers, the Austrian and German soldiers, the Don and Kuban Cossacks, etc.

"Conquer or die—such is the dilemma which faces the Ukrainian peasants and workers at this historic moment. But we cannot all die, for we are innumerable—we are mankind! Therefore, we will conquer. But we will not conquer in order to repeat the errors of the past years, the error of putting our fate into the hands of new masters; we will conquer in order to take our destinies into our own hands, to conduct our lives according to our own will and our own conception of the truth." (Taken from one of Makhno's first appeals.) This is how Makhno addressed the vast peasant masses. Soon he became the rallying point for all the insurgent masses. In every village the peasants created secret local groups, rallied to Makhno, supported him in all his undertakings, followed his advice and suggestions.

Many detachments of partisans—those already in existence as well as newly formed ones—joined his groups, seeking coordinated actions. The need for unity and activity on a general scale was recognized by all the revolutionary partisans, and all were of the opinion that this unity would be best achieved under Makhno's direction. Such was also the opinion of several large bands of insurgents who until then had been independent of one another. Notable among these were the large detachments commanded by Kurilenko, who operated in the Berdyansk region, that commanded by Shchus; in the Dibrivki region, and that of Petrenko-Platonov in the Grishino region. They all spontaneously joined Makhno. In this way the unification of the partisan units in the southern Ukraine into a single insurrectionary army came about naturally, through the force of events and the will of the masses.

It was at about this time, in September 1918, that Makhno received the nickname *Batko*—general leader of the revolutionary insurrection in the Ukraine. This took place in the following circumstances. Local *pomeshchiks* in the major centers, the *kulaks,* and the German authorities, decided to eliminate Makhno and his detachment at any cost. The *pomeshchiks* created a special volunteer detachment consisting of their own sons and those of *kulaks* for the decisive struggle against Makhno. On the 30th of September this detachment, with the help of the Austro-Germans, cornered Makhno in the region of Bol'shaya Mikhailovka, setting up strong military posts on all roads. At this time Makhno found himself with only 30 partisans and one machine gun. He was forced to make a fighting retreat, maneuvering in the midst of numerous enemy forces. Arriving in the forest of Dibrivki, Makhno found himself in an extremely difficult situation. The paths of retreat were occupied by the enemy. It was impossible for the detachment to break through, and escaping individually was beneath their revolutionary dignity. No one in the detachment would agree to abandon their leader so as to save himself. After some reflection, two days later, Makhno decided to return to the village of Bol'shaya Mikhailovka (Dibrivki). Leaving the forest the partisans met peasants who came to warn them that there were large enemy forces in Dibrivki and that they should make haste to go elsewhere. This information did not stop Makhno and his partisans. In spite of the tears of the women who tried to hold them back, they set out for Bol'shaya Mikhailovka. They approached the village guardedly. Makhno himself and a few of his comrades went on reconnaissance and saw a large enemy camp on the church square, dozens of machine guns, hundreds of saddled horses, and groups of cavalry. Peasants informed them that a batallion of Austrians and a special *pomeshchik* detachment were in the village. Retreat was impossible. Then Makhno, with his usual stubbornness and determination, said to his companions: "Well, my friends! We should all be ready to die on this spot. . ." The moment was ominous, the men were firm and full of enthusiasm. All 30 saw only one path before them—the path toward the enemy, who had about a thousand well-armed men, and they all realized that this meant certain death for them. All were moved, but none lost courage.

It was at this moment that one of the partisans, Shchus, turned to Makhno and said:

"From now on you will be *Batko* to all of us, and we vow to die with you in the ranks of the insurgents."

Then the whole detachment swore never to abandon the insurgent ranks, and to consider Makhno the general *Batko* of the entire revolutionary insurrection. Then they prepared to attack. Shchus' with five to seven men was assigned to go to attack the flank of the enemy. Makhno with the others attacked from the front. With a ferocious "Hurrah!" the partisans threw themselves headlong against the enemy, smiting the very center with sabres, rifles and revolvers. The attack had a shattering effect. The enemy, who were expecting nothing of the kind, were bowled over and began to flee in panic, saving themselves in groups and individually, abandoning arms, machine guns and horses. Without leaving them time to come to themselves, to become aware of the number of the attacking forces, and to pass to a counter-attack, the insurgents chased them in separate groups, cutting them down at full gallop. A part of the *pomeshchik* detachment fled to the Volchya River, where they were drowned by peasants who had joined the battle. The enemy's defeat was complete.

Local peasants and detachments of revolutionary insurgents came from all directions to triumphantly acclaim the heroes. They unanimously agreed to consider Makhno as *Batko* of the entire revolutionary insurrection in the Ukraine.

Two days after these events, Bol'shaya Mikhailovka was invaded by a mass of Austro-German troops and detachments of *pomeshchiks* and *kulaks* assembled from the entire region. On October 5, German troops began bombarding the

60

village with intense artillery fire, and when it was sufficiently destroyed by shells, infantry and *kulak* detachments entered the village and began to carry out executions and set fire to the entire village. Bol'shaya Mikhailovka burned for two days, and during those two days the *kulak* and German troops took fierce reprisals against the peasant population.

This fact further tightened the bonds among the peasants of the region and further strengthened their revolutionary relations.

The vast peasant masses, the majority of the inhabitants of the towns and villages, obviously were not in partisan detachments, but they were nevertheless tightly linked with the detachments. They supported them with supplies, furnished them with horses and fodder, brought them food in the forests when this was necessary, collected and transmitted to the partisans information on the enemy's movements; at times large masses of peasants joined the detachments to carry out in common some specific revolutionary task, battling alongside them for two or three days, then returning to their fields.

The occupation of Gulyai-Polye by the insurgents on the eve of the Hetman's downfall and the decomposition of the Austro-German troops is very typical of these relations. Makhno occupied the village with a small detachment. The Austrians stationed at Pologi sent troops. During a whole day Makhno received no help and was forced to leave the village. But in the evening several hundred peasants of Gulyai-Polye came to his aid, and with them he was able to hold out against an entire division of Austrian soldiers. At dawn the peasants returned home, fearing betrayal on the part of some villagers who might have seen them in the ranks of the insurgents. And during the day Makhno was again forced to leave the village because of the stronger and more numerous enemy forces. At night he once again began to attack, being notified by peasants that they would come to his help as soon as it was dark. He retook the village, chasing out the Austrians with the help of the local inhabitants. This continued for three or four days, after which Gulyai-Polye finally remained in the hands of the insurgent peasants.

Such vital links between the broad peasant masses and

Makhno's revolutionary detachments were established everywhere. These links were extremely important, since they gave the revolutionary insurrection the proportions and the character of a general peasant movement.

Chapter 4

The Fall of the Hetman.
Petliurism.
Bolshevism.

The counter-revolution of the Ukrainian *pomeshchiks,* personified by the Hetman, was without a doubt artificial, since it was implanted by the force of German and Austrian imperialism. The Ukrainian *pomeshchiks* and capitalists could not have held out for a single day during the tempestuous year of 1918 if they had not been supported by the power of the German army. According to one estimate, at least half a million Austro-German and Hungarian troops occupied the Ukraine. There may even have been more. All these troops were regularly spread out throughout the Ukraine in such a manner that more of them were assigned to revolutionary and turbulent regions. From the first day of the occupation, all these troops were placed at the service of counter-revolutionary interests, and in their relations with the working peasants they conducted themselves as conquerors in a vanquished country.

Thus, during the entire period of the counter-revolution the Ukrainian peasantry had to fight, not only against the Hetman's regime, but also against the entire mass of Austro-German soldiers. But in spite of this military support, the counter-revolution was not able to establish itself solidly, and with the growth of the peasant insurrection it began to disintegrate once and for all. Ultimately the insurrection also caused the disintegration of the Austro-German forces. When the troops, completely disoriented by the revolutionary insurrection on one hand, and by the political upheavals in Austria and Germany on the other, lost their purpose and were recalled to their countries, the entire Ukrainian reaction found itself suspended in mid-air. Its days, even its minutes, were numbered. Its weakness and its cowardice were such that it did not attempt any resistance. The Hetman simply

63

fled to regions less threatened by the peasant insurrection, returning to the place from which he had been artificially called to life by German imperialism. And the *pomeshchiks* had fled well in advance of the Hetman.

From this moment, three very different, basic forces were active in the Ukraine: Petliurism, Bolshevism and Makhnovism. Soon each of them became the avowed and irreconcilable enemy of the other two. In order to draw a more accurate picture of the character of the Makhnovist movement, we will first say a few words about the class and social nature of Petliurism. This is a movement of the Ukrainian national bourgeoisie striving to establish its political and economic domination in the country. Its program for the political organization of the country is modeled on the French or Swiss republics. This movement is in no way social but exclusively political and nationalist. Its promises to improve the social conditions of the workers, promises which are found in Petliura's program, are basically nothing more than a tribute to our revolutionary epoch, a token with which to achieve their own goals more easily.

From the first days of the March, 1917, revolution, the Ukrainian liberal bourgeoisie concerned itself with the problem of national separation from Russia. Large circles of *kulaks,* liberal intelligentsia, and educated Ukrainians in general, gave rise to a movement for political independence. From its beginning, its leaders paid serious attention to the masses of Ukrainian soldiers at the front and in the interior. They proceeded to organize the soldiers, on a national basis, into special Ukrainian regiments.

In May 1917, the leaders of the movement organized a military congress which elected a general military committee to direct the entire movement. Later this committee was enlarged and named the *Rada* (Council, in Ukrainian). In November, 1917, at the pan-Ukrainian Congress, this became the Central *Rada,* a kind of parliament of the new Ukrainian Democratic Republic. Finally, a month later, a "Universal" (Manifesto) of the *Rada* proclaimed the independence and autonomy of the Ukrainian Democratic Republic. Thus, during Kerensky's regime (in Great Russia), a new autonomous State was formed in the Ukraine, and began to establish itself throughout the country as the dominant force. This was

Petliurism, deriving its name from Simon Petliura, one of the active leaders of the movement.

The development and consolidation of Petliurism in the Ukraine was a serious blow to Bolshevism, which had just taken power in Great Russia and wanted to extend it to the Ukraine. The position of Bolshevism in Great Russia during those first days would have been even more difficult without the entire Ukraine. Therefore the Bolsheviks in all haste sent troops to Kiev. A furious struggle took place between the Bolsheviks and the Petliurists around Kiev from January 11 to January 25, 1918. On January 25 the Bolsheviks occupied Kiev and soon began to extend their power throughout the Ukraine. The Petliura government and the politicians of the separatist movement retired to the western part of the country, from where they protested against the occupation of the Ukraine by the Bolsheviks.

On this occasion the Bolsheviks did not remain in the Ukraine for a long time—two or three months at most—and they retreated to Great Russia in March-April, 1918, giving way to the Austro-German army of occupation. The Petliurists took advantage of this: their government, in the form of the Central *Rada* and the cabinet of ministers, returned to Kiev and reestablished itself. This time the Republic was not called Democratic, but rather the Ukrainian Peoples' Republic. The government of this Republic, obviously, like every other government, depended on its troops, and when it entered Kiev it did not make the slightest effort to ask whether or not the people needed this government. It took advantage of the situation, simply entered the country, and proclaimed itself the national government. Its main proof was the force of its arms.

But once again the Petliurists did not succeed in remaining at the head of the government for long. For the Austro-German forces which occupied the Ukraine it was much easier to deal with the former lords of the Ukraine—generals and *pomeshchiks*—than with the Petliurists. Consequently, on the basis of their military power, they unceremoniously replaced Petliura with the autocratic government of the Hetman Skoropadsky. This is when the reaction of the *pomeshchiks* and generals began in the Ukraine. In the face of this reaction, the Petliurists took a politically revolutionary position. They looked forward to its collapse so as to return to the head of the State. Petliura himself was imprisoned and thus disappeared from the political arena. But the Hetman's counter-revolution was coming to an end; it began to disintegrate under the blows of the generalized peasant insurrection. Sensing this, the Petliurists, even before the final collapse of the Hetman, began to organize their power in various regions of the Ukraine, and they began to form an army. Circumstances were extremely favorable to them. The peasantry was in a state of revolt, hundreds of thousands of spontaneous insurgents were only waiting for the first call to march against the Hetman's power. The Hetman was still in Kiev when a large number of southern Ukrainian cities had already passed to the hands of the Petliurists. It was there, in the provinces, that the central organ of Petliurist power, the Directorate, was established. The Petliurists hastened to extend and consolidate their power, taking advantage of the absence of other aspirants, especially the Bolsheviks. In December, 1918, Skoropadsky fled, and Petliura's Directorate solemnly entered Kiev, with Petliura himself at its head, together with other members of the government of the People's Republic.

This event aroused great enthusiasm in the country. The Petliurists did everything they could to magnify their success, and posed as national heroes. In a short time their power again extended over most of the Ukraine. It was only in the south, in the region of the Makhnovist peasant movement, that they had no success; on the contrary, they encountered serious resistance and experienced major setbacks. But in all the major centers of the country the Petliurists triumphed, and proudly displayed their banners. This time the domination of the separatist bourgeoisie seemed assured. But this success was illusory.

The new power had hardly had time to install itself before it began to disintegrate because of its contradictory class interests. Millions of peasants and workers who, at the moment of the overthrow of the Hetman, were within the orbit of the Petliurists, were soon disillusioned and began to leave Petliura's ranks in large numbers: they sought another vehicle for their interests and aspirations. The major part dispersed into the cities and villages and there adopted a hostile attitude toward the new power. Others joined the insurrectionary detachments of the Makhnovists with slogans calling for struggle against the ideas and power of the Petliurists. The Petliurists were thus as quickly disarmed as they had been armed by the march of events. Their idea of bourgeois independence, bourgeois national unity, could only last for a few hours among the revolutionary people. The burning breath of the popular revolution reduced this false idea to ashes and left its supporters in complete impotence. And at the same time, military Bolshevism was rapidly approaching from the North, expert in methods of class agitation and firmly resolved to take power in the Ukraine. Just one month after the entry of Petliura's Directorate into Kiev, the Bolshevik troops entered. From that time the Communist power of the Bolsheviks was extended over most of the Ukraine.

Bolshevism. Its Class Character.

We have already said, in the first chapter, that all the so-called socialist construction, the entire Soviet statist and governmental apparatus, all the new social-political relations, in short, everything that was carried out by Bolshevism in the Russian revolution, is nothing more than the realization of the vital interests of the socialist democracy, the establishment of its class domination in the country. The peasants and the workers, whose name was invoked millions of times during the entire Russian revolution, are only the bridge to power for the new caste of rulers, the new masters, the fourth estate.

At the time of the 1905 revolution this caste experienced a defeat. It had hoped to establish its leadership over the workers' movement, and to realize its goals by means of the well-trodden path of politics, starting with its well-known minimum program. At first they proposed the overthrow of the Tsarist regime and the establishment of a republican regime in the country. Then they would proceed to the conquest of State power by parliamentary means, as is done by democrats in Western European and American states. As is known, the plans of the democrats failed completely in Russia in 1905; the peasants and the workers did not give them the necessary support. Some erroneously hold that the defeat of the 1905 revolution was caused by the power and brutality of Tsarism. The causes of this defeat are much more profound; they reside in the very character of the revolution.

From 1900 to 1903, a whole series of massive economic strikes took place in the south of Russia, then in the north and elsewhere. At first this movement did not clearly formulate its goals; nevertheless, its class character soon revealed itself. The socialist democracy entered this movement from outside and attempted to lead it along the path of purely political struggle. Thanks to its numerous and marvelously organized parties, which occupied the entire field of political propaganda, it succeeded in obliterating all the vivid social slogans and in replacing them with the political slogans of the democracy. They determined the course of the 1905 revolution. It was precisely because the revolution took place under slogans foreign to the people that it met defeat. Having excluded from the revolution its social elements, the social program of the workers, the democracy took from it even its sap, because it killed the powerful revolutionary thrust of the people. The 1905 revolution failed, not because Tsarism was too powerful, but because, due to its narrowly political character, it could not arouse the great masses of the people. The revolution aroused only a part of the proletariat of the cities; the entire mass of peasants hardly budged. Tsarism, which had already begun to make concessions, quickly retracted them as soon as it understood the true state of affairs, and it crushed this revolution of half-measures. The revolutionary democracy which led the movement found refuge abroad. But the lesson learned from this defeat could not pass unnoticed. The lesson was completely absorbed by Bolshevism, the left wing of the democracy. The Bolsheviks understood that a purely political revolution was no longer possible in Russia, they saw that the attention of the masses had turned to social problems, and they concluded that a victorious revolution was possible in Russia only as a social movement of workers and peasants which was directed towards overturning the political as well as the *economic* regime. The imperialist war of 1914 to 1917 only accentuated and strengthened this direction of the revolution. By revealing the true face of the democracy, the war showed that the monarchy and the democracy well deserved each other; the one as well as the other showed itself to be a plunderer and murderer of the popular masses. If a purely political revolution was no longer possible in Russia already before the war, the imperialist war killed the very idea of such a revolution.

Throughout the world a volcanic tremor had long ago created an enormous chasm, dividing contemporary society into two distinct and hostile camps: capital and labor. This chasm put an end to the political differences among the various exploiter-States. The destruction of capital, the foundation of slavery—this is the idea which motivates the masses as soon as they turn their attention toward revolution. They are absolutely indifferent to the political upheavals of the past. This was the situation in Russia. This is also the situation in Western Europe and America. Not to see this, not to take it into account, means remaining hopelessly removed from life.

Bolshevism took this aspect of reality into account and promptly revised its political program. The Bolsheviks saw the coming mass revolution in Russia as a revolution directed against the very foundations of modern society: against agricultural, industrial and commercial capital. They saw that the class of proprietors in the cities and the countryside was condemned, and they drew their conclusion: if this is so, if a powerful social explosion is inevitable in Russia, then the democracy must realize its historic task on the terrain of this explosion. The democracy must profit from and make use of the revolutionary forces of the people, place itself at their head during the overthrow of the bourgeoisie, take state power and build the edifice of its domination on the basis of State socialism. And this is what Bolshevism successfully accomplished in the revolutionary mass movement before and during October. All their further activity in the course of the Russian revolution will only be a realization of the details of the democracy's statist domination.

Without a doubt, Bolshevism is a historic event in Russian and international life. It is not only a social, but also a psychological manifestation. It inspired a large number of individuals—stubborn, authoritarian, lacking all social or moral sentimentality and prepared to make use of any means in the struggle for their triumph. Bolshevism also pushed forward a leader perfectly suited to this task. Lenin is not only the leader of a party; he is, more importantly, the leader of a certain psychological type of people. In Lenin this human type finds its most perfect and most powerful personification. It is on this model that the selection and grouping of the combative and offensive forces of the democracy are made throughout the whole world. The basic psychological trait of Bolshevism is the realization of its will by means of the violent elimination of all other wills, the absolute destruction of all individuality, to the point where it becomes an inanimate object. It is not difficult to recognize in these traits an ancient breed of masters. And in fact, it is exclusively by authoritarian acts that Bolshevism makes its presence felt throughout the Russian revolution. It lacks even the shadow of what will constitute the essential trait of the real working class social revolution of the future: the *ardent desire to work,* to work unceasingly, without rest, until one's last breath, with complete disregard for oneself, for the good of the people. All the efforts of Bolshevism, at times enormous and persistent, are nothing more than the creation of authoritarian organs which, in relation to the people, represent only the threats and brutality of former masters.

Let us look briefly at the changes brought about by Bolshevism—in the lives of workers and peasants—which conform to its Communist ideology.

The nationalization of industry, land, urban dwellings, commerce; workers' and peasants' right to vote—these are the fundamentals of pure Bolshevik communism. In reality "nationalization" resulted in the absolute Statification of all forms of social life. Not only industry, transportation, education, distribution networks, etc., became the property of the State, but the entire working class, every worker individually, his work and his energy, trade union organizations and workers' and peasants' cooperatives came under the State. The State is everything, the individual worker—nothing. This is the main precept of Bolshevism. For the State is personified by functionaries, and in fact it is they who are everything; the working class is nothing.

70

The nationalization of industry, removing the workers from the hands of individual capitalists, delivered them to the yet more rapacious hands of a single ever-present capitalist boss, the State. The relations between the workers and this new boss are the same as earlier relations between labor and capital, with the sole difference that the Communist boss, the State, not only exploits the workers, but also punishes them himself, since both of these functions—exploitation and punishment—are combined in him. Wage labor has remained what it was before, except that it has taken on the character of an obligation to the State. Trade unions lost all their natural rights and were transformed into organs of police surveillance of the working masses. The establishment of taxes, wage rates, the right to hire and fire workers, the general management of enterprises, their internal organization, etc.—all this is the exclusive right of the Party, of its organs or of its agents. As for the role of trade unions in all fields of production, it is purely ceremonial: they *must* sign the decrees of the Party, which can neither be challenged nor changed.

It is clear that in all this we are dealing with a simple substitution of State capitalism for private capitalism. The Communist nationalization of industry represents a new type of production relations in which economic slavery, the economic dependence of the working class, is concentrated in a single fist, the State. In essence this in no way improves the situation of the working class. Obligatory labor (for workers, naturally) and the militarization of labor are the spirit of the nationalized factory. Let us give an example. In August, 1918, the workers of the former Prokhorov factory in Moscow became agitated and threatened to rebel against the inadequate wages and the police regime in the factory. They organized several meetings in the factory itself, evicted the factory committee, which was merely a party cell, and took as their wages part of what they had produced. Members of the central administration of the textile workers' union declared, after the mass of workers refused to deal with them: the behavior of the workers in the Prokhorov factory throws a shadow on the authority of Soviet power; all further action of these workers would defame Soviet power in the eyes of workers in other enterprises; this cannot be allowed, and consequently the Prokhorov factory must be closed, the workers must be sent away, a commission should be created which will be able to establish a firm regime in the factory; after which it will be necessary to recruit a new staff of workers. And this was done. It can be asked: who were these people, these three or four men who so freely determined the destiny of thousands of workers? Were they placed in their posts by the masses? Did the people give them such enormous power? Not at all. It was the Party that appointed them, and this was their power. This example is one of thousands. This example, like a drop of water, reflects the true situation of the working class in nationalized industry.

What remains to the workers and to their organizations? A very narrow berth—the right to elect this or that delegate to a soviet completely subservient to the Party.

The situation of the laborers in the countryside is even worse. The peasants made good use of the land of former *pomeshchiks,* princes and other landlords. However, this well-being was not given to them by the Communist power, but by the revolution. For dozens of years they had desired the land and in 1917 they took it, long before the Soviet power was established. If Bolshevism marched with the peasants in their seizure of the *pomeshchiks'* lands, it was only in order to defeat the agrarian bourgeoisie. But this in no way indicated that the future Communist power had the intention of furnishing the peasants land. On the contrary. The ideal of this power is the organization of a single agricultural economy belonging altogether to the same lord, the State. Soviet agricultural estates cultivated by wage workers and peasants—this is the model for the State agriculture which the Communist power strives to extend to the entire country. The leaders of Bolshevism announced this very clearly and simply after the first days of the revolution. In No. 13 of the "Communist International," notably in the resolution on the agrarian problem (pp. 2435-2445, Russian edition) are given detailed descriptions of the organization of State agriculture on this model. In the same resolution it is stated that it is necessary to proceed with the organization of collective (namely, State-capitalist) agriculture gradually and with the greatest prudence. Naturally. The abrupt transformation of tens of millions of peasants from independent farmers into wage workers for the State would inevitably have provoked a dangerous storm which could have led the Communist State to a catastrophe. The concrete activity of the Communist power in the countryside has until today been limited exclusively to the requisition of food and raw materials, and to the struggle against peasant movements which opposed the Communists.

The political rights of peasants. They consist of the compulsory establishment of village and district soviets entirely subordinate to the Party. The peasants have no other rights. The millions of peasants of a particular region, placed on one side of the political scale, will always weigh less than the smallest regional committee of the Party. In short, instead of rights we find a scandalous absence of rights among the peasants.

The Soviet State apparatus is organized in such a way that all the levers of power of the apparatus are in the hands of the democracy, which falsely presents itself as the vanguard of the proletariat. No matter what domain of State administration we examine, everywhere we find the principal places invariably occupied by the same, ever-present democrat.

Who directs all the newspapers, the journals and other publications? Politicians who come out of the privileged democratic circles.

Who writes and manages the central publications which claim to lead the world proletariat, like the *Izvestia* of the V.Ts.I.K. (All-Russian Central Executive Committee), *Communist International,* or the organ of the central committee of the Party? Exclusively hand-picked groups of intellectual-democrats.

And who heads the political organs created, as even their names show, not for the needs of the working class, but for the needs of politics, of domination? In whose hands is the central committee of the Party, the "Sovnarkom" (Council of People's Commissars), the V.Ts.I.K., etc.? Entirely in the hands of those who have been brought up in politics, far from the working class, and who invoke the name of the proletariat the same way as an unbelieving priest invokes the empty name of god. And all the economic organs, beginning with the *Sovnarkhoz* (Council of the National Economy) and ending with the less important "centrals" and "subsidiaries," are also in the same hands.

Thus we see the entire democratic social group occupying the main positions of leadership in the State.

Human history has never known an instance when a specific social group, with its class interests and its class goals, approached the workers in order to help them. No, such groups always go to the people with the sole aim of placing them under their thumb. The democratic group is no exception to this general social rule. On the contrary, it completely and definitively confirms this rule.

If some important posts in the Communist State are occupied by workers, this is only because it is useful to the slave regime; it gives the democratic power an *appearance of popularity* and serves to consolidate, to cement, the edifice of domination of the socialist democracy. The role of these workers is secondary; they mainly carry out orders. In addition, they enjoy privileges at the expense of the entire subjugated working class; they are recruited from among the so-called "conscious workers," namely those who uncritically accept the principles of Marxism and of the socialist movement of the intelligentsia.

In the Communist State the workers and peasants are socially enslaved, economically plundered, and politically deprived of all rights. But this is still not all. Having embarked on the road of general statification, Bolshevism inevitably had to place its hand on the spiritual life of the workers as well. In fact, it would be difficult to find another country where the thought of the workers is oppressed as completely as in the Communist State. Under the pretext of struggling against bourgeois and counter-revolutionary ideas, all publications which do not express the Communist viewpoint are suppressed, even when these publications are published and supported by broad masses of the proletariat. No one is able to express his thoughts out loud. Just as the Bolsheviks have arranged the social and economic life of the country in conformity with their program, they have also driven the spiritual life of the people into the framework of this program. The lively field of popular thought and popular exploration is transformed into the gloomy barracks of military basic training. The mind and soul of the proletariat are shaped in party schools. Any desire to see beyond the walls of this school is proclaimed harmful and counter-revolutionary.

But this still is not all. The distortion of the revolution and its perspectives carried out by Bolshevism with its dictatorship could not pass without protests on the part of the masses and without their attempt to struggle against this distortion. All these protests have not weakened the political oppression, but rather strengthened it. A long period of governmental terror transformed all of Russia into an immense prison, where fear became a virtue and lying became compulsory. Crushed by the political oppression, frightened by the governmental terror, adults lie, young people lie, five-year-old children lie.

The question which arises is why the Communist State has created such an impossible social, political and moral situation. Might the socialist democracy be worse than its predecessor, the capitalist bourgeoisie? Is it possible that the socialist democracy would not even concede the illusory freedoms with which the European and American bourgeoisie preserve an appearance of equilibrium in their States? The problem lies elsewhere. Although the democratic class has its own independent existence, until recently it was materially poor, even indigent. This is why, from the first days of its political activity, it was not able to find within itself the unity and universality which ruling classes enjoy because of their privileged material situation. The democracy produced only a detachment of fighting partisans, represented by the Communist Party, and this detachment had to devote more than three years to the enormous task of building the new State. Having no *natural* support in any of the classes of current society—neither among workers, nor among peasants, nor among the nobility or the bourgeoisie (among whom the democracy itself cannot be included, since it was not economically organized), the Communist Party naturally resorted to terror and to a regime of general oppression.

From what has been shown about the terrorist position of Bolshevism in Russia it is easy to understand why the Communist Party so openly and hurriedly enlarged and solidified the new bourgeoisie personified by the Communist Party, the leading functionaries, and the commanding staff of the army. This bourgeoisie is indispensable to Bolshevism as a natural soil which furnishes it with its vital sap, and as a permanent class support in its struggle against the working masses.

We do not explain the Communist construction we have mentioned, which brings slavery to workers and peasants, in terms of errors or deviations of Bolshevism, but in terms of its conscious aspiration to subordinate the masses, in terms of its domineering and exploitative essence.

But how does it happen that this group, foreign and hostile to the working masses, has succeeded in imposing itself as the leader of the revolutionary forces of the people, making its way to power in the name of the people, and consolidating its domination?

There are two causes: the atomized, disorganized condition of the masses in the days of the revolution, and the deception of the socialist slogans.

The professional organizations of workers and peasants which existed before 1917 were far behind the fiery revolutionary spirit of the masses. The revolutionary outburst of the masses went far beyond the limits of these organizations, surpassing and submerging them. The immense mass of workers and peasants faced the spreading social revolution without the necessary support or assistance of their own class organizations. And alongside this mass operated a marvelously organized socialist party (the Bolsheviks). Together with the workers and peasants this Party directly participated in the overthrow of the industrial and agrarian bourgeoisie, calling on the masses to carry this out, assuring them that this revolution would be the social—the last—revolution leading the enslaved to the free realm of socialism and communism. To the vast masses, inexperienced in politics, this seemed to be the obvious truth. The participation of the Communist Party in the destruction of the capitalist regime gave rise to enormous confidence in it. The stratum of intellectual workers who were the carriers of the ideals of the democracy was always so thin and sparse that the masses knew nothing of its existence as a specific economic category. Consequently, at the moment of the overthrow of the bourgeoisie, the masses saw no one other than themselves who might replace the bourgeoisie. And it was precisely at this moment that the bourgeoisie was in fact replaced by these accidental leaders, the deceitful Bolsheviks, experienced in political demagogy.

76

Shamelessly exploiting the revolutionary aspirations of workers and peasants for freedom, equality and social independence, Bolshevism very skillfully substituted its idea of soviet power.

In many parts of revolutionary Russia in the early days of the October upheaval, workers understood the idea of soviet power as the idea of their social and economic independence.

Thanks to its revolutionary energy and its demagogic confusion of the revolutionary idea of the workers with its own idea of political domination, Bolshevism drew the masses to itself and made extensive use of their confidence.

The misfortune of the masses consisted of the fact that they accepted the doctrines of socialism and communism completely and straightforwardly, as the people always accept the ideas of truth, justice and goodness. However, in these doctrines truth is nothing more than a lure, a beautiful promise which moves and exalts the soul of the people. As in all other State systems, the essence of this "truth" is the capture and distribution of the people's forces and their labor by a small but well-organized group of parasites.

In the whirlwind of events which swept across Russia and the Ukraine, in the avalanche of political, military and other operations, the rise to power of a new group of exploiters was not at first clearly perceived by the vast masses of the people. In addition, the definitive consolidation of this power took several years. Furthermore, this development was extensive and was skillfully masked by the interested group. A certain time was needed before it could reveal itself to the broad masses.

At the time of the great French revolution, when feudalism—the monarchy of kings and nobles—was definitively destroyed, the masses thought that they were engaged in this great destruction for the sake of their freedom, and that the political parties at the forefront were only friends and helpers. Several years passed before the working people, looking carefully around them, realized that what had taken place was a simple replacement of the authorities, that the places of the king and the nobles were now occupied by a new class of exploitative masters: the industrial and commercial bourgeoisie. Such historical facts always need a certain time to become visible and comprehensible to the large masses.

* * *

We have given a broad outline of the political and social foundations of Bolshevism, its real content. After two years of its dictatorship in Russia, Bolshevism made its content plainly visible. This became evident to isolated groups of workers and peasants at first, and later to the vast masses of people. This was the youthful force, full of authoritarian aspirations, which, after the fall of the Hetman, set out with an unbending will to establish its power in the Ukraine, cost what it may.

At the time of the Hetman Skoropadsky, the Bolsheviks did not have enough power in the Ukraine to enable them to organize the immediate seizure of power in the Ukraine when the Hetman fell.[1] Nearly all their forces were in Great Russia, and it is from there that they kept their eyes on the Ukraine, waiting for the opportune moment to move on the Ukraine and proclaim their power. It was in Great Russia, in the city of Kursk, that the Bolsheviks' Ukrainian government was prepared in advance; it included Pyatakov, Kviring, and others. In spite of all their vigilance, they did not succeed in attacking the Ukraine at the moment of Skoropadsky's fall, and this enabled the Petliurists to seize power first. But this circumstance led them to take even more energetic military measures. The atmosphere was revolutionary, the situation was extremely mixed up because of

[1] Actually, at the time of the Hetman, the Bolsheviks tried to have partisan detachments of their type in the country which were to carry out the orders of the Party. Such was the detachment of Kolosov in the Pavlograd region. But the number of these detachments was small, and they were submerged by the large mass of insurgents who followed a path independent of the Party. In addition, these rare Party-type detachments were infected by the general spirit of the revolutionary insurrection. The detachment of Kolosov did not draw a sharp line between its insurrectional activity and that of Makhno. They often worked together.

78

the massive insurrectionary movement of the peasants. In these circumstances the six weeks gained by the Petliurists over the Bolsheviks were easily swallowed by the march of events. What was needed was quick action. And the Bolsheviks rushed into action.

While the seat of their Ukrainian government was moved from Kursk to Khar'kov, which was first liberated and occupied by the insurrectionary detachment of the anarchist Cherednyakov,[2] and there proceeded to create a center of civil administration, their military divisions advanced through the already liberated regions into the depths of the Ukraine and established organs of Communist power throughout, by military force. We said: already liberated regions. Actually, the entire expanse of the Ukraine from the government of Kursk to the Sea of Azov and the Black Sea, had already been liberated from the Hetman's forces by peasant revolutionary insurrectionary detachments. With the fall of the Hetman these detachments partially dispersed throughout the villages, and partially retired to the coastal regions of the Sea of Azov, where there was already a threat of a new counter-revolution, that of General Denikin.

In most of the Ukraine the Bolsheviks found that the terrain had already been cleared. In the places where they encountered Petliurists, they defeated them by military force and took their place. The decisive encounter between the Bolsheviks and the Petliurists took place in the region of Kiev, which from the time of the entry of the Directorate had been the center of Petliurist political activity and the rallying point for Petliura's troops. At the end of January 1919, the Bolsheviks began a general attack against Kiev. At the beginning of February they occupied Kiev. The government of the Ukrainian People's Republic retreated, as usual,

[2]*Cherednyakov* was a peasant and an anarchist who was soon outlawed by the Bolshevik authorities. He and his detachment joined the general insurrectionary army of Makhno, and he fought on the Azov front against Denikin. At the time of Denikin's invasion of the Gulyai-Polye region in June, 1919, he was captured and given 300 blows of the whip. He escaped. In the summer of 1919 he again fell into the hands of Denikin's troops in the region of Poltava, and was shot.

toward the western frontiers of the Ukraine. State power passed to the Bolsheviks.

It is important to note that the Communist power installed itself by military force, not only when the Bolsheviks occupied a place after a battle to drive out the Petliurists, but also in places where the region was already free and the peasants were on their own. The workers' and peasants' soviets (councils), which had supposedly created this power, appeared after the power was already established. Before the soviets there were Party "revolutionary committees." And before the "revolutionary committees" there were simply military divisions.

Chapter 5

The Makhnovshchina.

The revolutionary insurrectionary movement of the Ukrainian peasants and workers at first had the character of a tempestuous sea. Throughout the immense stretches of the Ukraine, the masses seethed, rushing into revolt and struggle. High-handed *pomeshchiks* and representatives of power were killed or chased from their midst. The destructive side of the movement was dominant. The positive side seemed to be lacking. The movement did not yet offer a clear and precise plan for the organization of the free life of the peasants and workers. But gradually, in the process of its development, the real content of the movement was revealed and formed. After the unification of the majority of the insurrectionary currents under Makhno's leadership, the movement found the unity which it had lacked, its backbone. From this time on it represents an accomplished and clearly defined social movement with its specific ideology and its own plan for the organization of the life of the people. It is the most powerful and the highest point of the revolutionary insurrection, the Makhnovshchina.

The characteristic traits specific to this movement are: a profound distrust of non-working or privileged social groups; suspicion of political parties; rejection of all dictatorships over the people by any and all organizations; rejection of the principle of the State; complete self-direction of the working people in all their affairs. The primary and concrete form of this self-direction consists of free working councils of peasants' and workers' organizations. "Free" means that they would be absolutely independent of all forms of central power, taking part in the general economic system on the basis of equality. "Working" means that these councils would be based on the principle of work, composed only of workers, serving their interests and their will, and giving no access to political organizations. (See "The General Positions

81

of Makhnovists on the Free Councils of Workers' and Peasants' Organizations.'') This was the banner under which the Makhnovshchina entered the arena of social struggle.

The Makhnovshchina originated in the stormy era of contemporary Ukrainian life in the summer of 1918, when the entire peasantry thundered in revolt. From the first days of its existence until its very last moments, it did not have a single day of peace. As a result its growth and its entire evolution followed a specific, double path—the path of introducing its basic ideas to the vast masses of the people, and the path of enlarging and consolidating its military forces. From the day when all the military-revolutionary detachments were united in a single army, this army became the sole revolutionary army of the masses. The fact that the Ukraine was in a constant state of war was the reason why the best organizational powers of the movement were engaged in the army. This army involuntarily became both the armed self-defense of the peasants, and the leader of their entire movement, their revolutionary avant-garde. The army organized and actively led the offensive against the *pomeshchik* counter-revolution, drew up the plan for the struggle, and coined the slogans of the day. Nevertheless, the army was never a self-sufficient force. It always derived its revolutionary ideas from the vast masses, and defended their interests. The peasant masses, on their side, considered this army as the leading organ in all facets of their existence.[1]

The attitude of the Makhnovshchina toward State power, toward political parties, toward unproductive groups, became the attitude of the peasants, and conversely, the interests of the poorest peasants and workers, their hardships and their thoughts, became the interests, the hardships and

---

[1] Certain characteristic facts can serve as examples. Very often the peasants of different villages on the Azov seacoast stopped trains with food supplies and verified the documents. If they lacked the papers of the staff of the Makhnovist army, the trains were delayed until information was received from the Makhnovists. It also frequently happened that the peasants of many villages responded to the appeal of Bolshevik organizations to deliver grain to the State at a fixed price by telling the Bolsheviks that they would be happy to furnish the grain, if the Makhnovist organization agreed.

82

the thoughts of the Makhnovshchina. Thus the Makhnovist movement developed through mutual interaction, and soon became an immense social phenomenon in Russian life.

* * *

In October and November 1918, Makhno's detachments began a general attack against the Hetman's counter-revolution. At this time the Austro-German troops, influenced by the political events taking place in their countries, were already disorganized, and lacked their former force and energy. Makhno took advantage of this. He negotiated, and established relations of neutrality with units of soldiers who had caught the revolutionary spirit. These units allowed themselves to be disarmed, and the Makhnovists were able to arm themselves at their expense. Where Makhno failed to get on good terms with the Austro-Germans, he chased them from the region by force. After a fierce three-day battle Makhno definitively occupied Gulyai-Polye. There he consolidated his position and organized the general staff of his army. Everywhere people sensed the approaching end of the Hetman's reign, and the peasant youth thronged in large numbers toward Makhno. Already at this time his army consisted of several infantry and cavalry regiments with one battery and numerous machine guns.

None of the Hetman's troops were in the region. The State *Varta* (Guard) scattered in the face of the extraordinary growth of the insurrectionary army. Makhno's army remained the sole army in this enormous region. But the Hetman still held Kiev. So Makhno and his troops headed north, occupying the railway junctions of Chaplino, Grishino, Sinel'nikovo, reaching the city of Pavlograd, where he turned west in the direction of Ekaterinoslav. There he encountered the forces of Petliura.

The Petliurists, having seized power in a number of cities, considered themselves the real masters of the country. They formed their army by gathering a number of peasant detachments; then they decreed a general mobilization with the aim of creating a regular national army. They considered the Makhnovist movement an important episode in the Ukrainian revolution and hoped to attract it into their sphere of influence and bring it under their direction. They sent Makhno a series of political questions: what was his opinion of the Petliurist movement and of Petliura's government; how did he envision the political structure of the Ukraine; would he not find it desirable and useful to work in common with Petliura for the creation of an independent Ukraine? The response of Makhno and his staff was brief. They declared that in their opinion the Petliurist movement was a bourgeois nationalist movement whose road was entirely different from that of the revolutionary peasants; that the Ukraine should be organized on the basis of free labor and the independence of the peasants and workers from every political power. Not union, but only struggle was possible between the Makhnovist movement of the working people and the Petliurist movement of the bourgeoisie.

Shortly after, Makhno marched toward Ekaterinoslav in order to throw out the Petliurist government. Petliura had large military forces there. Protected by the Dnieper River, the Petliurists were almost invincible in this city. Makhno's detachments stopped at Nizhne-Dneprovsk, where there was a city committee of the Communist Party which disposed of some local armed forces. Makhno, being known in the region as a valiant revolutionary hero and a very gifted military guide, was offered the command of the Party's workers' detachments by this Committee. Makhno accepted.

As he often did, Makhno had recourse to a military ruse. He loaded a train with his troops and sent it across the Dnieper bridge straight into the city, disguised as a workers' [commuter] train. The risk was great. If the Petliurists had discovered this ruse a few minutes before the train stopped, the whole troop would have been captured. But the same risk cleared the Makhnovists' path to victory. The train entered the central station, where the revolutionary troops unexpectedly disembarked and immediately occupied the station as well as its surroundings. In the city itself a fierce battle broke out in which the Petliurists were defeated. But a few days later, due to the faulty vigilance of a Makhnovist garrison, the city was retaken by the Petliurists, who had returned with new forces from Zaporozh'e. During the retreat, there were two assassination attempts against Makhno in Nizhne-Dneprovsk. Both times the bombs thrown at him failed to go off. The Makhnovist army retreated to the Sinel'nikovo region, where it dug in and established a front between itself and the Petliurists on the north-west frontier of the insurgent region. Petliura's troops, composed chiefly of insurgent peasants or conscripts, rapidly disintegrated upon contact with the Makhnovists. And soon this front melted away without a battle. An immense space of several thousand miles was liberated from all authority and all troops.

* * *

Statists fear free people. They claim that without authority people will lose the anchor of sociability, will dissipate themselves, and will return to savagery. This is obviously rubbish. It is taken seriously by idlers, lovers of authority and of the labor of others, or by the blind thinkers of bourgeois society. The liberation of the people in reality leads to the degeneration and return to savagery, not of the people, but of those who, thanks to power and privilege, live from the labor of the people's arms and from the blood of the people's veins. The Russian revolution gives an example of how thousands of families from the privileged class—clean, well nourished and well groomed—fell to decadence and savagery. The revolution deprived them of their servants, and in a month or two they were covered with dirt, they were mangy. The liberation of the people leads to the savagery of those who live from its enslavement. As for the working people, it is precisely from the day when they become really and completely free that they begin to live and to develop intensely. The peasants of the Gulyai-Polye region made this plainly visible. For more than six months—from November 1918 to June 1919—they lived without any external political authority. They not only maintained social bonds with each other, but they also created new and higher forms of social relations—free workers' communes and free councils of working people.

85

After the expulsion of the *pomeshchiks* from the liberated regions, the land came into the hands of the peasants. But many of the peasants understood that the task was not finished, that it was not enough to appropriate a plot of land and be content with it. From the hardships of their lives they learned that enemies were watching them from all sides, and that they must stick together. In several places there were attempts to organize social life communally. In spite of the hostility of the peasants toward the official communes, in many places in the Gulyai-Polye region peasant communes were formed, called "working" communes and "free" communes. The first free commune, called Rosa Luxemburg, was organized near the village of Pokrovskoe. All of its members were indigent. At first it only contained a few dozen members, but later the number exceeded three hundred. This commune was created by the poorest local peasants. In consecrating it to the memory of Rosa Luxemburg, they gave witness to their impartiality. With a simplicity and generosity typical of peasants, they honored the memory of a revolutionary heroine, unknown to them, who had been a martyr in the revolutionary struggle. The internal life of the commune had nothing in common with the doctrine for which Rosa Luxemburg had struggled. The commune was based on anti-authoritarian principles. Its development and growth began to exercise great influence over the local peasants. The Communist authorities tried to intervene in the internal life of the commune, but they were not admitted. The commune firmly called itself free, working, and foreign to all authority.[2]

About five miles from Gulyai-Polye, on a former estate, another commune was formed, which consisted of poor peasants of Gulyai-Polye. It was called simply Commune No. 1 of the Gulyai-Polye peasants. About thirteen

---

[2]This commune was destroyed on June 9th and 10th, 1919, by the Bolsheviks, during their general campaign against the Makhnovist region. At that time, Comrade Kir'yakov, well-known local revolutionary peasant, as well as other organizers of the commune, were declared outlaws. Some days later, when the village of Pokrovskoe was occupied by Denikin's troops, the commune was completely destroyed and Kir'yakov was publicly shot.

miles away were Commune No. 2 and Commune No. 3. There were communes in a number of other places. Admittedly, the communes were not numerous, and included only a minority of the population—especially those who did not have well-established farmlands. But what was most precious was that these communes were formed on the initiative of the poor peasants themselves. The Makhnovists never exerted any pressure on the peasants, confining themselves to propagating the idea of free communes.

The communes were not created on the basis of example or caprice, but exclusively on the basis of the vital needs of peasants who had possessed nothing before the revolution and who, after their victory, set about organizing their economic life on a communal basis. These were not at all the artificial communes of the Communist Party, in which people assembled by chance worked together—people who only wasted the grain and damaged the soil, who enjoyed the support of the State and thus lived from the labor of those whom they pretended to teach how to work. These were real working communes of peasants who, themselves accustomed to work, valued work in themselves and in others. The peasants worked in these communes first of all to provide their daily bread. In addition, each found there whatever moral and material support he needed. The principles of brotherhood and equality permeated the communes. Everyone—men, women and children—worked according to his or her abilities. Organizational work was assigned to one or two comrades who, after finishing it, took up the remaining tasks together with the other members of the commune. It is evident that these communes had these traits because they grew out of a working milieu and that their development followed a natural course.

However, these seeds of free communism did not nearly represent all the constructive economic and social activities of the peasants. On the contrary, they only grew slowly and gradually, whereas the political situation demanded from the peasants immediate and general attention. It was indispensable to establish institutions which unified first a district composed of various villages, and then the districts and departments which composed the liberated region. It was indispensable to find general solutions for problems common to the entire region. It was indispensable to create organs suitable for these tasks. And the peasants did not fail to create them. These organs were the regional congresses of peasants and workers. During the period when the region remained free, there were three such congresses. Here the peasants strengthened their contacts, oriented themselves, and defined the economic and political tasks which they faced. At the first regional congress which took place on January 23, 1918, in the town of Bol'shaya Mikhailovka, the peasants directed their attention mainly to the danger from the movements of Petliura and Denikin.

The Petliurists were in the process of organizing a new government in the country. Making use of a misleading slogan, "defense of the country," they carried out a general mobilization, thus tightening the knot of a new slavery around the revolutionary people. The revolutionary peasantry of the entire Azov seacoast decided to struggle energetically against this danger. They organized several detachments and commissions and sent them to the region occupied by Petliura's Directorate with the aim of explaining to the broad masses the falsity of the new democratic power, calling on them to disobey this authority, to boycott the mobilization and to continue the insurrection until the overthrow of this power.

The counter-revolution of Denikin represented an even greater danger for the liberated region. It declared war on the entire Russian revolution in all its aspects and represented one of the general counter-revolutionary currents which aimed at the restoration of the deposed monarchy. This counter-revolution appeared as soon as the nobility came to itself and looked around after the fall of Tsarism. Generals Kornilov, Kaledin, Krasnov, Alekseev, Kolchak and Denikin were all leaders of the same general monarchist counter-revolution in Russia. They were the living debris of the overthrown monarchy. If many of them had recourse to democratic slogans and marched under constitutional banners, they did this only for tactical reasons. They made these concessions because of the requirements of the times in order to carry through successfully the first stages of the restoration of the monarchy. Any form of republican spirit was absolutely foreign to them.

The second regional congress of peasants, workers and insurgents was held three weeks after the first congress, on February 12, 1919 in Gulyai-Polye. At this congress, the danger which the impending counter-revolution of Denikin represented for the liberated region was thoroughly examined. Denikin's army consisted of varied counter-revolutionary elements: former Tsarist officers and Imperial Cossacks. The peasants were perfectly aware of the nature of the confrontation between them and this army. They took all the measures necessary to reinforce their self-defense. The insurrectionary army of the Makhnovists at this time numbered around 20,000 volunteer fighters. But many of them were worn out by fatigue, having engaged in incessant battles for five or six months. Moreover, Denikin's troops were rapidly growing stronger, immensely endangering the free region. The second congress of peasants, workers and insurgents thus resolved to call the inhabitants of the region to a ten-year, *voluntary* and *egalitarian* mobilization. The mobilization was to be voluntary, based on the conscience and good will of each. The decree of the congress had no other meaning than to *emphasize,* to sanction by its moral authority, the need to strengthen the insurrectionary army with new soldiers.[3] "Egalitarian" mobilization meant that the peasants of various villages, towns or districts were expected to take on themselves the obligation of furnishing soldiers on an egalitarian basis.

Once the resolutions of the second congress were made known to the peasants of the region, each village began to send to Gulyai-Polye masses of new volunteers desiring to go to the front against Denikin. The number of such fighters was enormous. Unfortunately, there was a shortage of arms in the region, and as a result new insurrectionary detachments could not be formed at the opportune moment. This had un-

---

[3]Some members of the army, as well as some peasants, later interpreted this mobilization as compulsory. In their opinion the decree of the congress, which reflected the will of the working people of the entire region, and which was expressed in the form of an invitation, was to be strictly carried out. This was an error and a misinterpretation on the part of some individuals. The mobilization decree of the congress was simply an appeal to join the army voluntarily.

avoidable consequences for the region during Denikin's general offensive in June, 1919. We will return to this later.

To coordinate the struggle against Petliura and Denikin, to maintain and support the social relations among the working people of the region, to take care of the needs for information and communication, and finally to put into practice the various measures which were adopted by the congress, the second congress established a *Regional* Revolutionary Military Council (Soviet) of peasants, workers and insurgents. It was made up of representatives from 32 districts from the governments of Ekaterinoslav and Tauride, as well as insurrectionary detachments. This Council embraced the whole free region. It was supposed to carry out all the economic, political, social and military decisions made at the congress, and thus was, in a sense, the supreme executive organ of the whole movement. But it was not at all an authoritarian organ. Only strictly executive functions were assigned to it. Its role was to carry out the instructions and decisions of the congress of workers and peasants. At any moment it could be dissolved by the congress and cease to exist.

After the creation of the Regional Council the social activity of the region became more intense. In all the towns and villages, problems common to the entire area were examined and resolved. These included principally the military problem, the problem of provisions, and the question of local self-management. We have already spoken of the military measures taken by the peasants with a view to the needs of the moment and of the region. The problem of provisions was not yet resolved on an extensive scale with a view to the interests of the whole population of the region. This problem was to be resolved on this scale at the 4th regional congress of peasants, workers, insurgents and soldiers of the Red Army called for June 15, 1919, but outlawed by the Soviet authorities. We will speak of this later. As for the insurrectionary army, the peasants undertook to supply it. A central supply depot for the army was organized at Gulyai-Polye, where food and forage were brought from all parts of the region, to be taken from there to the front.

With respect to the organs of social self-government, the peasants and workers of the entire region held to the idea of Free Working Soviets. Unlike the political soviets of the Bolsheviks and other socialists, the free soviets of workers and peasants were to be organs of social-economic self-management. Each soviet was only to carry out the will of the local workers and their organizations. Among themselves the local soviets established indispensable links and thus formed larger economic and territorial relations, organs of popular self-management.

Nevertheless, the constant state of war in the entire region made the creation and functioning of these organs very difficult, and the organization was never carried through to its logical conclusions.

The general statutes on the Free Soviets of peasants and workers were not published until 1920. Before that date, the general principles of these soviets appeared in the "Declaration" of the revolutionary military council of the Makhnovist army, in the chapter on the system of Free Soviets.

Thus we see that the vast peasant masses and some of the workers, having liberated themselves from the regime of the Hetman and other authorities, undertook the immense task of constructing a new life in theory and in practice. We see that, although surrounded on all sides by various hostile forces, the working masses took healthy and reasonable measures for the defense of their region and its spark of freedom. The creation of a whole series of free working communes, the desire to create organs for social and economic self-management, were the first steps of the peasants and workers toward the construction of a free and independent life. There is no doubt that the entire mass of working people, if they had remained free, would have followed this path and would have carried out this construction with many healthy, original and wise elements, thus laying the foundation for a truly free workers' society.

But already the mortal enemy of freedom and labor—Authority—approached the region. From the north came the State army of the Bolshevik-Communists, and from the southeast, the army of General Denikin.

Denikin arrived first. Already in the period of the peasant struggle against the Hetman, and especially during the first days after his fall, several counter-revolutionary detachments commanded by General Shkuro had infiltrated into the Ukraine along the Don and Kuban Rivers and had approached Pologi and Gulyai-Polye. This was the first threat of the new counter-revolution against the liberated region. Naturally the Makhnovist insurgent army moved its forces in this direction. At this time it consisted of several extremely well-organized infantry and cavalry regiments. The Makhnovist infantry was equipped in a very unusual and original way. They moved like cavalry, with the aid of horses, not on horseback but in light carriages with springs, called *Tachanka* in the southern Ukraine. This infantry, forming one or two rows, usually travelled at a rapid trot together with the cavalry, covering 40 to 50 miles a day, and if necessary 60 to 70.

Denikin was counting on the confused general situation in the Ukraine, and especially on the struggle between the Petliurist Directorate and the Bolsheviks; he hoped to occupy most of the Ukraine without much difficulty, and to establish his front, at least at the beginning, beyond the northern limits of the government of Ekaterinoslav. But he unexpectedly encountered the well-organized and tenacious army of Makhnovist insurgents. After several battles, Denikin's detachments had to beat a retreat in the direction of the Don River and the Sea of Azov. In a short time all the territory from Pologi to the sea was liberated. The Makhnovists occupied several important railway stations and the cities of Berdyansk and Mariupol'. It was from this moment —January 1919—that the first front against Denikin was established—a front along which the Makhnovist army for six months contained the flood of the counter-revolution pouring in from the Caucasus. This front was later extended for more than 60 miles to the east and northeast of Mariupol'.

The fighting on this front was stubborn and fierce. Denikin's forces, following the example of the Makhnovists, used the partisans' tactics. Their cavalry detachments would penetrate deep into the region, then spread out rapidly, destroying, burning and massacring all they could reach; then they would vanish and appear suddenly in another place, to commit similar destruction. It was exclusively the laboring people who suffered from these incursions. Denikin's forces took revenge for the help which the peasants gave to the insurgent army and for their hostility toward the counter-revolutionaries; in this way they hoped to provoke a reaction against the revolution. The Jewish population which had lived for a very long time in independent colonies in the Azov region also suffered from these raids. Denikin's detachments massacred Jews on every visit, thus seeking to provoke an anti-Semitic movement which would have prepared the ground for their definitive invasion of the Ukraine. General Shkuro was particularly noteworthy in these counter-revolutionary incursions.

However, for more than four months, despite their well-trained and well-armed troops, despite their furious attacks, Denikin's forces could not subdue the insurgent troops who were full of revolutionary ardor and quite as skillful at guerrilla warfare. On the contrary, General Shkuro more than once received such blows from the Makhnovist regiments that only hasty retreats of 50 to 90 miles toward Taganrog and Rostov saved him from catastrophe. During this period the Makhnovists advanced at least five or six times to the walls of Taganrog. The hatred and fury of Denikin's officers toward the Makhnovists took incredible forms. They subjected Makhnovist prisoners to torture, mangled them by exploding shells, and there were instances when they burned prisoners alive on sheets of red-hot iron.[4]

During this bitter four-month struggle, Makhno's military talent was revealed in a striking manner. His reputation as a remarkable war leader was recognized even by his enemies, the Denikinists. This, obviously, did not prevent General Denikin from offering half a million roubles to whoever killed Makhno.

The revolutionary insurrection was an attempt of the masses of the people to carry out in practice the unrealized aspirations of the Russian revolution. The insurrection was an organic continuation of the massive movement of workers and peasants of October, 1917, and was propelled by the same goals as this movement and imbued with a profound sense of brotherhood toward working people of all nationalities and regions.

Let us describe a characteristic event. At the beginning

[4]See *Put' k Svobode,* No. 2 and No. 3.

of 1919, the Makhnovist insurgents, having thrown back Denikin's troops toward the Sea of Azov after a hard fight, captured a hundred carloads of wheat from them. The first thought of Makhno and the staff of the insurgent army was to send this booty to the starving workers of Moscow and Petrograd. This idea was enthusiastically accepted by the mass of insurgents. The hundred carloads of wheat were delivered to Petrograd and Moscow, accompanied by a Makhnovist delegation which was very warmly received by the Moscow Soviet.

* * *

The Bolsheviks entered the region of the Makhnovshchina much later than Denikin. The Makhnovist insurgents had already been fighting Denikin for three months; they had driven him out of their region and established their line of defense to the east of Mariupol' when the first Bolshevik division, commanded by Dybenko, arrived at Sinel'nikovo.

At this point Makhno himself, as well as the entire insurrectionary movement, were essentially unknown to the Bolsheviks. Until then he had been spoken of in the Communist press—in Moscow and in the provinces—as a bold insurgent of great promise for the future. His fight with Skoropadsky, then with Petliura and Denikin, brought him the good will of the Bolshevik leaders. They did not doubt that the Makhnovist revolutionary detachments, which had fought against so many different counter-revolutions in the Ukraine, would be incorporated into the Red Army. Consequently they sang Makhno's praises in advance, and devoted whole columns of their newspapers to him, without having made his acquaintance. The first meeting between the Bolshevik military command and Makhno took place in March 1919, under the same auspices of praise and good will. Makhno was immediately invited to join the Red Army with all his detachments in order to create a united front in the struggle against Denikin. The political and ideological differences between the Bolsheviks and the Makhnovist peasants were considered completely natural and were not in any way considered an obstacle to a union on the basis of a common cause. The Bolsheviks let it be understood that the specific characteristics of the insurrectionary army would not be violated.

Makhno and the staff of the insurrectionary army were perfectly aware that the arrival of Communist authority was a new threat to the liberty of the region; they saw it as an omen of a civil war of a new kind. But neither Makhno nor the staff of the army nor the Regional Council wanted this war, which might well have a fatal effect on the whole Ukrainian revolution. They did not lose sight of the open and well organized counter-revolution which was approaching from the Don and the Kuban, and with which there was only one possible relationship: that of armed conflict. This danger increased from day to day. The insurgents retained some hope that the struggle with the Bolsheviks could be confined to the realm of ideas, in which case they could feel perfectly secure about their region, for the vigor of the revolutionary ideas together with the revolutionary common sense of the peasants and their defiance of elements foreign to their free movement were the best guarantee of the region's freedom. According to the general opinion of the leaders of the insurrection, it was necessary for the movement to concentrate all forces against the monarchist counter-revolution, and not to be concerned with ideological disagreements with the Bolsheviks until that was liquidated. It was in this context that the union between the Makhnovists and the Red Army took place. We will see later that the leaders of the Makhnovshchina were mistaken in their hope to find in the Bolsheviks only ideological adversaries. They failed to take into account the fact that they were dealing with accomplished and violent statists. Mistakes which do not lead to ruin may be useful. And this mistake did the Makhnovists some good.

The insurrectionary army became part of the Red Army under the following conditions: a) the insurrectionary army will retain its internal organization intact; b) it will receive political commissars appointed by the Communist authorities; c) it will only be subordinated to the Red supreme command in strictly military matters; d) it cannot be removed from the front against Denikin; e) it will receive munitions and supplies equal to those of the Red Army; f) it will retain its name of Revolutionary Insurrectionary Army, and its black flag.

The Makhnovist insurrectionary army was organized according to three fundamental principles: voluntary enlistment, the electoral principle, and self-discipline.

Voluntary enlistment meant that the army was composed only of revolutionary fighters who entered it of their own free will.

The electoral principle meant that the commanders of all the units of the army, including the staff, as well as all the men who held other positions in the army, were either elected or accepted by the insurgents of the unit in question or by the whole army.

Self-discipline meant that all the rules of discipline were drawn up by commissions of insurgents, then approved by general assemblies of the various units; once approved, they had to be rigorously observed on the individual responsibility of each insurgent and each commander.

All these principles were maintained by the Makhnovist army when it joined the Red Army. It was first called the Third Brigade, then the First Revolutionary-Insurrectionary Ukrainian Division, and still later it became the "Revolutionary Insurrectionary Army of the Ukraine (Makhnovist)." All political questions were excluded from the alliance, which remained exclusively military. As a result, the life of the region, its social and revolutionary development, continued to follow the same path—the path of self-activity of the working people who did not allow any authority to enter the region. We will see later that this was the sole reason for the Bolsheviks' armed aggression against this region.

Since the creation of the Regional Council in February, 1919, the region had been solidly united. The idea of free working soviets reached the most distant towns of the region. In the circumstances of the time, the creation of these soviets proceeded slowly, but the peasants held consistently to this idea, feeling that it was the only sound basis on which a really free community could be constructed. At the same time the problem of direct and solid union between the peasants and the urban workers arose. Such a union was to be established directly with the workers' enterprises and organizations, outside of State organs. This union was indispensable for the consolidation and subsequent development of the revolution. The peasants were perfectly aware that its accomplishment would inevitably provoke a struggle with the State and governmental Party, who would certainly not renounce its hold over the masses without a struggle. However, the peasants did not feel that this danger was too serious, for they considered that once they and the workers were *united,* they could easily defy any political power. And above all, forms of union with the workers which were not direct and which did not lead to the suppression of authority and thus to its opposition, were out of the question. For it was precisely *this* form of union between city and village which made possible the consolidation and further development of the revolution. "Worker, give us your hand"—such was the call of the Gulyai-Polye revolutionary peasants to the city. For the peasants of the liberated region this was the only reasonable appeal. In their village they were completely free; they disposed of themselves, and of the product of their labor, independently. Naturally they wanted to see the urban workers in the same situation and sought to approach them directly, avoiding all political, governmental or other unproductive organizations which had caused them too much suffering in the past. They also wanted the workers to come to them just as directly.

This is how the problem of union with the city workers was raised and discussed, until it finally became an objective of the whole insurrectionary region.

It is obvious that in the face of such attitudes, political parties could have no success in the area. When they appeared with statist plans of organization, they were received coldly, indifferently, sometimes even with hostility, as people who came uninvited to meddle in other people's affairs. The Communist authorities who penetrated into all parts of the region were received as foreigners and intruders.

At first the Bolsheviks hoped to absorb the Makhnovists into the ranks of Bolshevism. This was a vain hope. The insurgent masses obstinately followed their own path. They wanted nothing to do with the governmental organs of the Bolsheviks. In certain places armed peasants drove the "Extra-

97

ordinary Commissions" (Chekas) out of their villages, and at Gulyai-Polye the Communists did not even dare to establish such an institution. Elsewhere the attempts to implant Communist institutions resulted in bloody collisions between the population and the authorities, whose situation became very difficult.

It was then that the Bolsheviks began an organized struggle against the Makhnovshchina, both as an idea and as a social movement.

They began the campaign in the press. The Communist press began to treat the Makhnovist movement as a *kulak* (wealthy peasant) movement, its slogans as counter-revolutionary, and its activity as harmful to the revolution.

Direct threats to the guides of the movement were made by the newspapers and by the central authorities. The region was definitively blockaded. All the revolutionary militants leaving Gulyai-Polye or returning to it were arrested. Supplies of ammunition and cartridges were reduced considerably. All this was a bad omen.

On April 10, 1919, the Revolutionary Military Council convened the third regional congress of peasants, workers and insurgents. The congress was to determine the immediate tasks and to consider the perspectives of revolutionary life in the region. The delegates of 72 districts, representing more than two million people, took part in the work of the congress. This work took place in a lively atmosphere. I regret that I have no transcripts of the proceedings, for from them one would have been able to see clearly with what wisdom and clarity the people sought their own course in the revolution and their own popular forms for a new life. Toward the end of its session the Congress received a telegram from Dybenko, commander of the Bolshevik division, which declared the organizers of the Congress outlaws, and the Congress itself, counter-revolutionary.

This was the first direct assault of the Bolsheviks on the freedom of the region. The entire Congress understood perfectly the full significance of this attack and immediately voted an indignant resolution protesting this attack. The protest was immediately printed and distributed among the peasants and workers of the region. Several days later the Revolutionary Military Council of the region gave a detailed reply to the Communist authorities (in the person of Dybenko) in which they emphasized the role of the Gulyai-Polye region in the revolution, and unmasked those who in reality were engaged in counter-revolutionary practice. This response characterizes the positions of both parties, and we include it in its entirety:

COUNTER-REVOLUTIONARY?

"Comrade" Dybenko declares that the Congress called at Gulyai-Polye for the 10th of April is counter-revolutionary, and puts its organizers outside the law. According to him, the severest repression should strike them. We quote his telegram verbatim:

"Novoalekseevka, No. 283, April 10, 2:45 p.m. Forward to Comrade Batko Makhno, General Staff of the Aleksandrovsk Division. Copy to Volnovakha, Mariupol', to transmit to Comrade Makhno. Copy to the Gulyai-Polye Soviet:

"Any Congress called in the name of the Revolutionary Military General Staff, which is now dissolved by my order, shall be considered manifestly counter-revolutionary, and its organizers will expose themselves to the severest repressive measures, to the extent of their being declared outlaws. I order that steps be taken immediately so that such measures may not be necessary. Signed: *Dybenko.*"

Before declaring the congress counter-revolutionary, "Comrade" Dybenko has not even taken the trouble to find out by whom and for what purpose this congress was called. Thus he says that it was called by the dissolved Revolutionary Staff of Gulyai-Polye, whereas in reality it was called by the Executive Committee of the Revolutionary Military Council. Consequently, having called the congress, the members of the Council do not know whether they have been declared outlaws, or whether the congress is considered counter-revolutionary by "Comrade" Dybenko.

If this is the case, permit us to explain to "Your Excellency," by whom and for what purpose this congress—in your opinion counter-revolutionary—was called, and then it might not seem as terrible as you represent it.

As has already been said, the Congress was called by the Executive Committee of the Revolutionary Military Council of the Gulyai-Polye region, at Gulyai-Polye itself, on April 10. It was the Third Regional Congress of Gulyai-Polye, called for the purpose of determining the future free conduct of the Revolutionary Military Council. (You will see, "Comrade" Dybenko, that three of these "counter-revolutionary" congresses have taken place.) A question now arises —where does the Revolutionary Military Council come from, and for what purpose was it created? If you do not already know that, "Comrade" Dybenko, we are going to tell you. The Regional Revolutionary Military Council was formed following a resolution of the Second Congress, which took place at Gulyai-Polye on February 12 of this year (you see that it was a long time ago—you were not even here yet). The Council was created to organize the fighting men and to proceed to a voluntary mobilization, for the region was surrounded by *Kadets,* and the insurrectionary detachments, composed of the first volunteers, did not suffice to hold a very extended front. There were no Soviet troops in our region at that time. Furthermore the population did not count very much on their intervention, considering that the defense of its region was its own duty. It is for this purpose that the Revolutionary Military Council was created. It was composed, following the resolution of the Second Congress, of a delegate from each district; in all there were 32 members, each representing the districts of the governments of Ekaterinoslav and Tauride.

We will give you later some more details about the Revolutionary Military Council. For the moment, the question arises: where did the second regional congress come from? Who called it? Who authorized it? Were those who called it outlaws? And if not, why not? The second regional congress was in fact called at Gulyai-Polye by an initiating group composed of five persons elected by the first congress. This second congress took place on February 12, and to our great astonishment, the persons who called it were not outlawed. For, you see, at that time there were no heroes here who dared to suppress the rights of the people, rights won with their own blood. Thus another question arises: where did the first congress come from and who called it? Were those who called it outlawed? And if not, why not? "Comrade" Dybenko, you are still, it seems, rather new to the revolutionary movement of the Ukraine, and we shall have to tell you about its very beginnings. That is what we are going to do, and after learning these facts, you will perhaps shift your sights a little.

The first regional congress took place on January 23 of this year at the insurrectionary camp at Bol'shaya Mikhailovka. It was composed of delegates from the districts situated near the front against Denikin. The Soviet troops were then far away, very far away. Our region was isolated from the whole world, on one side by Denikin's troops, on the other by the Petliurists. At that time there were only the insurgent detachments, with Batko Makhno and Shchus'at their head, and these dealt continuous blows to the Petliurist and White armies. The organizations and social institutions in the various towns and villages did not at that time always bear the same name. In one town there was a Soviet, in another a Popular Administration, in a third a Revolutionary Military Staff, in a fourth a Provincial Administration, and so forth. But the spirit was equally revolutionary everywhere. The first congress was organized to consolidate the front and to create a certain uniformity of organization and action in the whole region.

No one called it; it met spontaneously. By the wish and with the approval of the population. At this congress the proposal was made to rescue from the Petliurist army our brothers who had been mobilized by force. To this end a delegation composed of five persons was elected. It was given the task of presenting itself to Batko Makhno's staff and to other staffs if need be, and of entering the army of the Ukrainian Directorate (of Petliura), in order to explain to our brothers that they had been fooled and that they should leave that army. In addition, the delegation was instructed, upon its return, to call a second, larger congress, for the purpose of organizing the whole region which had been delivered from the counter-revolutionary bands, and of creating a more powerful defense front. The delegates, on returning from their mission, therefore called the second regional congress, outside of any party, any authority, or any law. You,

101

"Comrade" Dybenko, and the other lovers of laws, were then far, far away, and since the heroic guides of the insurrectionary movement did not want power over the people who had just broken with their own hands the chains of slavery, the Congress was not proclaimed counter-revolutionary, and those who called it were not declared outlaws.

Let us return to the Regional Council. At the time of the creation of the Revolutionary Military Council of the Gulyai-Polye region, the Soviet Power appeared in our region. Following the resolution passed by the Second Congress, the Regional Council did not drop its work when the Soviet authorities appeared. It had to carry out the instructions of the congress. The Council was not an organ of command, but an executive organ. It thus continued to work to the best of its ability, and as always followed the revolutionary course in its work. Little by little, the Soviet authority began to erect obstacles to the activity of the Revolutionary Military Council. The Commissars and other high functionaries of the Soviet government began to treat the Council as a counter-revolutionary organization. It was then that the members of the Council decided to call a third regional congress on April 10 at Gulyai-Polye to determine the future conduct of the Council, or to liquidate it if the congress considered this necessary. And so the congress took place. Those who came to the congress were not counter-revolutionaries, but people who had been the first to raise the flag of the insurrection and social revolution. They came to it to help coordinate the general struggle of the region against all oppressors. The representatives of the 72 districts, as well as those of several insurgent units, participated in the congress. All of them found that the Military Revolutionary Council was necessary; they even enlarged its Executive Committee and instructed the latter to carry out a voluntary and egalitarian mobilization of the region. This congress was somewhat astonished to receive "Comrade" Dybenko's telegram declaring it "counter-revolutionary," inasmuch as this region had been the first to raise the flag of insurrection. That is why the congress voted a lively protest against this telegram.

Such is the picture that should open your eyes, "Comrade" Dybenko. Come to your senses! Think!

Have you, a single person, the right to declare counter-revolutionary a population of a million workers, a population which by itself, with its own calloused hands, threw off the chains of slavery, and which is now in the process of building its own life, according to its own will?

No! If you are really a revolutionary, you should come to help this people in its fight against the oppressors, and in its work in building a new, free life.

Can there exist laws made by a few people who call themselves revolutionaries which permit them to outlaw a whole people who are more revolutionary than they are themselves? (For the Executive Committee of the Council represents the whole mass of the people.)

Is it permissible, is it admissible, that they should come to the country to establish laws of violence, to subjugate a people who have just overthrown all law-makers and all laws?

Does there exist a law according to which a revolutionary has the right to apply the most severe penalties to a revolutionary mass, of which he calls himself the defender, simply because this mass has taken the good things which the revolution has promised them, freedom and equality, without his permission?

Should the mass of revolutionary people perhaps be silent when such a revolutionary takes away the freedom which they have just conquered?

Do the laws of the revolution order the shooting of a delegate because he believes he ought to carry out the mandate given him by the revolutionary mass which elected him?

Whose interests should the revolutionary defend: those of the Party or those of the people who set the revolution in motion with their blood?

The Revolutionary Military Council of the Gulyai-Polye region holds itself above the pressure and influence of all parties, and only recognizes the people who elected it. Its duty is to accomplish what the people have instructed it to do, and to create no obstacles to any left socialist party in the propagation of ideas. Consequently, if one day the Bolshevik idea succeeds among the workers, the Revolutionary Military Council—from the Bolshevik point of view a manifestly counter-revolutionary organization—will necessarily be replaced by another organization, "more revolutionary" and more Bolshevik. But meanwhile, do not interfere with us, do not try to stifle us.

If you and your like, "Comrade" Dybenko, continue to carry on the same policy as before, if you believe it good and conscientious, then carry your dirty little business to its conclusion. Outlaw all the organizers of the regional congresses called when you and your Party were at Kursk. Proclaim counter-revolutionary all those who first raised the flag of the insurrection, of the social revolution in the Ukraine, and who thus acted without waiting for your permission, without following your program to the letter. Also outlaw all those who sent their delegates to the regional congresses which you call counter-revolutionary. Finally, outlaw all the vanished comrades who, without your permission, took part in the insurrectionary movements for the liberation of all the working people. Proclaim forever illegal and counter-revolutionary any congress called without your permission, but know that in the end truth will triumph over force. Despite your threats, the Council did not abandon its duties, because it has no right to do this and because it has no right to usurp the rights of the people.

> Revolutionary Military Council
> of the Gulyai-Polye region:
> *Chernoknizhnyi,* president
> *Kogan,* vice-president
> *Karabet,* secretary
> *Koval', Petrenko, Dotsenko*
> and other members.

After this, the question of the Makhnovshchina was treated in high Bolshevik circles in a clear and definite manner. The official press, which already earlier had misrepresented the Makhnovist movement, now set out to abuse it systematically, deliberately inventing and attributing to it all types of absurdities, villainies and crimes. The following example will give a fair notion of the Bolshevik way of behaving. At the end of April or the beginning of May, 1919, General Shkuro, misled by a Makhnovist prisoner, sent a letter to Makhno in which, after praising his innate military talents and expressing regret that this talent had been engaged on a false revolutionary path, suggested to Makhno that his army be united with Denikin's for the salvation of the Russian people. When this letter was read at a large meeting of revolutionary insurgents, everyone ridiculed the naivety and the stupidity of the counter-revolutionary general, who did not even know the ABCs about the revolution in Russia and in the Ukraine. They published this letter in their newspaper *Put' k Svobode* for the purpose of ridicule. The entire letter, followed by derisive comments, was published in *Put' k Svobode* No. 3. What did the Communist-Bolsheviks do then? They found this letter in the Makhnovist newspaper, reprinted it in their newspapers and declared shamelessly that they had intercepted this letter, that negotiations about an alliance were taking place between Makhno and Shkuro, and even that this alliance had been formed. The entire Bolshevik war of ideas against the Makhnovists was carried out in this form.

* * *

In mid-April, 1919, high officials in the Communist government began a thorough investigation of the insurgent region. On April 29, the Commander of the southern front, Antonov, arrived in Gulyai-Polye in order to become acquainted with Makhno himself, with the Makhnovist front and the disposition of the insurrection. On May 4 and 5, the Extraordinary Plenipotentiary of the National Defense Council, L. Kamenev, arrived together with other government officials from Khar'kov. Kamenev's entry into Gulyai-Polye was friendly and left nothing to be desired. He complimented the assembled peasants and insurgents as heroes who had liberated the region from the Hetman's power on their own, and had defended it successfully against Petliura and Denikin. It seemed that the revolutionary self-activity of the peasants had found in Kamenev its greatest admirer. However, in his official interview with Makhno, the members of the staff, and the Regional Council, Kamenev spoke a language which had nothing in common with the self-activity of the working people. When the question of the Revolutionary Military

Council was raised, Kamenev found the existence of this Council absolutely inadmissible under Soviet power, and demanded that it be dissolved.

As can be expected from a statist, Kamenev confused two completely different institutions: the Revolutionary Military Council of the Republic, created by the ruling Party, and the Revolutionary Military Council of the working masses, *directly* created by them as their executive organ. The first of these councils could, in fact, be dissolved very easily: by order of the Central Committee of the Party; but the second council cannot be dissolved except by the masses who created it. Only counter-revolutionary power could dissolve it despite the masses, but in no case could revolutionaries do so.

And this was what Kamenev was told. This answer was obviously disagreeable to him, and gave rise to a heated discussion. Nevertheless, Kamenev as well as Antonov parted warmly, expressed to the Makhnovists their deep appreciation, and wished them well. Kamenev embraced Makhno and assured the Makhnovists that the Bolsheviks would always find a common language with them as with all true revolutionaries, and that they could and should work together.

Were the visits of these high Bolshevik People's Commissars to Gulyai-Polye really as friendly as their warm wishes suggested, or did their friendliness already then hide their irreconcilable hostility toward the insurgent region? More likely the second. The developments which took place in the region soon after this meeting showed that the idea of a military campaign against the region and the free insurrectionary movement had already been ripening for a long time in the Bolshevik world. The visits of Antonov and Kamenev to Gulyai-Polye can only be considered as reconnaissance before aggression. These visits brought no changes in the relations between the Bolsheviks and the Makhnovshchina. The agitation carried out by their press did not diminish; on the contrary, it became more violent. They did not cease to invent lies, each more shameful and abominable than the preceding one. All this revealed that the Bolsheviks wanted to prepare the workers and the Red Army troops to accept their armed attack against the free region. A month earlier they had made an attempt to assassinate

Makhno. The commander of an insurgent regiment, Padalka, bribed by the Bolsheviks, accepted their "commission" to attack Gulyai-Polye from the side of Pokrovskoe, and to capture Makhno and his staff. The plot was discovered by Makhno himself while he was at Berdyansk, minutes before he was to leave for Gulyai-Polye. It was possible to foil this plan only thanks to an airplane which was found at hand and with which Makhno succeeded in covering the distance between Berdyansk and Gulyai-Polye in two hours and some minutes. The organizers of the plot were unexpectedly caught and executed.

More than once Makhno was warned by comrades employed in Bolshevik institutions not to go either to Ekaterinoslav or to Khar'kov, or anywhere else if he were called, since any official summons would be a trap where death would await him. In short, every new day made it increasingly obvious that the Bolsheviks were preparing to resolve the question of ideological influence in the Ukraine by military means. The revolt of Grigor'ev unexpectedly stopped them, and caused them to temporarily change their attitude toward the Makhnovshchina.

Chapter 6

The Makhnovshchina (Continuation).

Grigor'ev's Revolt.
The Bolsheviks' First Assault on Gulyai-Polye.

On May 12, 1919, the following telegram was received at the Makhnovist headquarters in Gulyai-Polye:

"Gulyai-Polye, forward to Batko Makhno.
"The traitor Grigor'ev has delivered the front to the enemy. Refusing to execute battle orders, he turned his guns around. The decisive moment has come: either you will march with the workers and peasants of all of Russia, or else you will in practice open the front to the enemy. There can be no hesitation. Send immediate information on the disposition of your troops and issue a proclamation against Grigor'ev, sending me a copy at Khar'kov. A lack of response will be considered a declaration of war. I have faith in the honor of revolutionaries—yours, Arshinov's, Veretel'nikov's, and that of others.

"(Signed)
Kamenev.
No. 277
Revolutionary Military Inspector,
Lob'ye."

The Staff immediately called a session, inviting representatives of the Revolutionary Military Council, and after serious consideration of the telegram and the event which it announced, reached the following conclusion. On the eve of the Hetman's overthrow Grigor'ev, former Tsarist officer, was in the ranks of the Petliurists and commanded numerous insurrectionary troops under the Petliurist authorities. When the Petliurist army disintegrated because of the influence of

109

class contradictions, Grigor'ev and his troops joined up with the Bolsheviks, who had just arrived from Central Russia. He collaborated with the Bolsheviks against the Petliurists, while retaining a certain autonomy and freedom of action for his troops. He was largely responsible for liberating the government of Kherson from the Petliurists. He occupied Odessa. Subsequently he and his detachments held the Bessarabian front.

Grigor'ev's insurrectionary detachments were organizationally, and particularly ideologically, retarded in comparison with the Makhnovist insurgents. Throughout the entire period, they remained in the first stages of their development. At the beginning of the general insurrection they had been imbued with a revolutionary spirit, but they, unlike the Makhnovists, were unable to find, either in themselves or in the peasant environment from which they came, the historic tasks of labor or its vivid social aspirations. In spite of their initial revolutionary impetus, their social ideals were irresolute and undetermined, and as a result they fell under the influence of Petliura, then of Grigor'ev, then of the Bolsheviks.

Grigor'ev himself had never been a revolutionary. There was a great deal of adventurism in his joining the ranks of the Petliurists and then the ranks of the Red Army. He was above all a warrior for whom the spontaneity of the popular insurrectionary movement provided a role. His temperament was extraordinarily variegated; it consisted of a certain amount of sympathy for oppressed peasants, authoritarianism, the extravagance of a Cossack chieftain, nationalist sentiments and anti-Semitism. What had induced him to turn against the Bolsheviks? The Makhnovist staff did not know. There were many indications that the Bolsheviks themselves had provoked him in order to disband his autonomous insurrectionary detachments which did not pursue independent revolutionary goals, as did the Makhnovists, but whose form and content were nevertheless hostile to the idea of Bolshevism. In any case, in the eyes of the Makhnovists, Grigor'ev's move against the Bolsheviks did not appear to be in the spirit of the revolution or the working people, but seemed purely military and political, and consequently did not merit their serious attention. This became particularly clear after Grigor'ev published his "Universal" (Appeal), filled with the notion of national hatred among the working people. The only element of this movement worthy of attention and compassion, in the view of the Makhnovists, were the insurgent masses misled into political adventure by Grigor'ev.

This was the conclusion reached by the Makhnovists after their consideration of Grigor'ev's movement. In conformity with this view, the staff of the army began to respond to the event. First of all, it sent the following orders to the front:

"Mariupol'. Field Staff of the Makhnovist Army. Copies to all heads of combat units, to all commanders of regiments, batallions, companies and platoons. Order to be read to all units of the army known as Batko Makhno's. Copy to Khar'kov, to the Extra-ordinary Plenipotentiary of the National Defense Council, Kamenev.

"The most energetic measures will need to be adopted for the defense of the front. A weakening of the external front of the revolution is absolutely inadmissible. Revolutionary honor and dignity oblige us to remain true to the revolution and to the people, and the rivalry for power between Grigor'ev and the Bolsheviks cannot be allowed to make us weaken the front which the Whites seek to penetrate in order to re-enslave the people. As long as we have not achieved victory over our common enemy personified by the Don Whites, and as long as we have not guaranteed the freedom won with our own hands and weapons, we will remain at our front and will continue to struggle for the freedom of the people, but under no circumstances will we struggle for the power or for the intrigues of charlatan politicians.

"Brigade Commander, *Batko Makhno*
"Members of the Staff (Signatures)"

At the same time, the Staff answered Kamenev with the following telegram:

"Khar'kov. Extraordinary Plenipotentiary of the National Defense Council, Kamenev. Copy to Mariupol'. Field Staff.

"Upon receipt of your and Roshchin's[1] telegrams informing us about Grigor'ev, I immediately gave the order to maintain the front firmly and not to give an inch to Denikin or any other counter-revolutionary gang, fulfilling our revolutionary obligations toward the workers and peasants of Russia and of the entire world. But you should know that my troops and I will remain resolutely true to the workers' and peasants' revolution, but not to the institutions of violence personified by your Commissariats and your Extraordinary Commissions *(Chekas)* which tyrannize the working population. If Grigor'ev has actually abandoned the front and moved his troops in order to seize power, then this is a criminal adventure and a betrayal of the people's revolution, and I will widely publicize my view of this matter. But as yet I do not have exact information on Grigor'ev or on the movement linked with him; I do not know what he has done nor for what purpose; consequently for the time being I will refrain from publishing a proclamation against him, until I receive clearer information about him. As a revolutionary and an anarchist, I let it be known that I cannot in any way support the seizure of power by Grigor'ev or by anyone else; as earlier my insurgent comrades and I will continue to pursue Denikin's bands, while at the same time doing the utmost to allow the liberated region to establish networks of free unions of peasants and workers who are themselves the possessors of all power. In terms of these relations, the *Chekas* and Commissariats, which are only instruments of constraint and violence serving to establish a Party dictatorship—extending their violence to anarchist federations and the anarchist press—will find in us energetic adversaries.

> "Brigade Commander, *Batko Makhno*.
> "Members of the Staff (Signatures).
> "President of the Cultural Section, *Arshinov*."

[1]In addition to L. Kamenev's telegram, a telegram addressed to Makhno was received from Grossman-Roshchin (Soviet anarchist), referring to the same event.

A commission of representatives of the staff and the Revolutionary Military Council was formed and sent to the region of Grigor'ev's movement in order to unmask him in the eyes of the insurgents and to invite them to enlist under the revolutionary flag of the Makhnovists. In the meantime Grigor'ev, who had already occupied Aleksandriya, Znamenka, Elisavetgrad, approached Ekaterinoslav, which seriously alarmed the Communist authorities residing at Khar'kov. The Communists looked toward the Gulyai-Polye region with apprehension. Every sound from Gulyai-Polye, every telegram from Makhno, was eagerly received and printed in the Soviet press. Naturally these apprehensions had no other foundation than the profound ignorance of Soviet government functionaries, who imagined that the revolutionary anarchist Makhno would suddenly turn against them and join forces with Grigor'ev. The Makhnovshchina always held principled positions and was always guided by the ideals of social revolution, ideals of the stateless working community. Consequently the Makhnovshchina could never have united with just any anti-Bolshevik position solely on the ground that the Makhnovshchina also opposed Bolshevism. On the contrary, a movement like Grigor'ev's represented an additional threat to the freedom of the workers and, consequently, was as much an enemy to the Makhnovists as to the Bolsheviks. And in fact, during its entire existence, the Makhnovshchina did not collaborate with a single anti-Bolshevik movement, but fought with the same heroism and the same spirit of sacrifice against Bolshevism as against Petliura, Grigor'ev, Denikin, Wrangel, considering all these movements to be authoritarian groups seeking to enslave and exploit the working masses. The Makhnovshchina even turned down the advances made by certain groups of left-wing SRs (Socialist-Revolutionaries) to struggle together agianst the Bolsheviks; these advances were turned down because the left SR, as a political movement, in essence represented the same thing as Bolshevism, namely statist domination of the people by the socialist democracy.

Grigor'ev himself, at the time of his rebellion, had tried several times to establish ties with Makhno. But of all his telegrams to Gulyai-Polye, only one arrived, with the following content: "Batko! Why are you looking toward the Communists? Thrash them!—*Ataman*[2] *Grigor'ev."* This telegram was obviously left unanswered, and two or three days later the staff, together with representatives of the insurrectionary troops at the front, definitively condemned Grigor'ev, and published the following proclamation:

WHO IS GRIGOR'EV?

Fellow Workers! When, a year ago, we set out on a relentless struggle against the Austro-German invasion and the domination of the Hetman, and then against Petliura and Denikin, we were perfectly clear about the direction of this struggle and from the first day we marched under a banner which proclaimed: the liberation of the workers is the task of the workers themselves. This struggle led us to numerous victories which were profoundly significant: we chased out the Germans, overturned the Hetman, kept the petit-bourgeois regime of Petliura from establishing itself, and began creative work in the regions we liberated. At the same time we continually urged the vast popular masses to pay close attention to what was going on around them; we warned them that numerous beasts of prey stalked them, waiting only for the opportune moment to seize power and to attach themselves to the backs of the people. A new predator of this type has just made his appearance, the Ataman Grigor'ev who, while shouting about the sufferings, the burdens and the oppression of the people, in practice reestablishes the old regime of violence and brigandage which plunders the people's labor, increases their misery, reinforces tyranny and abolishes freedom. Let us examine the Ataman Grigor'ev himself.

Grigor'ev is a former Tsarist officer. At the beginning of the revolution in the Ukraine he fought with Petliura against the Soviet power, and then he took sides with the Soviet authorities; now he has turned against the Soviets and against the revolution in general. What does Grigor'ev have to say? In the first

---

[2] [Cossack chieftain.]

114

lines of his "Universal" he says that the Ukraine is ruled by those who crucified Christ, by those who came out of the "lower depths of Moscow." Brothers, do you not hear in these words a somber call for a pogrom of Jews? Do you not sense the desire of Ataman Grigor'ev to shatter the living fraternal links which unite revolutionary Ukraine with revolutionary Russia? Grigor'ev speaks of calloused hands, of the holy worker, etc. But who today does not speak of sacred work, of the good of the people? Even the Whites, while attacking us and our country, declare that they are fighting for the cause of the working people. But we know what kind of wellbeing they give the people when they have power over them.

Grigor'ev says that he is fighting against the commissars for the true power of the soviets. But in the same "Universal" he writes: "I, Ataman Grigor'ev. . . here are my orders—choose your commissars." And further on, declaring that he is against bloodshed, Grigor'ev announces in the same "Universal" that he is calling for a general conscription, and sends messages to Khar'kov and Kiev in which he writes: "I demand that my orders be executed; I will take care of all the rest." What is this? The direct power of the people? Tsar Nicholas also considered his authority to be the power of the people. Or does Ataman Grigor'ev believe that his orders will not represent a power over the people and that his commissars will not be commisars but angels? Brothers! Don't you see that a band of adventurers is turning you one against the other, disrupting your revolutionary ranks, and trying to enslave you behind your backs and with your own help? Be on your guard! The traitor Grigor'ev, who has struck a major blow from within against the revolution, has at the same time revived the bourgeoisie. Taking advantage of Grigor'ev's pogromist movement, Petliura is already trying to break through our front from Galicia, and Denikin from the Don. The worse for the Ukrainian people if they do not put an immediate stop to these internal and external adventures.

Fellow peasants, workers and insurgents! Many among you will wonder what to make of the numerous insurgents who loyally battled for the cause of the revolution and who, because of Grigor'ev's

115

treachery, are now enrolled in his shameful ranks. Should they be considered counter-revolutionaries? No. These comrades are victims of deceit. We believe that their healthy revolutionary sense will inform them that Grigor'ev has misled them and they will abandon him to rejoin the ranks of the revolution.

We should also point out that the causes which gave rise to Grigor'ev's movement have their origin, not only in Grigor'ev himself, but mainly in the disorder which has plagued the Ukraine in recent times. Since the arrival of the Bolsheviks the dictatorship of their Party has been established here. As a party of statists, the Bolshevik Party everywhere set up state organs for the purpose of governing the revolutionary people. Everything has to be submitted to their authority and take place under their vigilant eye. All opposition, protest, or even independent initiative has been stifled by their Extraordinary Commissions. Furthermore, all these institutions are composed of people who are far removed from labor and from revolution. In other words, what has been created is a situation in which the laboring and revolutionary people have fallen under the surveillance and rule of people who are alien to the working classes, people who are inclined to exercise arbitrariness and violence over the workers. Such is the dictatorship of the Bolshevik-Communist Party. Among the masses this dictatorship has aroused irritation, protest and animosity toward the existing order. Grigor'ev takes advantage of this situation to carry on his adventure. Grigor'ev is a traitor to the revolution and an enemy of the people, but the Bolshevik-Communist Party is no less an enemy of labor. With its irresponsible dictatorship this Party has aroused in the masses a hatred from which Grigor'ev benefits today, and from which another adventurer will benefit tomorrow. Consequently, while unmasking Grigor'ev's treason to the cause of the revolution, we must call the Communist Party to answer for Grigor'ev's movement.

We again remind the working people that they will liberate themselves from oppression, misery and violence only through their own efforts. No change in power will help them in this. Only by means of their own free worker-peasant organizations can the workers reach the summit of the social revolution

—complete freedom and real equality. Death and destruction to traitors and enemies of the people! Down with national hatred! Down with provocateurs! Long live the solidarity of the workers and peasants! Long live the universal free working commune!

Signed:
Staff Council of the Military Division known as Batko Makhno's. Members of the Council: *Batko Makhno, A. Chubenko, Mikhalev-Pavlenko, A. Ol'khovik, I.M. Chuchko, E. Karpenko, M. Puzanov, V. Sharovskii, P. Arshinov, B. Veretel'nikov.*

Joined by:
Members of the Executive Committee of the Council of Deputies of Workers, Peasants and Red Guards of the City of Aleksandrovsk: *Andryushchenko,* President of the Executive Council of the District; *Shpota,* Head of the Administrative Section; *Gavrilov,* Member; *A. Bondar',* Member of the City Executive Committee and Political Commissar.

A large number of copies of this proclamation was distributed among the peasants and at the front; it was also printed in the main publication of the Makhnovist insurgents, *Put' k Svobode,* as well as in the anarchist journal *Nabat (Alarm).*

Grigor'ev's adventure sank as quickly as it had risen. It caused several pogroms of Jews, among which one, in Elisavetgrad, was extremely widespread. As a result, a large number of insurgents quickly abandoned Grigor'ev. The peasantry could not support him for long because it realized how superficial he was. Grigor'ev retained only a few thousand men; they entrenched themselves in the district of Aleksandriya in the government of Kherson. Nevertheless this adventure caused great anxiety among the Bolsheviks. But as soon as they learned the attitude of the Gulyai-Polye region, they breathed freely and regained their assurance. The Soviet authorities loudly announced that the Makhnovists had condemned Grigor'ev's revolt. The Soviets sought to take advantage of the Makhnovists' attitude in order to launch a vast propaganda campaign against Grigor'ev. Makhno's name was cited constantly by the Soviet press. His telegrams were continually reprinted. He was praised as a real guardian of the workers' and peasants' revolution. They even sought to frighten Grigor'ev by making up the story that Grigor'ev was surrounded on all sides by Makhno's troops and would either be imprisoned or completely annihilated by them.

However, all this admiration of Makhno was two-faced and did not last long. As soon as the danger from Grigor'ev disappeared, the previous propaganda of the Bolsheviks against the Makhnovists resumed. At this time Trotsky arrived in the Ukraine; he set the tone of this propaganda: —the insurrection is nothing but a movement of rich *kulaks* trying to establish their power in the country; all the Makhnovist and anarchist talk about the stateless workers' commune is merely a tactic of war; in practice the Makhnovists and the anarchists hope to establish their own anarchist power which is the power of the rich *kulaks* (from the newspaper *V Puti (On the Road)*, No. 51, Trotsky's article, "The Makhnovshchina."). Together with this deliberately false agitational campaign, the blockade of the region was carried to the limit. Revolutionary workers from the furthest localities of Russia—from Ivanovo-Voznesensk, Moscow, Petrograd, from the Volga, the Urals and Siberia, who were attracted to the region by its independence and pride, were able to penetrate the blockade only with the greatest difficulty. The provisioning of shells, cartridges and other indispensable equipment which was used up daily at the front, ceased completely. Two weeks earlier, at the time of Grigor'ev's revolt, Grossman-Roshchin had come to Gulyai-Polye from Khar'kov and had been told about the difficult situation at the front which resulted from the lack of shells and cartridges. Roshchin attentively received this information and committed himself to do his utmost in Khar'kov so that the indispensable equipment would be sent to the front immediately. But two weeks passed, no shipment of munitions arrived, and the situation at the front became catastrophic. And this at a time when Denikin's troops were being reinforced on this front by the arrival of Cossacks from Kuban and contingents formed in the Caucasus.

Did the Bolsheviks realize what they were doing and

what results their line of action would have on the complicated Ukrainian situation?

They obviously realized what they were doing. They had adopted the tactic of the blockade for the purpose of destroying, annihilating, the military power of the region. It is easier to struggle against disarmed adversaries than against armed ones. Insurgents without cartridges and facing Denikin's solid front would be easier to subdue than the same insurgents armed with cartridges. But at the same time the Bolsheviks were not at all aware of the situation in the entire Donets region. They did not have any notion of Denikin's front or of Denikin's forces. They were also completely ignorant of Denikin's immediate plans. Yet large and well trained contingents had been formed in the Caucasus, in the Don region and in the Kuban, with the aim of a general campaign against the revolution. The four-month long resistance of the Gulyai-Polye insurgents had prevented Denikin's troops from carrying out their northern offensive, since the Gulyai-Polye insurgents constituted a permanent danger to their left flank. All the desperate attacks of General Shkuro, carried on for four months, failed to decrease this danger. Thus the Whites prepared their second campaign with all the more energy; this campaign began in May, 1919, and its scope surprised even the Makhnovists. The Bolsheviks knew nothing of all this, or rather they did not want to know anything about it, being preoccupied with the struggle against the Makhnovshchina.

Thus the free region, as well as the rest of the revolutionary Ukraine, were threatened from two sides at once. It was then that the Revolutionary Military Council of Gulyai-Polye, in view of the gravity of the situation, decided to call an extraordinary congress of peasants, workers, insurgents and red soldiers *from several regions:* Ekaterinoslav, Khar'-kov, Tauride, Kherson and the Donets. This congress was to examine the general situation in view of the mortal danger represented by Denikin's counter-revolution and in view of the inability of the Soviet authorities to undertake any action at all to avert this danger. The congress was to determine the immediate tasks and the practical measures to be taken by the workers to remedy this state of affairs.

Here is the text of the call to this congress issued by

the Revolutionary Military Council to the workers of the Ukraine:

CONVOCATION OF
THE FOURTH EXTRAORDINARY CONGRESS
OF WORKERS', PEASANTS',
AND INSURGENTS' DELEGATES.
Telegram No. 416.

> To all the Executive Committees of the districts, towns and villages of the governments of Ekaterinoslav, Tauride and neighboring regions; to all the units of the First Insurrectionary Division known as Batko Makhno's; to all the troops of the Red Army located in the same region. To all! To all!

In its session of May 30, the Executive Committee of the Revolutionary Military Council, after having examined the situation at the front, created by the offensive of the White bands, and also the situation in general—political and economic—of the Soviet power, reached the conclusion that only the working masses themselves could find a solution, and not individuals or parties. That is why the Executive Committee of the Revolutionary Military Council of the Gulyai-Polye region has decided to call an extraordinary congress for June 15, 1919, at Gulyai-Polye. *Method of Election:* 1) The peasants and workers will send a delegate for each three thousand inhabitants. 2) The insurgents and Red soldiers will delegate a representative from each unit (regiment, division, etc.). 3) The staffs: Batko Makhno's division, two delegates; the brigades, one delegate from each brigade staff. 4) The executive committees of the districts will send one delegate from each faction. 5) The district party organizations which adhere to the program of the *Soviet regime* will send one delegate from each organization.

Remarks: a) the elections of delegates of peasants and workers will take place at general assemblies of villages, towns, factories and workshops; b) separate meetings of members of soviets and factory committees will not take place; c) since the Revolutionary Military

Council does not have the necessary means, the delegates should come provided with food and money.

Agenda: a) Report of the Executive Committee of the Revolutionary Military Council and reports of the delegates; b) the current situation; c) the role, tasks and aims of the Soviet of Peasants', Workers', Insurgents', and Red Soldiers' Delegates of the Gulyai-Polye Region; d) reorganization of the Revolutionary Military Council of the region; e) organization of military activity in the region; f) the problem of food supply; g) the agrarian problem; h) financial questions; i) union of working peasants and workers; j) public security; k) exercise of justice in the region; l) current matters.

> Executive Committee of the Revolutionary Military Council.
> Gulyai-Polye, May 31, 1919.

As soon as this call was sent out, the Bolsheviks began a military campaign against the Gulyai-Polye region.

While the insurgent troops were marching to their death, resisting the furious assault of Denikin's Cossacks, Bolshevik regiments invaded the insurgent region from the north, striking the Makhnovists in the rear. Invading the villages, the Bolsheviks seized the militants and executed them on the spot; they destroyed the free communes and similar organizations. Trotsky, who arrived in the Ukraine at this time, played a leading role in this attack. It can easily be imagined how he felt when he got a good view of a perfectly independent region, when he heard the language of people who lived freely and did not pay the slightest attention to the new power, when he read the newspapers of these people who spoke of him, without fear or respect, as nothing more than a State functionary. Trotsky, who was going to rid Russia of anarchism with an "iron broom," could only have felt the fierce and blind hatred appropriate to statists of his type. This hatred pervades a whole series of orders issued by Trotsky against the Makhnovshchina.

With an unbelievable lack of constraint, Trotsky set out to liquidate the Makhnovist movement.

121

First of all, he issued the following order in response to the call of the Gulyai-Polye Revolutionary Military Council:

ORDER NO. 1824
OF THE REVOLUTIONARY MILITARY COUNCIL
OF THE REPUBLIC.
KHAR'KOV, JUNE 4, 1919.

To all Military Commissars and to all Executive Committees of the districts of Aleksandrovsk, Mariupol', Berdyansk, Bakhmut, Pavlograd and Kherson.

The Executive Committee of Gulyai-Polye, with the collaboration of the staff of Makhno's brigade, is trying to call, for the 15th of this month, a congress of soviets and insurgents of the districts of Aleksandrovsk, Mariupol', Berdyansk, Melitopol', Bakhmut and Pavlograd. This congress is squarely directed against the Soviet Power in the Ukraine and against the organization of the southern front, where Makhno's brigade is stationed. This congress can have no other result than to excite some new disgraceful revolt like that of Grigor'ev, and to open the front to the Whites, before whom Makhno's brigade can only retreat incessantly, on account of the incompetence, criminal designs and treason of its commanders.

1. By the present order this congress is forbidden, and will in no case be allowed to take place.

2. All the peasant and working class population shall be warned, orally and in writing, that participation in the said congress shall be considered an act of high treason against the Soviet Republic and the Soviet front.

3. All the delegates to the said congress shall be arrested immediately and brought before the Revolutionary Military Tribunal of the 14th, formerly 2nd, Army of the Ukraine.

4. The persons spreading the call of Makhno and the Gulyai-Polye Executive Committee shall likewise be arrested.

5. The present order shall have the force of law as soon as it is telegraphed. It should be widely distributed, displayed in all public places, and sent to the representatives of the executive committees of towns

and villages, as well as to all the representatives of Soviet authority, and to commanders and commissars of military units.

> *Trotsky,* President of the Revolutionary Military Council of the Republic;
> *Vatsetis,* Commander in Chief;
> *Aralov,* Member of the Revolutionary Military Council of the Republic;
> *Koshkarev,* Military Commissar of the Khar'kov region.

This document is truly classic. Whoever studies the Russian revolution should learn it by heart. How farsighted and discerning had the Gulyai-Polye revolutionary peasants been two months earlier when, in their famous reply to Dybenko (cited earlier) they virtually foresaw this order! They had unceremoniously asked the Bolsheviks the following questions: (p. 103)

"Can there exist laws made by a few people who call themselves revolutionaries which permit them to outlaw a whole people who are more revolutionary than they are themselves?"

Article 2 of Trotsky's order replies clearly that such laws can exist, and that Order No. 1824 is proof of this.

"Does there exist a law," had asked the Gulyai-Polye insurgents, "according to which a revolutionary has the right to apply the most severe penalties to a revolutionary mass, of which he calls himself the defender, simply because this mass has taken the good things which the revolution has promised them, freedom and equality, without his permission?"

The same Article 2 replies in the affirmative. The entire peasant and laboring population are declared guilty of high treason if they dare to participate in their own free congress.

"Do the laws of the Revolution order the shooting of a delegate because he believes he ought to carry out the mandate given him by the revolutionary mass which elected him?"

Articles 3 and 4 of Trotsky's order declare that not

only delegates carrying out their mandates, but even those who have not yet begun to carry them out, should be arrested and brought before the Revolutionary Military Tribunal of the Army; which means they are to be shot (as in fact happened to Kostin, Polynin, Dobrolyubov and others who were brought before the military tribunal and shot on the charge of having *discussed* the call of the Revolutionary Military Council of Gulyai-Polye).

This entire document represents such a crying usurpation of the rights of the workers that it is pointless to comment further on it.

Guided by institutional clichés, Trotsky considered Makhno the culprit who was responsible for all that happened in Gulyai-Polye, and for all the measures that were taken in the region. He had even failed to notice that the Congress had not been called by the Staff of Makhno's brigade nor by the Executive Committee of Gulyai-Polye, but by an organ completely independent from these—the Revolutionary Military Council of the Region. It is significant that in this order Trotsky already harped on the treachery of the Makhnovist commanders, whom he accused of "retreating incessantly before the Whites." A few days later Trotsky and the entire Communist press loudly proclaimed that the Makhnovists had opened the front to Denikin.

We already know that this front had been formed only through the efforts and sacrifices of the insurgent peasants themselves. It was born at a heroic moment of their history —at the moment when the region was liberated from all forms of authority. The front was established in the southeast as a heroic sentinel and defender of the freedom they had won. For more than six months the revolutionary insurgents maintained an unbreakable barrier against the most vigorous assaults of the monarchist counter-revolution, sacrificing several thousand of their best sons. They mobilized all the resources of the region and prepared to defend their freedom to the end, by resisting the counter-revolution which was unleashing a general offensive. The extent to which the front was held mainly by the insurgents—during the entire period—is shown by L. Kamenev's telegram about Grigor'ev's revolt, cited earlier. In it this Extraordinary Plenipotentiary from Moscow had asked Makhno to tell him about the disposition of the insurrectionary troops at the front against Denikin. He obviously addressed such a question to Makhno only because in Khar'kov, where he was at the time, he was unable to obtain this necessary information from the Military Commissariat or from the Commander at the front. It is obvious that Trotsky, who arrived in the Ukraine when it was being attacked from several sides by the counter-revolution, had even less of an idea of what was happening at the southern front against Denikin. But Trotsky needed a formal justification for his criminal campaign against the revolutionary people, and it was with monstrous cynicism and unimaginable insolence that he declared the congress of peasants, workers and insurgents, projected for June 15, harmful to the organization of the southern front. Thus it would appear that the peasants and insurgents who were doing everything in their power to maintain this front, who had invited all who were capable of carrying arms to voluntarily and immediately enlist in the front against Denikin (Resolutions adopted by the Second Regional Congress of February 12, 1919, on voluntary and egalitarian 10-year mobilization)—it would appear that these same peasants and insurgents were organizing a conspiracy against their own front. It might be thought that such assertions are made by mentally deranged individuals. No, they are the assertions of individuals who are sane, but who are accustomed to treating the people with unbounded cynicism.

This order of Trotsky's was not communicated by the Soviet authorities to the staff of the Makhnovist army, and the Makhnovists only heard of it by chance two or three days later. Makhno immediately sent a telegram declaring that he wanted to give up his post as commander in view of the awkward and impossible situation. Unfortunately we do not have the text of this telegram.

Trotsky's order acquired the force of law by telegram. The Bolsheviks set out to execute every point in Trotsky's order in a militaristic fashion. Workers from Aleksandrovsk factories who met to discuss the call issued by the Revolutionary Military Council of the Gulyai-Polye region were dispersed by force and declared outlaws. The peasants were threatened with shooting and hanging. In various places individuals—Kostin, Polynin, Dobrolyubov and others—were seized, accused of having publicized the call of the Revolutionary Military Council, and were executed after a summary trial by the Revolutionary Military Tribunal. This order was followed by numerous others in which Trotsky commanded the units of the Red Army to destroy the Makhnovshchina by every method and at its very source. Moreover, he gave secret orders to capture, at any cost, not only Makhno and the members of his staff, but even the peaceful militants of the cultural section. The instructions were to bring them all before the Revolutionary Military Tribunal, i.e., to execute them.

According to an individual who commanded several divisions of the Red Army, and to several Bolshevik military leaders who held high posts, Trotsky formulated his relationship to the Makhnovshchina in the following terms: it would be better to yield the whole Ukraine to Denikin than to permit a further development of the Makhnovshchina. Denikin's movement, being frankly counter-revolutionary, can be undermined later by means of class propaganda, whereas the Makhnovshchina develops in the depths of the masses and arouses the masses themselves against us. . .

A few days before these events, Makhno reported to the staff and to the Council that the Bolsheviks had withdrawn some of their troops in the Grishino sector, and had thus offered Denikin's troops free access to the Gulyai-Polye region from the northeast. And in fact, hoards of Cossacks had overrun the region, *not through the insurrectionary front but from the left flank where the Red Army was stationed.* As a result, the Makhnovist army, which held the front on the Mariupol'—Kuteinikovo—Taganrog line, was bypassed by Denikin's troops, who invaded the very heart of the region with enormous forces.

We said earlier that the peasants throughout the region anticipated a general attack by Denikin; that they were preparing for it with a voluntary ten-year mobilization. Already in April peasants in numerous villages sent large numbers of new fighters to Gulyai-Polye. But weapons were lacking in the region. Even the older units at the front were out of cartridges and often attacked Denikin's troops solely in order to obtain them. The Bolsheviks, who were obliged by their treaty to provide supplies to the insurgents, already in April began their blockade and sabotage. This is why, in spite of the arrival of volunteers, it was impossible to organize new units in time, and now the region had to pay for this.

In a single day the peasants of Gulyai-Polye formed a regiment to try to save their village. They armed themselves with domestic utensils: axes, picks, old rifles, shot guns, etc. They set out to meet the Cossacks with the aim of breaking their thrust. About ten miles from Gulyai-Polye, near the village of Svyatodukhovka in the district of Aleksandrovsk, they encountered a considerable number of Don and Kuban Cossacks. The Gulyai-Polye insurgents engaged in a heroic and murderous battle with them, and were nearly all killed, including their commander B. Veretel'nikov, a worker from the Putilov Works in Petrograd who was born in Gulyai-Polye. Then an avalanche of Cossacks swooped down on Gulyai-Polye and occupied it on June 6, 1919. Makhno, with the army staff and a small detachment of troops with only one battery, retreated to the railway station situated about five miles from the village, but in the evening was forced to abandon the station as well. Regrouping all the forces he could still muster, Makhno vigorously counter-attacked the next day and succeeded in dislodging the enemy from Gulyai-Polye. However, a new wave of Cossacks forced him to abandon the village once again.

It should be pointed out that the Bolsheviks, although they had directed several orders against the Makhnovists, feigned friendship with them during the first days, as if nothing had happened. This was a tactic to capture the leaders of the Makhnovshchina. On June 7 they sent Makhno an armored train, asking him to resist to the end, and they promised other reinforcements. In fact, two days later, several detachments of Red Army troops arrived at the station of Gyaichur near Chaplino, thirteen miles from Gulyai-Polye. With them arrived the military Commissars Mezhlauk, Voroshilov and others. Contacts were established between the Red command and the insurgents; a kind of joint staff was created. Mezhlauk and Voroshilov were on the same armored train with Makhno, and they directed the military operations together with him. But at the same time Voroshilov had in his hand an order signed by Trotsky commanding him to capture Makhno and all the other responsible leaders of the Makhnovshchina, to disarm the insurgent troops, and to shoot anyone who resisted. Voroshilov was only waiting for the most appropriate moment. Makhno was warned in time, and knew what he had to do. He took account of the situation, saw that a bloody struggle could break out at any moment, and sought a satisfactory way out. He thought it would be best for him to abandon his post as commander of the insurrectionary army. He informed the staff of the insurrectionary army of this decision, and added that for the time being his work as a simple fighter in the ranks of the insurgents would be more useful under the circumstances. This is what he did. He sent the Soviet high command a written explanatory statement, which follows:

> To Voroshilov, Staff of the 14th Army.
> To Trotsky, President of the Revolutionary Military Council, at Khar'kov.
> To Lenin, Kamenev, in Moscow.

As a result of Order No. 1824 of the Revolutionary Military Council of the Republic, I sent the Staff of the 2nd Army and Trotsky a telegram requesting that I be relieved of the post I now occupy. I repeat my request. Here are the reasons which I believe should justify it. Although I have made war with the insurgents against the White bands of Denikin, preaching nothing to the people other than the love of freedom and self-activity, the entire official Soviet press as well as that of the Communist-Bolshevik Party has spread rumors attributing to me actions which are unworthy of a revolutionary. They wish to make me seem a bandit, an accomplice of Grigor'ev, a conspirator against the Soviet Republic, whose aim is to reestablish capitalism. Thus in an article entitled "The Makhnovshchina," published in *V Puti (On the Road)* No. 51, Trotsky poses the question: "Against whom did the Makhnovist insurgents arise?" and throughout his article he occupies himself with demonstrating that the Makhnovshchina is nothing but a battlefront against the power of the Soviets. He does not say a word about the real front against the Whites, which is more than seventy miles long, where the insurgents

128

have been suffering enormous losses for the last six months. Order No. 1824 calls me a conspirator against the Soviet Republic and the organizer of a revolt like Grigor'ev's.

I consider it an inviolable right of the workers and peasants, a right won by the revolution, to call congresses on their own account, to discuss their affairs. That is why the prohibition by the central authorities on the calling of such congresses, and the declaration proclaiming them illegal (Order No. 1824), represent a direct and insolent violation of the rights of the workers.

I understand perfectly the attitude of the central authorities with regard to me. I am absolutely convinced that these authorities consider the insurrectionary movement incompatible with their statist activity. At the same time they believe that this movement is closely tied to me personally and they honor me with all the resentment and hatred they feel for the whole insurrectionary movement. Nothing could demonstrate this better than the article by Trotsky mentioned above, in which, deliberately accumulating lies and slanders, he gives evidence of personal animosity towards me.

This hostile attitude—which now becomes aggressive—of the central authorities toward the insurrectionary movement leads unavoidably to the creation of a special internal front, on both sides of which are the working masses who have faith in the revolution. I consider this circumstance an immense, unpardonable crime against the workers and I believe it my duty to do what I can to avert it. The most effective means of preventing the central authorities from committing this crime is, in my opinion, evident. I must leave the post I occupy. I presume that, having done this, I and the revolutionary insurgents will cease to be suspected of engaging in anti-Soviet conspiracies by the central authorities, and the latter will come to consider the insurrection in the Ukraine an important phenomenon, a living, active manifestation of the social revolution of the masses, and not a hostile movement with which they can only have, as they have shown up to now, relations of distrust and deception, going as far as to haggle over every case of munitions and even sabotaging necessary supplies, which has caused the insurgents innumerable losses in men and territory won by the revolution, losses which would easily have been avoided if the central authorities had adopted another attitude. I request that I be relieved of my post and my duties.

Gyaichur Station,
June 9, 1919.
Batko Makhno.

* * *

At this time the insurgent detachments stationed near Mariupol' retreated to Pologi and Aleksandrovsk. Makhno unexpectedly joined them, saving himself from the trap which the Bolsheviks had set for him at Gyaichur. The Bolsheviks immediately seized and executed Ozerov, Chief of Staff of the Makhnovist Army, staff members Mikhalev-Pavlenko and Burbyga, as well as several members of the Revolutionary Military Council. This was the signal for the execution of numerous other Makhnovists who fell into the hands of the Bolsheviks at this time.

Makhno's situation became increasingly untenable. He either had to completely abandon his detachments, with whom he had lived through the most difficult moments of the Ukrainian revolution, or else call them to a struggle against the Bolsheviks. But the second course was impossible because of Denikin's powerful offensive. With his usual far-sightedness and revolutionary sensitivity, Makhno found a way out of this predicament. He turned to the insurrectionary army with an explanatory proclamation in which he described the new situation, explaining that he had to leave his post as commander for the time being, and calling on the insurgents to continue fighting with the same energy against Denikin's troops without being disturbed by the fact that they would temporarily be under the command of the Bolshevik Staff.

In answer to this appeal the majority of the Makhnovist units remained where they were, accepting the Red command and their incorporation into the Bolshevik Army.

130

But at the same time the commanders of insurrectionary detachments agreed to wait for the opportune moment to reunite themselves under Makhno's command, so long as this act did not endanger the external front. (As we will see below, this moment was chosen by the insurgents with amazing foresight and accuracy.)

After this, Makhno disappeared with a small cavalry detachment.

The insurgent regiments, transformed into Red units and remaining under their regular commanders—Kalashnikov, Kurilenko, Klein, Dermendzhi and others—continued to hold off Denikin's troops, preventing them from taking Aleksandrovsk and Ekaterinoslav.

* * *

Until the last moment the Bolshevik high officials were not aware of the true proportions of Denikin's invasion. Only a few days before the fall of Ekaterinoslav and Khar'kov, Trotsky declared that Denikin did not represent a serious threat, and that the Ukraine was not at all in danger. It is true that the following day, on the basis of new information, he was forced to retract his previous assertions and to recognize that Khar'kov was seriously threatened. But he only admitted this after it was already obvious to everyone that the entire Ukraine was threatened. Ekaterinoslav fell at the end of June, and Khar'kov fell two weeks later.

The Bolsheviks did not try to regain the offensive or even to organize a defense; they hurriedly evacuated the Ukraine. All the Red Army units were involved in this operation. The entire Ukraine was delivered to the reaction literally without a blow being struck.

It was then, when it became clear to everyone that the Bolsheviks were abandoning the Ukraine and were concerned only with taking with them as many men and as much rolling stock as possible, that Makhno decided that the time had come to once again take up the initiative in the struggle against the counter-revolution, and to act as an independent revolutionary force against both Denikin and the Bolsheviks. The word was given to the insurgent detachments who had temporarily been under the command of the Red Army to rid themselves of the Red commanders and to regroup under Makhno's general command.

Chapter 7

The Long Retreat of the Makhnovists
And Their Victory.

Execution of Grigor'ev.
Battle of Peregonovka.
Rout of Denikin's Troops.
Period of Freedom.

As we already mentioned, Makhno retired with a small cavalry detachment when he left his post as commander of the insurrectionary army. He went to Aleksandrovsk. There, in spite of the fact that the Bolsheviks sought his head on the front in the vicinity of the Gyaichur Station, he succeeded in officially turning over the command as well as the affairs of the insurrectionary division to the new brigade commander who had just been appointed by the Bolsheviks. Makhno did this because he desired to leave his post openly and honestly so that the Bolsheviks would have no pretext for accusing him of anything with regard to the affairs of the division he commanded. Makhno needed to act with prudence. Forced to play their game, Makhno did it honorably.

In the meantime Denikin's offensive dealt a heavy blow to the laboring masses. A large number of fleeing peasants set out to look for Makhno whom they considered their popular leader. Numerous insurgents, scattered throughout the region, converged toward him. At the end of two weeks a completely new insurrectionary detachment was formed under Makhno's command. With this detachment, as well as some parts of the original insurrectionary army who arrived in the vicinity of Aleksandrovsk, Makhno prepared to stop Denikin's divisions, retreating step by step, seeking to orient himself and take stock of the situation.

Rapidly overrunning the Ukraine, Denikin's army did not forget about Makhno's presence; they remembered the enormous efforts and losses he had caused them during the previous winter. They assigned a whole army corps consisting of 12 to 15 regiments of cavalry, infantry and artillery, to fight against Makhno. But this was not only a war against the Makhnovist army. Nearly every village which was occupied by Denikin's troops was the scene of fire and bloodshed. Peasants were plundered, violently abused, and killed. This was the officers' revenge against the revolution.

From the first days of Denikin's occupation of Gulyai-Polye, a large number of peasants were shot, dwellings were destroyed, and hundreds of carts and wagons filled with food and other possessions of the Gulyai-Polye inhabitants were sent by Shkuro's Cossacks to the Don and the Kuban. Almost all the Jewish women of the village were raped.

This is why Makhno's retreating army was followed by thousands of peasant families who abandoned their villages, bringing with them their livestock and their belongings. A veritable migration stretched over hundreds of miles. A vast "empire on wheels" followed the army on its march westward. In the course of the retreat this enormous mass of refugees spread throughout the whole Ukraine. Most of them lost their homes and belongings forever; many lost their lives.

Makhno began by digging in on the Dnieper, near Aleksandrovsk, and for some time held the Kichkass bridge.[1] However, overwhelmed by the superior forces of the enemy, he retreated to Dolinskaya and from there toward Elisavetgrad. Meanwhile the Red Army troops lost all their importance in the Ukraine. Many of them were transferred to Great Russia, and the rest began to vacillate and to show distrust of their commanders.

For Makhno, the time had come to call them to his ranks.

But his attention was turned elsewhere.

Already for a long time a dark stain had marred the face of the Ukrainian revolution, a stain which Makhno never lost from view. This was Grigor'ev's movement.

Grigor'ev's forces had begun to dwindle shortly after he had rebelled against the Soviet power; however, he was far from having lost all of them. With several detachments he set

---

[1] One of the most important railway bridges in Russia, spanning the Dnieper near Aleksandrovsk.

up his defenses in the government of Kherson and carried on guerrilla warfare against the Bolsheviks. The total number of detachments under his command or under his influence included several thousand men. These troops carried out frequent raids against small Red Army units stationed in the important villages of the region, disarmed them, occupied the villages, and destroyed railroad tracks. The destruction of railways was their most common practice. Grigor'ev used the following technique to damage railways: at a junction, where the rails came close to each other, he removed all the spikes from a tie under two or three rails; he then hitched several pairs of healthy oxen to the loosened rails, which caused all the rails freed from the tie to bend into a semi-circle.

Grigor'ev was quite skillful in guerrilla warfare. It was he rather than the Bolsheviks who held power in the region of Znamenka, Aleksandriya and Elisavetgrad. The war which Grigor'ev had declared against the Soviets was not inspired by revolutionary motives, but first of all by personal motives and later by counter-revolutionary ones. Lacking any stable ideology, he held on to whatever was nearest at hand: first Petliura, then Bolshevism, then Petliura again, and finally Denikin.

Grigor'ev himself was without a doubt a counter-revolutionary adventurer, but the region and the masses which he led were revolutionary. This is why Makhno decided to include these masses among the revolutionary forces. This could only be done if Grigor'ev and his staff were removed. With his usual skill and energy, Makhno set out to unmask and publicly execute Grigor'ev. The Bolshevik statists who had fought for several months against Grigor'ev had found nothing better to do than put a price on his head (half a million roubles for the person who killed him; half of this sum was offered to the person who killed one of his accomplices, as was announced in June 1919 in several Ukrainian journals). The revolutionary peasant Makhno, with a view to the needs of the revolution, decided to expose and denounce Grigor'ev publicly and in a revolutionary manner. In order to gain access to him, Makhno established relations with Grigor'ev and his detachments, as if to unify all the guerrilla forces.

On Makhno's initiative, a congress of insurgents from

the governments of Ekaterinoslav, Kherson and Tauride was called for July 27, 1919, in the village of Sentovo near Aleksandriya. The agenda of the congress included the establishment of a program of action for the entire insurrectionary Ukraine which would correspond to the needs of the moment. Nearly 20,000 people came—peasants and insurgents, Grigor'ev's detachments and Makhno's troops. Among the many scheduled orators were Grigor'ev, Makhno, and other representatives of the two movements. Grigor'ev was the first to speak. He invited the peasants and the insurgents to devote all their forces to chasing the Bolsheviks out of the country, without rejecting any allies. Grigor'ev said that for this purpose he was even ready to ally with Denikin. Afterward, when the yoke of Bolshevism was broken, the people would themselves see what they had to do. This declaration was fatal to Grigor'ev. Makhno and his comrade Chubenko spoke immediately after Grigor'ev, and declared that the struggle against the Bolsheviks could be revolutionary only if it were carried out in the name of the social revolution. An alliance with the worst enemies of the people—with generals —could only be a counter-revolutionary and criminal adventure. Grigor'ev invited participation in this counter-revolution, and consequently he was an enemy of the people. Following this, Makhno demanded before the entire congress that Grigor'ev immediately answer for the appalling pogrom of Jews which he had organized in Elisavetgrad in May, 1919, as well as other anti-Semitic actions. "Scoundrels like Grigor'ev are the shame of all the Ukrainian insurgents; they cannot be tolerated in the ranks of honest revolutionary workers." Such was Makhno's final indictment of Grigor'ev. Grigor'ev saw that the situation was going badly for him. He reached for weapons. But it was too late. Simon Karetnik —Makhno's comrade—shot him with a Colt revolver, while Makhno himself shouted "Death to the Ataman!" and also shot him. Grigor'ev's assistants and the members of his staff ran to his help, but they were shot on the spot by a group of Makhnovists who had been placed on guard. All this happened during two or three minutes before the eyes of the entire congress.

After the initial agitation over the events that have just been described, the congress heard the declarations of

Makhno, Chubenko and other representatives of the Makhnovshchina, and approved the act, considering it historically necessary. According to the record of the proceedings of the congress, the Makhnovshchina assumed all responsibility for the events which had just taken place and for their consequences. The assembly also decided that the partisan detachments formerly under Grigor'ev's command would henceforth be part of the general insurrectionary army of the Makhnovists.[2]

* * *

We have already mentioned that the small numbers of Soviet troops who had remained in various parts of the Ukraine were suspicious of their commanders. They considered the shameful flight of the Soviet authorities from the Ukraine to be a defection from the revolutionary cause. Makhno was considered the only revolutionary hope in the country. All those who desired to struggle for freedom converged toward Makhno. This spirit also pervaded the Red Army units that had remained in the Ukraine. At the end of July, Bolshevik detachments in the Crimea mutinied, deposed their commanders, and set out to join Makhno's army. This mutiny was organized by Makhnovist commanders who had remained in the ranks of the Red Army: Kalashnikov, Dermendzhi and Budanov. Large numbers of Red Army soldiers advanced from Novi Bug to Pomoshchnaya looking for Makhno, bringing with them, as captives, their former commanders: Kochergin, Dybets and others. These troops met the Makhnovists at Dobrovelichkovka in the government of Kherson at the beginning of August, 1919. For the Bolsheviks this defection was a major blow, since it reduced their military forces in the Ukraine to almost nothing.

Makhno halted for the first time in the region between

---

[2]The record of the proceedings of the congress, the record of Makhno's and Grigor'ev's speeches, as well as a number of other documents, were lost during the armed struggles of 1920.

Pomoshchnaya, Elisavetgrad and Voznesensk (near Odessa) in order to regroup the troops which were arriving from all sides. Four infantry and cavalry brigades, an artillery division and a regiment of machine-gunners were formed here, consisting of about 15,000 soldiers. A special cavalry squad of 150 to 200 always accompanied Makhno, and are not counted in the total number of soldiers. It was with these forces that the Makhnovists undertook an offensive against Denikin's troops. The encounters took on a desperate character. Several times Denikin's army was pushed back thirty to fifty miles eastward. During the struggles the Makhnovists captured from Denikin's troops three or four armored trains, one of which was enormous—the "Invincible." But supported by new reinforcements, Denikin's troops once again pushed the Makhnovists westward. Denikin had great superiority in numbers and weapons. On the other hand, Makhno's army was almost completely out of cartridges. Two out of three of their attacks against Denikin's troops had the sole aim of capturing munitions. In addition the Makhnovists had to battle against some Bolshevik troops retreating from Odessa to the north. This is why it became necessary to retreat further and leave the region of Elisavetgrad-Pomoshchnaya-Voznesensk.

The retreat took place in the midst of incessant combat. The troops Denikin sent against Makhno distinguished themselves by their energy and obstinacy. The regiments of officers were particularly remarkable for their bravery —especially the First Simferopol' and the Second Labinski regiments. Entering into battles against them, Makhno could not help admiring their courage and their defiance of death. Denikin's cavalry merited the highest praise. As Makhno declared, it was truly a cavalry that justified its name. The very numerous cavalry of the Red Army, organized later, was a cavalry in name only; it was never able to carry on hand -to-hand combat, and engaged in combat only when the enemy was already disoriented by the fire of cannons and machine guns. During the entire civil war the Red cavalry always avoided a confrontation with the Makhnovist cavalry, even though the Red cavalry always outnumbered the Makhnovist. The Caucasian cavalry regiments and Denikin's Cossacks always accepted combat with sabres and charged on the enemy at full speed, without waiting for the enemy to be disorganized by cannon fire.

But even these elite troops succumbed more than once in combat against the Makhnovists. The commanders of Denikin's regiments said in their papers, which often fell into the hands of Makhnovists, that nothing in their entire campaign had been as difficult and more horrible for them than these fierce battles against Makhno's cavalry and artillery.

From the middle of August, 1919, this corps of Denikin's army began to exert powerful pressure on Makhno's troops, seeking to encircle them on all sides. Makhno saw that the smallest error on his part could be fatal for his entire army. That is why he carefully sought the moment when he could deal a decisive blow to the enemy. In the north Denikin's troops were already nearing Kursk. Makhno took this circumstance into account, and considered that the further they moved in this direction, the easier it would be to attack them from the rear. In addition to these considerations, Makhno was forced to retreat westward because of the pressure of the enemy's numerically superior forces. Near the end of August, Denikin's army corps, which already weighed so heavily on Makhno, was reinforced by new troops from near Odessa and Voznesensk. The situation worsened. The insurgent army then decided to abandon the vicinity of the railroads, and blew up all the armored trains accessible to them. The retreat continued along country roads, from village to village. Denikin's troops continued to follow. Their goal was not only to defeat, but to liquidate Makhno's army altogether.

This retreat, carried out in the midst of daily battles, lasted more than a month, until Makhno's army arrived near the city of Uman, occupied by the troops of Petliura. Petliura was in a state of war with Denikin. The question was raised —what was to be done about Petliura's army? Declare war on them, or adopt some other tactic toward them? At this time Makhno's army had about 8000 wounded soldiers who were deprived of all medical aid and who comprised an enormous train in the rear of the army, which seriously hindered its movements and its military operations. After an examination of all sides of the question, it was decided that military neutrality be proposed to the Petliurists. In the meantime, a

Petliurist delegation arrived from Uman to Makhno's camp and described the point of view of the Petliurist command about the general situation: being at war with Denikin, the Petliurists wanted to avoid the formation of a new front and hoped to avoid a military encounter with the Makhnovists. This corresponded perfectly with the wishes of the Makhnovists. A Makhnovist delegation was sent to Zhmerinka to conclude a pact according to which both sides agreed to maintain strict military neutrality toward each other, disregarding the political differences which divided them. Furthermore, the Petliurists agreed to take the wounded Makhnovists into their hospitals.

Makhno as well as the rest of the army were obviously aware that this neutrality was superficial, and that any day Petliura could be expected to make common cause with Denikin for a united attack against the Makhnovists. But for the Makhnovists it was a question of gaining one or two weeks of respite, to avoid an attack from the rear—the western flank—and not to be caught in a military trap. In fact, the Makhnovists' attitude toward the Petliurists had hardly changed. While relating to the Petliurist soldiers as brothers, the Makhnovists continued their earlier propaganda against the Petliurist authorities. The Revolutionary Military Council of the Makhnovist Army published a pamphlet entitled "Who is Petliura?" in which Petliura is unmasked as a defender of the privileged classes who deserves to be destroyed by the workers. Many of Petliura's soldiers were Makhnovists in spirit and by tradition, and if Denikin's offensive had not taken such a fierce course, many of them would undoubtedly have been drawn to the ranks of the Makhnovists. The Makhnovists thought about this constantly; the Petliurist leaders suspected it and, recalling the case of Grigor'ev, they maintained a guarded attitude toward the Makhnovists.

The Makhnovist suspicions about the Petliurists' intention to establish relations with Denikin for the purpose of joint action against Makhno started to be confirmed. According to the pact with the Petliurists, the Makhnovist Army was to occupy a territory of 7 square miles near the village of Tekuche in the vicinity of Uman. Petliura's forces were dispersed to the north and west; Denikin's to the east and south, around Golta. This part of the pact, which had been arranged by the Petliurists, soon began to arouse suspicion. And after a few days, information arrived that the Petliurists were negotiating with Denikinist commanders to work out a plan for cooperating to surround and exterminate Makhno's troops. At the same time, on September 24–25, four or five Denikinist regiments appeared at the rear of the Makhnovists, on their western side. These regiments could only have gotten there by passing through the territory occupied by the Petliurists, namely with the help or at least the acquiescence of the Petliurists.

On the evening of September 25, the Makhnovists were completely surrounded by Denikin's troops. The bulk of Denikin's forces remained concentrated to the east, but the city of Uman was also in Denikin's power. The Makhnovists had to act quickly. The fate of the entire insurgent army was in question.

* * *

The Makhnovist retreat had covered more than 400 miles and had lasted close to four months. It had been unimaginably difficult. The insurgents lacked clothes and shoes. Through torrid heat, enveloped by clouds of dust, under a hail of bullets and shells, they went further and further away from their own region toward an unknown destination. But they were all animated by the idea of victory over the enemy, and they valiantly endured the rigors of the retreat. Only occasionally did the least patient among them cry out: "Turn around! Toward the Dnieper!" But implacable necessity kept pushing them further from the Dnieper and their birthplace, their proud region. With inexhaustible patience, with their will stretched to the limit, they rallied around their leader under continual enemy fire. Uman was the end of the retreat. It was impossible to go anywhere else. The enemy was on all sides. It was there that Makhno, with the usual simplicity with which he was able to evoke heroism in his comrades, declared that the retreat had only been a necessary strategic measure, and that the real war was about

141

to begin, not later than the following day, September 26th.

The disposition of Denikin's troops in the north as well as on other fronts was learned. Makhno became convinced that fate was offering him a marvelous opportunity—the possibility of dealing a deathblow to the entire counter-revolution of Denikin. It seemed to him that this could actually be carried out. It was only a question of breaking the fist which, right here at Uman, pressed down on the Makhnovist army.

On the evening of September 25 the Makhnovist troops, who until then had been marching westward, suddenly turned all their forces eastward and marched straight toward the main forces of Denikin's army. The first encounter took place late in the evening near the village of Kruten'koe, where the Makhnovist first brigade attacked a Denikinist unit. Denikin's troops retreated to take up better positions and to draw the Makhnovists after them. But the Makhnovists did not pursue them. This misled the vigilance of the enemy, who concluded that the insurgents were still moving westward. However, in the middle of the night, all the Makhnovist forces, stationed in several villages, began marching eastward. The enemy's principal forces were concentrated near the village of Peregonovka; the village itself was occupied by the Makhnovists. (See map, pp. 156-157.)

The fighting started between 3 and 4 a.m. It kept mounting in intensity and reached its peak by 8 a.m., in a hurricane of machine gun fire on both sides. Makhno himself, with his cavalry escort, had disappeared at nightfall, seeking to turn the enemy's flank. During the whole battle that ensued there was no further news of him. By 9 in the morning the outnumbered and exhausted Makhnovists began to lose ground. They were already fighting on the outskirts of the village. From all sides enemy reinforcements brought new bursts of fire to bear on the Makhnovists. The staff of the insurrectionary army as well as everyone in the village who could handle a rifle, armed themselves and joined in the fighting. This was the critical moment, when it seemed that the battle and with it the whole cause of the insurgents was lost. The order was given for everyone, even the women, to be ready to fire on the enemy in the village streets. All prepared for the supreme hour of the battle and of their lives.

But suddenly the machine-gun fire of the enemy and their frantic cheers began to grow weaker, and then to recede into the distance. The defenders of the village realized that the enemy was retreating, and that the battle was now taking place some distance away. It was Makhno who, appearing unexpectedly, at the very moment when his troops were driven back and were preparing to fight in the streets of Peregonovka, had decided the fate of the battle. Covered with dust and fatigued from his exertions, he reached the enemy flank through a deep ravine. Without a cry, but with a burning resolve fixed on his features, he threw himself on the Denikinists at full gallop, followed by his escort, and broke into their ranks. All exhaustion, all discouragement disappeared from among the Makhnovists. —"Batko is here! Batko is fighting with his sabre!"—could he heard everywhere. And with redoubled energy they all pushed forward, following their beloved leader, who seemed doomed to death. A hand-to-hand combat of incredible ferocity, a "hacking," as the Makhnovists called it, followed. However brave the First Officers' Regiment of Simferopol' may have been, they were thrown into retreat, at first slowly and in an orderly manner, trying to halt the impetus of the Makhnovists, but then they simply ran. The other regiments, seized by panic, followed them, and finally all of Denikin's troops were routed, and tried to save themselves by swimming across the Sinyukha River.

Makhno hastened to take advantage of this situation, which he understood perfectly. He sent his cavalry and artillery at full speed in pursuit of the retreating enemy, and himself went at the head of the best mounted regiment by a shortcut which would enable him to catch the fugitives from behind. The pursuit continued for 8 to 12 miles. At the critical moment when Denikin's troops reached the river, they were overtaken by the Makhnovist cavalry, and hundreds of them perished in the river. Most of them, however, had time to cross to the other bank, but there Makhno himself was waiting for them. The Denikinist staff and the reserve regiment which was with it were surprised and taken prisoners. Only an insignificant part of these troops, who had raged for months in the stubborn pursuit of Makhno, managed to save themselves. The First Simferopol' Regiment

INSURGENT UKRAINE.
UKRAINIAN PEASANT: "You want my bread? Here's bread for you!"
(Signed: *Pugachev*)

144

of officers and several others were entirely cut down by the insurgents' sabres. The route of their retreat was strewn with corpses for over two miles. However horrible this spectacle was to some, it was only the natural outcome of the duel between Denikin's army and the Makhnovists. During the entire pursuit, the Denikinists had had no thought except to exterminate the insurgents. The slightest error on Makhno's part would inevitably have led to the same fate for the revolutionary insurrectionary army. Even the women who supported the Makhnovist army or fought alongside the men would not have been spared. The Makhnovists were experienced enough to know this.

* * *

The following legend about Pugachev is told among the peasants of Great Russia. After his uprising he fell into the hands of the authorities. He told the noblemen sitting around him: "In this uprising I only gave you a foretaste. But wait: soon after me will come the real *broom* — it will sweep all of you away." Makhno showed himself to be this historic broom of the people in all his revolutionary insurrectionary activity, and especially when he defeated the Denikinists.

Once Denikin's fist was broken, the Makhnovists immediately set out in three directions. They literally swept through villages, towns and cities like an enormous broom, removing every vestige of exploitation and servitude. The returned *pomeshchiks,* the *kulaks,* the police, the priests, the Denikinist mayors and officers in hiding—all these were swept out of the victorious path of the Makhnovist movement. Prisons, police stations and posts—all these symbols of the people's servitude were destroyed. All those who were known to be active enemies of the peasants and workers were condemned to death. *Pomeshchiks* and major *kulaks* perished in great numbers. This fact suffices to show the mendacity of the myth spread by the Bolsheviks about the so-called *kulak* character of the Makhnovshchina. In fact, wherever the Makhnovist movement developed, the *kulaks* sought the protection of the Soviet authorities, and found it there.

145

The army returned to the Dnieper at an incredible pace. The day after the defeat of Denikin's troops at Peregonovka, Makhno was already more than 60 miles away from the scene of the battle. Accompanied by his escort, he marched about thirty miles ahead of the rest of the troops. On the following day the Makhnovists occupied Dolinskaya, Krivoi Rog and Nikopol'. The day after, the Kichkass Bridge across the Dnieper was taken at a trot, and the city of Aleksandrovsk was occupied. In their furious advance, it seemed as though they were entering an enchanted kingdom: no one had yet heard of the events at Uman; no one knew where the Makhnovists were; the authorities had taken no precautionary measures and were caught in the lethargy that characterizes the rearguard. This is why the Makhnovists everywhere struck their enemies unexpectedly, like a bolt of lightning. Aleksandrovsk was followed by Pologi, Gulyai-Polye, Berdyansk, Melitopol', Mariupol'. At the end of ten days the entire southern Ukraine was freed of Denikin's troops and authorities.

The Makhnovists' occupation of the southern Ukraine, especially the regions bordering on the Sea of Azov, represented a mortal danger to Denikin's entire counter-revolutionary campaign. In fact, the supply base of Denikin's army was located in the region between Mariupol' and Volnovakha. When Berdyansk and Mariupol' were taken, immense stores of munitions were gained. At Volnovakha shells were stacked in tiers. To be sure, all these supplies did not fall immediately into the hands of the Makhnovists; the battle around Volnovakha raged for five days. But, since all the railroads of the region were in the insurgents' hands, no war material could reach Denikin's troops. Denikinist reserve regiments stationed throughout the region were annihilated. Consequently all this gigantic base of artillery was blockaded by the Makhnovists, and not a single shell could be sent to Denikin's northern front or to any other front.

The Denikinists hurriedly sent against Makhno the reserve troops stationed near Taganrog; but these troops were also routed and the flood of the Makhnovshchina flowed toward the bottom of the Donets Basin and northward. By October 20th the Makhnovists occupied Ekaterinoslav and its surroundings. It was then that the Denikinists recognized the situation as it was. They announced that the center of their campaign had to shift from the north to the south; that the fate of their campaign would be decided in the south. General Mai-Maevsky told the Cossacks: Our lands are directly threatened; the enemy rages in the south endangering our homes; we must rush there to protect our lands (Mai-Maevsky's speech was published in a Denikinist newspaper).

In view of the situation, Denikin's best cavalry troops, commanded by Mamontov and Shkuro, were transferred from the northern front to the Gulyai-Polye region. But it was already too late. The fire was raging throughout the whole country, from the shores of the Black Sea and the Sea of Azov to Khar'kov and Poltava. Due to fresh reinforcements and numerous armored cars, the Whites momentarily succeeded in making the Makhnovists retreat from Mariupol', Berdyansk and Gulyai-Polye. But the Makhnovists, in turn, occupied Sinel'nikovo, Pavlograd, Ekaterinoslav and other cities and localities. During October and November, the struggle again became fierce, and Denikin's troops again underwent some enormous defeats. Denikin's Caucasian regiments suffered the greatest losses, especially the Chechen cavalry and others, who perished by the thousands. Toward the end of November these troops declared categorically that they refused to continue fighting against Makhno. They abandoned their posts in Denikin's army and returned home to the Caucasus. Thus began the general disintegration of Denikin's army.

The complete defeat of the Denikinists in their struggle against the Makhnovshchina in southern Russia determined the fate of their entire campaign against the Russian revolution.

It is necessary to emphasize the historic fact that the honor of having annihilated the Denikinist counter-revolution in the autumn of 1919 belongs almost entirely to the Makhnovists. If the insurgents had not won the decisive victory at Peregonovka, and had not destroyed the Denikinist supply lines for artillery, food and ammunition, the Whites would probably have entered Moscow in December, 1919. The battle between the Whites and the Reds near Orel was relatively insignificant. In fact, Denikin's southern retreat had already begun before this battle, having been provoked precisely by the defeat of its rearguard. All the subsequent military operations of the Denikinists had the sole purpose of protecting their retreat and evacuating their munitions and supplies. Along the whole length of the route from Orel through Kursk to the shores of the Black Sea and the Sea of Azov, the Red Army advanced almost without resistance. Its entry into the Ukraine and the Caucasus was carried out exactly the same way as its entry had been carried out a year earlier, at the time of the fall of the Hetman—along paths that were already cleared.

* * *

Purely military concerns absorbed nearly all the forces of the Makhnovists at this time. The state of war in the region was absolutely unfavorable to internal creative activities. Even so, the Makhnovists demonstrated the necessary initiative and diligence in this domain as well. First of all, wherever they went they undertook to prevent an important misunderstanding: the possibility of being taken for a new power or party. As soon as they entered a city, they declared that they did not represent any kind of authority, that their armed forces obliged no one to any sort of obligation and had no other aim than to protect the freedom of the working people. The freedom of the peasants and the workers, said the Makhnovists, resides in the peasants and workers themselves and may not be restricted. In all fields of their lives it is up to the workers and peasants themselves to construct whatever they consider necessary. As for the Makhnovists —they can only assist them with advice, by putting at their disposal the intellectual or military forces they need, but under no circumstances can the Makhnovists prescribe for them in any manner.[3]

[3] In certain cities the Makhnovists appointed a commander. His function consisted only of serving as a contact man between the troops and the population, and of informing the population about measures taken by the army which might have repercussions on the life of the inhabitants and which the military command felt it opportune to take. These commanders had no authority over the population and did not interfere in any way with their civil life.

Aleksandrovsk and the surrounding region were the first places where the Makhnovists remained for a fairly long time. They immediately invited the working population to participate in a general conference of the workers of the city. When the conference met, a detailed report was given on the military situation in the region and it was proposed that the workers organize the life of the city and the functioning of the factories with their own forces and their own organizations, basing themselves on the principles of labor and equality. The workers enthusiastically acclaimed all these suggestions; but they hesitated to carry them out, troubled by their novelty, and troubled mainly by the nearness of the front, which made them fear that the situation of the city was uncertain and unstable. The first conference was followed by a second. The problems of organizing life according to the principles of self-management by the workers were examined and discussed with animation by the masses of workers, who all welcomed this idea with the greatest enthusiasm, but who only with difficulty succeeded in giving it concrete forms. Railroad workers took the first step in this direction. They formed a committee charged with organizing the railway network of the region, establishing a detailed plan for the movement of trains, the transport of passengers, the system of payments, etc. From this point on, the proletariat of Aleksandrovsk began to turn systematically to the problem of creating organs of self-management.

Shortly after the workers' meetings, a regional congress of peasants and workers was called at Aleksandrovsk for October 20, 1919. More than 200 delegates took part, among whom 180 were peasants, and the rest workers. The congress dealt with: a) military questions (the struggle against Denikin; reinforcement and maintenance of the insurrectionary army); b) questions dealing with constructive activity in the region.

The congress continued for nearly a week and was characterized by a remarkable spirit on the part of those present. This was largely due to specific circumstances. First of all, the return of the victorious Makhnovist army to its own region was an extremely important event for the peasants, since nearly every family had one or two of its members among the insurgents. But still more important was

149

the fact that this congress met in conditions of absolute freedom. There was no influence emanating from above. Besides all this, the congress had an excellent militant and speaker in the anarchist Voline, who, to the amazement of the peasants, lucidly expressed their own thoughts and wishes. The idea of free soviets genuinely functioning in the interests of the working population; the question of direct relations between peasants and city workers, based on mutual exchange of the products of their labor; the launching of a stateless and egalitarian social organization in the cities and the country—all these ideas which Voline developed in his lectures, represented the very ideas of the peasantry. This was precisely the way the peasants conceived the revolution and creative revolutionary work.

During the first day the representatives of political parties naturally attempted to introduce a spirit of discord into the work of the congress, but they were censured by the entire congress, and the work of the congress continued with complete harmony among the participants.

The final days of the congress resembled a beautiful poem. Concrete resolutions were followed by magnificent bursts of enthusiasm. All were moved by confidence in their own strength and by faith in the power of the revolution. A spirit of true freedom, such as is rarely experienced, was present in the hall. Everyone saw before him and really grasped the enormous project which was worthy of all one's energy and for which one would willingly die. The peasants, among whom there were old and even ancient men, said that this was the first congress where they felt not only perfectly free, but also real brothers in relation to each other, and that they would never forget it. And indeed it is hardly likely that anyone who took part in that congress could ever forget it. It remained engraved forever on the memories of many, if not of all, as a beautiful dream about a life in which true liberty would bring people together, giving them the opportunity to live united at heart, joined by a feeling of love and brotherhood.

The congress resolved numerous problems concerning the insurrectionary army, its organization and reinforcement. It was proposed that men up to the age of 48 enlist in this army. In keeping with the spirit of the congress, this enrollment would be voluntary, but as general as possible, in view of the extremely dangerous situation of the region. Earlier we already mentioned the meaning of the voluntary 10-year mobilization which was proposed at the second regional congress on February 12, 1919. The resolution on mobilization passed by the October congress had the same meaning. The congress decided that the supplying of the army would be done primarily by free gifts from the peasants, in addition to spoils of victory and requisitions from privileged groups. In the domain of internal constructive activity, the congress limited itself for the time being to indicating general guidelines—that the workers, without any authority, should themselves organize their lives by their own efforts and means.

When the peasants left, they emphasized the need to put the decisions of the congress into practice. The delegates took away with them copies of the resolutions in order to make them known all over the countryside. It is certain that at the end of three or four weeks the results of the congress would have been known all over the region and that the next congress, called on the initiative of the workers and peasants themselves, would not have failed to attract the interest and active participation of great masses of workers. Unfortunately, the freedom of the working masses is continually threatened by its worst enemy—authority. The delegates hardly had time to return to their homes when many of their villages were again occupied by Denikin's troops, coming by forced marches from the northern front. To be sure, this time the invasion was only of short duration; it was the death agony of a dying enemy. But it halted the constructive work of the peasants at the most vital moment, and since another authority, equally hostile to the freedom of the masses —Bolshevism—was approaching from the north, this invasion did irreparable harm to the workers' cause: not only was it impossible to assemble a new congress, but even the decisions of the first could not be put into practice.

In the city of Ekaterinoslav, which was occupied by the insurgent army at the time of the congress, conditions were even less favorable for constructive activity in the economic sphere. Denikin's troops, who were driven out of the city, managed to dig in on the left bank of the Dnieper River. Daily, for a whole month, they bombarded the city from their numerous armored trains. Each time the cultural section of the insurrectionary army managed to call a meeting of the city's workers, the Denikinists, who were well informed, fired great numbers of shells, especially on the places where the sessions were to be held. No serious work, no systematic organization was possible. It was possible to hold only a few meetings in the center and the suburbs of the city. The Makhnovists did, however, succeed in publishing their daily newspaper, *Put' k Svobode,* which was soon supplemented by a daily edition in the Ukrainian language, *Shlyakh do Voli.*[4]

* * *

Throughout the liberated region, the Makhnovists were the only organization powerful enough to impose its will on the enemy. But they never used this power for the purpose of

[4]One of the favorite arguments of the Bolsheviks against the Makhnovists is the claim that the insurgents did nothing during their stay at Ekaterinoslav to achieve a constructive organization of the life of that city. But in saying this, the Bolsheviks hide from the masses two circumstances of extraordinary importance. In the first place, the Makhnovists were neither a party nor an authority. In Ekaterinoslav, they acted as a revolutionary military detachment, guaranteeing the freedom of the city. In this capacity, they were *in no way obliged* to try to achieve a constructive revolutionary program. This task could only be carried out by the workers of the place. The Makhnovist army could at most help them with its opinions and advice, with its spirit of initiative and its organizational ability, and it did this.

Secondly, the Bolsheviks in their arguments hide from the masses the exceptional situation of the city at that time: during the whole time that the Makhnovists remained there, it was not only in a state of siege, but actually under bombardment. Not an hour passed without shells bursting. It was *this situation,* and not the Makhnovist army, that prevented the workers from setting out, on the spot, to organize life according to the principles of self-management.

As for the fable according to which the Makhnovists declared to the railway workers who came to them for help that they (the Makhnovists) did not need railroads, since they had good horses as well as the Steppes—this gross invention was started by Denikin's newspapers in October, 1919, and from that source the Bolsheviks took it to serve their own ends.

domination or even to gain political influence; they never used it against their purely political or ideological opponents. The military opponents, the conspirators against the freedom of action of the workers and peasants, the state apparatus, the prisons—these were the elements against which the efforts of the Makhnovist army were directed.

Prisons are the symbol of the servitude of the people. They are always built only to subjugate the people, the workers and peasants. Throughout the centuries, the bourgeoisie in all countries crushed the spirit of rebellion or resistance of the masses by means of execution and imprisonment. And in our time, in the Communist and Socialist State, prisons devour mainly the proletariat of the city and the countryside. Free people have no use for prisons. Wherever prisons exist, the people are not free. Prisons represent a constant threat to the workers, an encroachment on their consciousness and will, and a visible sign of their servitude. This is how the Makhnovists defined their relationship to prisons. In keeping with this attitude, they demolished prisons wherever they went. In Berdyansk the prison was dynamited in the presence of an enormous crowd, which took an active part in its destruction. At Aleksandrovsk, Krivoi-Rog, Ekaterinoslav and elsewhere, prisons were demolished or burned by the Makhnovists. Everywhere the workers cheered this act.

* * *

It gives us great satisfaction to be able to state that the Makhnovists fully applied the revolutionary principles of freedom of speech, of thought, of the press, and of political association. In all the cities and towns occupied by the Makhnovists, they began by lifting all the prohibitions and repealing all the restrictions imposed on the press and on political organizations by one or another power. Complete freedom of speech, press, assembly and association of any kind and for everyone was immediately proclaimed. During the few weeks that the Makhnovists spent at Ekaterinoslav, five or six newspapers of various political orientations appeared: the right Socialist-Revolutionary paper, *Narodo-*

vlastie (The People's Power), the left Socialist-Revolutionary paper, *Znamya Vosstanya (The Standard of Revolt),* the Bolshevik *Zvezda (Star),* and others. However, the Bolsheviks hardly had the right to freedom of press and association because they had destroyed, wherever they had been able to, the freedom of press and association of the working class, and also because their organization at Ekaterinoslav had taken a direct part in the criminal invasion of the Gulyai-Polye region in June, 1919; it would only have been just to inflict a severe punishment on them. But, in order not to injure the great principles of freedom of speech and assembly, the Bolsheviks were not disturbed, and could enjoy, along with all the other political tendencies, all the rights inscribed on the banner of the proletarian revolution.

The only restriction that the Makhnovists considered necessary to impose on the Bolsheviks, the left Socialist-Revolutionaries and other statists was a prohibition on the formation of those "revolutionary committees" which sought to impose a dictatorship over the people. In Aleksandrovsk and Ekaterinoslav, right after the occupation of these cities by the Makhnovists, the Bolsheviks hastened to organize *Revkoms (Revolutionary Committees)* seeking through them to establish their political power and govern the population. At Aleksandrovsk, the members of the *Revkom* went so far as to propose to Makhno a division of spheres of action, leaving Makhno the military power, and reserving for the Committee full freedom of action and all political and civil authority. Makhno advised them to go and take up some honest trade instead of seeking to impose their will on the workers; he even threatened to put to death the members of the *Revkom* if they undertook any authoritarian measures against the working population. At Ekaterinoslav, a similar *Revkom* was dissolved the same way. In this context the Makhnovists' attitude was completely justified and consistent. To protect the full freedom of speech, press, and organization, they had to take measures against formations which sought to stifle this freedom, to suppress other organizations, and to impose their will and dictatorial authority on the workers. And when, in November, 1919, the commander of the Makhnovist Third (Crimean) Insurrectional Regiment, Polonsky, was implicated in the activities of an authoritarian organization of this type, he was executed along with other

154

members of the organization.

Here is the Makhnovist text regarding freedom of the press and of association:

1. All socialist political parties, organizations and tendencies have the right to propagate their ideas, theories, views and opinions freely, both orally and in writing. No restriction of socialist freedom of speech and press will be allowed, and no persecution may take place in this domain.

Remark. Military communiques may not be printed unless they are supplied by the editors of the central organ of the revolutionary insurgents, *Put' k Svobode.*

2. In allowing all political parties and organizations full and complete freedom to propagate their ideas, the Makhnovist insurgent army wishes to inform all the parties that any attempt to prepare, organize and impose a political authority over the working people will not be permitted by the revolutionary insurgents, such an act having nothing in common with the free dissemination of ideas.

> Ekaterinoslav. November 5, 1919.
> Revolutionary Military Council of
> the Makhnovist Insurgent Army.

In the course of the whole Russian revolution, the period of the Makhnovshchina was the only period in which the freedom of the working masses found full expression. However painful and unstable the situation in Aleksandrovsk, and especially in Ekaterinoslav, where shells from the armored trains of Denikin's army fell daily, the workers of these two cities could for the first time in their history say and do anything they wanted, and as they wanted. In addition, they at last held in their own hands the tremendous possibility to organize their life and their work themselves, according to their own judgments and their own understanding of justice and truth.

At the end of the month the Makhnovists were forced to leave Ekaterinoslav. But they had time to demonstrate to the working masses that true freedom resides in the hands of the workers themselves, and that it begins to radiate and develop as soon as statelessness and equality are established among them.

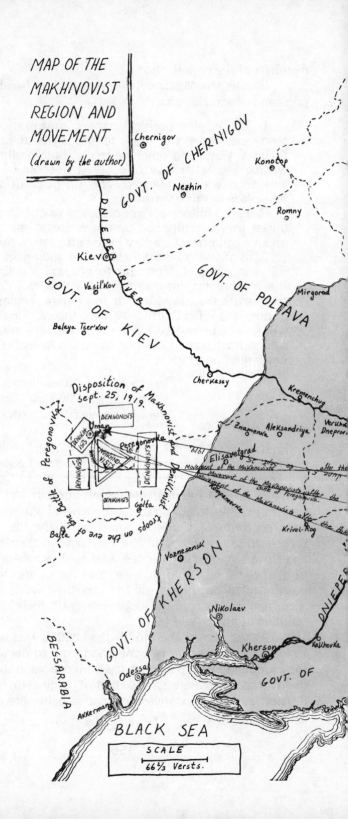

MAP OF THE
MAKHNOVIST
REGION AND
MOVEMENT
(drawn by the author)

Chernigov

GOVT. OF CHERNIGOV

Konotop

Nezhin

Romny

Kiev

Vasil'kov

GOVT. OF KIEV

GOVT. OF POLTAVA

Mirgorod

Belaya Tser'kov

Cherkassy

Kremenchug

Verkhn.
Dneprov.

Disposition of Makhnovist
Sept. 25, 1919.

DENIKINISTS

Uman

DENIKINISTS

Peregonovka

MAKHNO-
VISTS

DENIKINISTS

DENIKINISTS

Golta

Znamenka

Aleksandriya

Elisavetgrad

Movement of the Makhnovist
Movement of the Makhnovists after the
Movement of the Makhnovists after the
Battle of Peregonovka.

Kompaneevka

Krivoi-Rog

Balta to the eve of the Battle of Peregonovka.

Voznesensk

GOVT. OF KHERSON

Nikolaev

Kherson

Kakhovka

DNIEPER

BESSARABIA

Odessa

GOVT. OF

Akkerman

BLACK SEA

SCALE
66⅔ Versts.

Kursk

GOVT. OF KURSK

Oboyan

Korocha

Belgorod

my

Voronezh

GOVT. OF VORONEZH

Bobrov

tirka

GOVT. OF KHAR'KOV

Khar'kov

Chuguev

ava

Konstantinograd

Izyum

Starobel'sk

Slavyanoserbsk

Novomoskovsk

Pavlograd

Sinel'nikovo

Ekaterinoslav

ttle of Perey

GOV F EKATERINOSLAV

ovo

B. Mikhailovka

Pokrovskoe

B. Yanissel'

Konstantin

DON

REGION

Aleksandrovsk

Gulyai-Polye

Kermenchik

Orekhov

Pologi

pol'

Kirilovka

Taganrog

Chernigovka

Mariupol'

Tokmak

Novospasovie

Melitopol'

Berdyansk

Eisk

Nagolsk

AURIDE

Genichesk

SEA OF

AZOV

CAUCASUS

Denikin's Counter-Revolution

RIMEA

Limit of central Makhnovist region.
Limit of region under
strong Makhnovist influence.

Chapter 8

Errors of the Makhnovists.
Second Bolshevik Assault
on the Insurgent Region.

The exertions of the Makhnovists in their struggle against Denikin were colossal. The heroism of their six-month struggle had been visible to everyone. Throughout the extensive area of the liberated region, they alone carried the revolutionary thunder and prepared the grave for Denikin's counter-revolution. This is how the broad masses of the cities and villages understood the events which took place.

This circumstance led many Makhnovists to the conclusion that they were now protected from all Communist provocations in view of the understanding of the workers and peasants. It was thought that the Red Army, coming from the north, would now understand the falsity of the Communist Party's accusations of the Makhnovists; that this army would not be taken in by a new hoax or provocation by the Party, but would on the contrary make common cause with the Makhnovists as soon as the two met. Furthermore, the optimism of certain Makhnovists went so far as to consider it unlikely, in view of the widespread Makhnovist leanings among the people, that the Communist Party would dare to organize a new attack against the free people.

The military and revolutionary activity of the Makhnovists corresponded to this attitude. They limited themselves to occupying part of the region between the Dnieper and the Don, and did not seek to advance northward and consolidate themselves there, thinking that when the two armies met, an appropriate tactic would be worked out. In addition, some militants were convinced that exaggerated importance should not be given to the military, even if revolutionary, aspect, but that it was necessary to concentrate on the activity of the masses of workers and peasants, to encourage them in the work of revolutionary construction.

159

Congresses of workers and peasants—district, regional, provincial—these were to be the practical tasks of the day. This is how the revolution was to be helped and saved from the Bolshevik impasse.

The optimism of the Makhnovists and their attitude about the need to concentrate mainly on constructive work in the region were perfectly healthy, but did not in any way correspond to the situation which was developing in the Ukraine, and consequently did not lead to the anticipated results.

There was first of all Bolshevism. By its very nature it could never, under any circumstances, allow the free and open existence of a popular movement from below, such as the Makhnovshchina. Whatever the public opinion of the workers and peasants, Bolshevism, on first contact with the movement, would take all measures to annihilate it. This is why the Makhnovists, situated at the heart of the popular activity of the Ukraine, should have begun by protecting themselves from this threat. Their desire to devote themselves principally to positive work—a profoundly justified and revolutionary desire—was untenable in the specific circumstances of the Ukraine after 1918. The country had been traversed several times by Austro-Germans, by Petliurists, by Denikinists, by the Bolsheviks. In 1919 the insurgent region had been swept from one end to the other by a wave of Cossacks heading in one direction, and four months later by the same wave heading in the opposite direction, devastating everything in its path. This avalanche was followed immediately by the numerous troops of the Red Army, who inflicted on the revolutionary people the same unremitting devastation.

Consequently, in the summer of 1919 the situation in the insurgent region made large-scale revolutionary construction absolutely impossible. It seemed as though a gigantic grate composed of bayonets shuttled back and forth across the region, from north to south and back again, wiping out all traces of creative social construction. In these conditions the Makhnovists were forced to concentrate on military affairs, to combat enemy forces.

We must continue to take into account the conditions of life in the region.

160

In the autumn of 1919, the annihilation of Denikin's counter-revolution was the main task of the Makhnovists in the context of the Russian revolution. The Makhnovists completed this task. But this did not complete their historical mission in the Russian revolution at this time. The country in revolt, liberated from Denikin's troops, urgently required the immediate organization of defense throughout its whole territory. Without such defense, the country and all the revolutionary possibilities given to it by the liquidation of Denikin, were in constant danger of being wiped out by the statist army of the Bolsheviks, which had been sent into the Ukraine in pursuit of Denikin's retreating troops.

It is therefore incontestable that, in the autumn of 1919, one of the historic tasks imposed on the Makhnovshchina by the course of events was the creation of a revolutionary army strong enough to permit the revolutionary people to defend their freedom, not only in an isolated and limited area, but in the whole territory of the Ukrainian insurrection.

During the fierce struggle against Denikin, this would certainly not have been an easy task, but it was historically necessary and entirely possible, since the major part of the Ukraine was in the midst of revolution and was Makhnovist in spirit. The units of insurgents who flocked to join the Makhnovists came not only from the southern Ukraine, but also from the north—for example the insurrectional division of Bibik, who occupied Poltava. Furthermore, certain detachments of the Red Army came from Central Russia to the ranks of the Makhnovists, thirsting to fight for the social revolution under the banner of the Makhnovshchina. Among others, fairly numerous troops came from the government of Orel, under the command of Ogarkov. They arrived at Ekaterinoslav toward the end of October, 1919, having fought battles on the way against the Bolshevik as well as the Denikinist armies.

The banner of the Makhnovshchina rose spontaneously and floated over the whole Ukraine. It was only necessary to take certain measures in order to merge all the numerous armed formations which were wandering over the whole Ukraine into a single, powerful, popular and revolutionary army that could have stood guard around the territory of the revolution.

Such a force, defending the whole revolutionary territory, and not merely a narrow and limited region, would have been the most persuasive argument against the Bolsheviks, accustomed as they were to work and deal with force.

However, intoxication with the victories, as well as a certain carelessness, prevented the Makhnovists from creating a force of this sort in time. This is why, from the time the Bolsheviks entered the Ukraine, the Makhnovists were obliged to withdraw into the limited area of Gulyai-Polye. This was a serious military error, an error which the Bolsheviks were not slow in turning to their advantage, and an error whose consequences soon fell heavily on the Makhnovists and on the entire revolution in the Ukraine.

* * *

A typhus epidemic which spread all over Russia attacked the Makhnovist army as well. In October, half the men were sick. This was the main reason why the Makhnovists were obliged to abandon Ekaterinoslav when the city was attacked, toward the end of November, by a strong force of Denikin's army commanded by General Slashchev. These troops were retreating toward the Crimea, and their temporary occupation of Ekaterinoslav had no significance.

The Makhnovists regrouped in the region between the cities of Melitopol', Nikopol' and Aleksandrovsk. The staff of the army halted in Aleksandrovsk. News of the Red Army's approach had been heard for some time. Envisaging a fraternal meeting, the Makhnovists did not make any preparations for a collision.

At the end of December, several divisions of the Red Army arrived in the region of Ekaterinoslav and Aleksandrovsk. The encounter between the Makhnovists and the Red Army soldiers was warm and comradely. A general meeting was organized at which the combatants of both armies shook hands and declared that they would fight together against their common enemy: capitalism and counter-revolution. This alliance lasted for about a week. Some units

162

of the Red Army even showed a desire to go over to the Makhnovist ranks.

Then the commander of the Makhnovist army received an order from the Revolutionary Military Council of the 14th Corps of the Red Army to move the insurrectionary army to the Polish front. Everyone immediately understood that this was the first step of the Bolsheviks towards a new attack on the Makhnovists. Sending the insurrectionary army to the Polish front meant removing from the Ukraine the main nerve center of the revolutionary insurrection. This was precisely what the Bolsheviks wanted: they would then be absolute masters of the rebellious region, and the Makhnovists were perfectly aware of this. Furthermore, the order itself aroused the indignation of the Makhnovists: neither the 14th Corps nor any other unit of the Red Army had any ties whatsoever with the Makhnovist army; least of all were they in a position to give orders to the insurrectionary army, which alone had supported the whole weight of the struggle against the counter-revolution in the Ukraine.

The Revolutionary Military Council of the Makhnovist insurrectionary army replied immediately to the order issued by the 14th Army Corps. This response stated (lacking the written documents, we cite from memory): The Makhnovist insurrectionary army has demonstrated its revolutionary spirit better than anyone else. It will remain at its revolutionary combat post by staying in the Ukraine, and not by travelling to the Polish front, the significance of which they do not understand. Furthermore, this departure is physically impossible because half the men, the entire staff and the commander himself are in the hospital with typhus. The Revolutionary Military Council of the Makhnovist insurrectionary army considers the order of the 14th Army Corps misplaced and a provocation.

This reply of the Makhnovists was accompanied by an appeal to the soldiers of the Red Army calling on them not to be duped by the provocative maneuvers of their commanders. Having done this, the Makhnovists broke camp and set out for Gulyai-Polye. They arrived without hardships and without incidents. The soldiers of the Red Army showed no desire to oppose the move of the Makhnovists. Only a few small detachments and some isolated individuals who fell behind the rest of the movement were held by the Bolsheviks.

In the middle of January, 1920, the Bolsheviks declared Makhno and the members of his army outlaws for their refusal to go to the Polish front. This date marked the beginning of a violent struggle between the Makhnovists and the Communist power. We will not go into all the details of this struggle, which lasted nine months. We will only note that it was a merciless struggle on both sides. The Bolsheviks relied on their numerous well-armed and well-supplied divisions. In order to avert fraternization between the soldiers of the Red Army and the Makhnovists, the Bolshevik commander sent against the Makhnovists a division of Lettish sharpshooters and some Chinese detachments, that is to say, units whose members had not the slightest idea of the true meaning of the Russian revolution and who blindly obeyed the orders of the authorities.

* * *

In January the Makhnovists were disorganized by the typhus epidemic. All the members of the staff had typhoid fever. Makhno himself had contracted a particularly acute form of typhus. The majority of the soldiers of the army had to leave the ranks because of the illness, and were scattered in the villages. It was in these conditions that the Makhnovists had to face their numerous enemies and to care for Makhno, who was unconscious for many days. It was a moment of concern, sacrifice and devoted care for their leader. The insurgents, simple peasants from the surrounding villages, were deeply moved by Makhno's dangerous situation. Being sick, he could be taken prisoner by the Red Army from one day to the next. It was perfectly clear to all that the loss of Makhno would be a terrible blow to the entire peasantry, a loss with consequences that could not be imagined. So the peasants did everything they could to prevent this. One should have seen the solicitude with which they transported Makhno from one hut to another in Gulyai-Polye and other

164

villages, shielding him from the Red soldiers sent after him; one should have seen how, more than once, at the critical moment when Makhno's hiding place was discovered, the peasants sacrificed themselves, seeking to gain time to transport him to a safer place—one had to have seen all this in order to understand with what fanatic devotion the peasants were ready to defend their leader, and to what degree they valued him. It was only due to this exceptional devotion that Makhno's life was saved at this critical moment.

* * *

Though the Bolshevik troops were much more numerous, Makhno and his detachments constantly kept out of their reach. But the Bolsheviks managed to establish themselves solidly in several places, and to stop the free development of the region, which had begun in 1919. It was then that mass executions of peasants began.

Many will remember that the Soviet press, in articles on the struggle with Makhno, cited the number of Makhnovists defeated, captured or shot. But this press always neglected to mention that the victims were usually not insurgents in Makhno's army but local peasants of various villages who sympathized with the Makhnovshchina. The arrival of Red divisions in a village meant the immediate arrest of many peasants, who were later executed either as Makhnovist insurgents, or as hostages. The commanders of various Red divisions were particularly fond of this savage and vile method of struggle against the Makhnovshchina, preferring it to open struggle against Makhno. It was especially the units of the 42nd and 46th Red Rifle divisions who indulged in this type of activity. The village of Gulyai-Polye, which passed from one side to the other several times, suffered the most. Each time the Bolshevik troops entered the village or were obliged to leave, the commanders rounded up several dozen peasants, arresting them unexpectedly in the streets, and shot them. Every inhabitant of Gulyai-Polye can tell horrifying stories about this Bolshevik practice. According to the most moderate estimates, more than 200,000 peasants and workers were shot or seriously injured by the Soviet authorities in the Ukraine at that time. Nearly as many were imprisoned or deported to various parts of Russia and Siberia.

Naturally the Makhnovists—revolutionary sons of a people in revolution—could not remain indifferent to such a monstrous distortion of the revolution. They replied to the Bolshevik terror with blows no less severe. They employed against the Bolsheviks all methods of guerrilla warfare which they had formerly used in their struggle against the Hetman Skoropadsky. Whenever the Red Army units entered into combat with the Makhnovists, the battle followed all the rules of war, and it was unfortunately the simple soldiers of the Red Army who were the main victims of such encounters, soldiers who had been sent into the battle under compulsion and who in no way deserved such a fate. But this could not be avoided. When the Makhnovists captured Red prisoners they disarmed the soldiers and set them free; those who wished could join the insurgent ranks; but the commanders and Party functionaries were generally killed, except for the rare instances when the soldiers asked that they be spared.

The Soviet authorities and their agents often depicted the Makhnovists as pitiless assassins, giving long lists of soldiers of the Red Army and members of the Communist Party put to death by them. But the authorities were always silent about the essential fact, namely about the circumstances in which these soldiers or Party members had been killed. They were always *victims of combats* started or provoked by the Communists themselves, combats which were forced on the Makhnovists when they were cornered by the Bolsheviks. War is war; there are always victims on both sides. But the Makhnovists understood perfectly that they were making war, not against the soldiers of the Red Army as a group or against any of them individually, but against the handful of rulers who directed this mass, who disposed of them, and who valued the life of a Red soldier only to the extent that it was useful for the preservation of their power. This is why, although they often struggled bitterly against the Red Army units, once the battle was over the Makhnovists related to the soldiers of the Red Army with the same spirit of brotherhood and friendship which characterized relations among themselves. One can only admire the tact, the self-restraint and the revolutionary honor with which the Makhnovists turned to the soldiers of the Red Army: not one of the soldiers of this army taken prisoner by the Makhnovists was made to suffer by them. And this happened at a time when all the Makhnovists who fell into the hands of the Bolsheviks were invariably shot on the spot.

But the Makhnovists had completely different relations with the chiefs of the Red Army and with the Party aristocracy. They considered them the only real culprits of all the evils and all the horrors which the Soviet power imposed on the region. These chiefs had deliberately annihilated the freedom of the people and transformed the insurgent region into a wound from which the blood of the people flowed. And the Makhnovists treated them accordingly: when they were caught they were usually killed.

The Bolshevik terror against the Makhnovists contained all the symptoms of terror inherent in a ruling caste. If Makhnovist prisoners were not shot on the spot, they were imprisoned and subjected to all types of torture to force them to repudiate the movement, to denounce their comrades and to take employment with the police. The assistant to the commander of the 13th insurgent regiment, Berezovsky, was taken prisoner by the Bolsheviks and became an agent of the Special Section *(Cheka);* but according to him, he did this only after being subjected to torture. Similarly, the Bolsheviks more than once offered freedom to the commander of the engineering corps of the Makhnovist army, Chubenko, if he would agree to assist them in killing Makhno. Assassinating Makhno with the help of any imprisoned Makhnovist was the constant concern of the Bolsheviks during the entire summer of 1920. Here is a text of a document published by the Makhnovists after an unsuccessful attempt by the Bolsheviks to assassinate Makhno.

TREACHEROUS ATTEMPT
TO ASSASSINATE BATKO MAKHNO
ORGANIZED BY THE BOLSHEVIK-COMMUNISTS

For two months the staff headquarters of the Ukrainian revolutionary insurgents has been receiving information from many sources about the fact that the ruling Communist-Bolshevik Party, unable in spite of all its regiments and divisions to vanquish the independent and free insurrection of the Makhnov-shchina in open combat, has been plotting, with the help of mercenaries, to assassinate the leader of the revolutionary insurrection, comrade Nestor Makhno.

We possess precise information about the fact that a special section has been instituted for this purpose in the All-Ukrainian *Cheka,* headed by experienced Bol-shevik executioners Mantsev and Martynov. The per-sonnel of this special section is recruited exclusively among former *naletchiki* ("bandits") who are con-demned to death and buy their lives through services rendered to the *Cheka.*

Among the agents provocateurs, there are some who have had connections with the anarchist move-ment, for example: Peter Sidorov, Tima-Ivan Petrakov, Zhenya Ermakova (Anna Sukhova), Chaldon and Burtsev. Their links to the anarchist movement were mainly military. We have also been informed that one of these agents provocateurs is "Big Nicholas"—an individualist who last year edited the journal *K Svetu (Toward the Light)* in Khar'kov, and who is also known as Vasili.

There are no limits to the treachery of this band of provocateurs. Having learned many of the clandestine names and addresses of anarchists at the time of Denikin's invasion, they burst into the comrades' quar-ters and carried out outright pogroms; it goes without saying that all the anarchists whom they knew, and who were more or less hostile to the Bolshevik author-ities, were arrested and shot.

After having operated this way in Khar'kov and Odessa, this unsavory band, headed by its boss, Mantsev, moved to Ekaterinoslav in order to prepare the assassination of Batko Makhno from there, and to recruit collaborators.

However, the "revolutionary" Bolsheviks have evidently forgotten, during the three years they have ruled, the type of sincerity with which agents pro-vocateurs served the Tsarist government, and how many times a Petrov emerged from their ranks, who succeeded in redeeming his honor. Such is the case again. Among the provocateurs bought by the Bolsheviks in exchange for money and the promise to have their lives spared, there are people who, haunted by moral obligations or possibly by the awareness of their betrayal, manage to thwart all the ventures of Mister Mantsev and his friends.

THE CAPTURE OF MANTSEV'S AGENTS[1]

On June 20, one hour after the arrival of a group of revolutionary insurgents (Makhnovists) in Turkenovka, ten miles from Gulyai-Polye, a certain Fedya Glushchenko, who during the preceeding year had worked in counter-espionage for the insurrectionary army, and who had just arrived in the village, approached Comrade Makhno in the street and said to him nervously: "Batko, I have some very important information for you!. . ." Comrade Makhno instructed him to make his communication to Comrade Kurilenko, who was nearby. Fedya declared that he and another person, who at that time stood on the street close to Comrade Makhno, had been sent there to assassinate Batko Makhno. Kurilenko cautiously approached the other person and succeeded in disarming him. He was carrying a Mauser revolver, a Browning and two bombs, and Fedya himself had a Colt revolver.

The other individual was Yakov Kostykhin, a *naletchik* who had the nickname "Bad Yashka." He quickly described, in detail and with all sincerity, verbally as well as in writing, everything he was supposed to do at the instigation of Mister Mantsev, toward whom he showed no respect. They had received 13 thousand rubles in Tsarist paper money and a sum of Soviet money. A detailed plan of the projected assassination had been carefully worked out in Ekaterinoslav by Mantsev, Martynov and Fedya. Kostyukhin was under Fedya's orders. Fedya also had the mission of winning over to his side the former head of counter-espionage of the First (Donets) Makhnovist Corps, Lev Zadov. Kostyukhin, knowing that he deserved only to die, offered his services for any purpose whatever. Naturally this offer was re-

[1] Extract from the proceedings of a Council session.

jected, and he was executed the following day. Just before he died, he cursed Fedya for having led him here and then betrayed him.

Fedya declared that he had been arrested by Mantsev and had been offered the choice between death and working under the orders of the *Cheka* with a view to assassinating Makhno. He chose the latter proposition, with the intention, he said, of warning Comrade Makhno in time. He remained firm and declared that he deserved to die for his participation in the *Cheka;* but he repeated that he had done this in order to be able to warn his comrades and to die by their hands. The insurgents obviously could not let collaboration with the *Cheka* go unpunished, whatever the motives which had induced Fedya to do this, since a revolutionary cannot under any circumstances collaborate with the police. On June 21 Fedya Glushchenko was executed together with Kostyukhin. He died calmly, saying that he fully deserved to die, but he asked that his Makhnovist comrades be informed that he did not die as a villain, but as a true friend of the insurgents who had accepted service with the *Cheka* only so that his death would save the life of Batko Makhno. "God help you!" were his last words.

Thus ended the treacherous attempt of the All-Ukrainian *Cheka* to use mercenaries to assassinate the leader of the revolutionary insurrection, comrade Makhno.

Council of Ukrainian Revolutionary
Insurgents (Makhnovists)
June 21, 1920.

All through the year of 1920 and even later, the Soviet authorities carried on the fight against the Makhnovists pretending to be fighting banditry. They engaged in intense agitation to persuade the country of this, using their press and all their means of propaganda to uphold the slander both inside and outside of Russia. At the same time, numerous infantry and cavalry divisions were sent against the insurgents, for the purpose of destroying the movement and pushing its members toward the gulf of real banditry. The Makhnovist prisoners were pitilessly put to death, their families—fathers, mothers, wives, relatives—were tortured and killed, their property was pillaged or confiscated, their houses were destroyed. All this was practiced on a large scale. A superhuman will and heroic efforts were needed by the vast masses of insurgents, in the face of all these horrors committed daily by the authorities, to retain intact their rigorously revolutionary position, and not to fall, in exasperation, into the abyss of banditry. But the masses never lost their courage, they never lowered their revolutionary banner, but remained to the end faithful to their task. For those who saw it during this hard and painful period, this was a genuine miracle, demonstrating how deep was the faith of these working masses in the revolution, how strong their devotion to the cause whose ideas had won them over.

* * *

During the spring and summer of 1920, the Makhnovists had to carry on the struggle, not merely against detachments of the Red Army, but against the whole Bolshevik system, against all its governmental forces in the Ukraine and Great Russia. This is why the insurrectionary troops were sometimes obliged—so as to avoid encountering an enemy of too superior numbers—to leave their region and make forced marches of 600 miles or more. Sometimes they had to retreat to the Donets Basin, sometimes to the governments of Khar'kov and Poltava. These involuntary wanderings were put to considerable use by the insurgents for propaganda purposes, and every village in which they halted for a day or two became a vast Makhnovist auditorium.

It was during this nomadic period, in June-July, 1920, that a higher organ to direct the activity of the army and the entire movement was constructed: the Council of Ukrainian Revolutionary Insurgents (Makhnovists), consisting of seven members elected or ratified by the mass of the insurgents. This Council was divided into three sections: military affairs and operations, organization and general control, education and culture.

171

Chapter 9

Makhnovist Pact With the Soviet Government.
Third Bolshevik Assault.

During the summer of 1920, the Makhnovists more than once attempted to engage in battle against Wrangel. On two occasions they had military encounters with his troops, but each time the Red troops struck the Makhnovists from behind, and the Makhnovists had to abandon the firing line and retreat. The Soviet Authorities did not stop slandering the Makhnovists. Throughout the Ukraine, Soviet newspapers spread the false news of an alliance between Makhno and Wrangel. In the summer of 1920, the Plenipotentiary of the Khar'kov Government, Yakovlev, declared at the Plenary Session of the Ekaterinoslav Soviet, that the Soviet authorities had written proof of the alliance between Makhno and Wrangel. This was obviously an intentional lie. The Soviet authorities made use of this tactic in order to mislead the masses of workers who, disturbed by Wrangel's successes and the Red Army's retreat, began to look toward Makhno and to invoke his name more frequently.

No one among the workers and peasants believed the Bolshevik lies about an alliance between Makhno and Wrangel. The people knew Makhno too well, and they were also familiar with Bolshevik methods. But it was Wrangel who in the end believed the fable repeated daily by the Soviet press: the fact that Wrangel personally sent a messenger to Makhno can only be explained by the influence of the Soviet press, unless it was simply the result of General Wrangel's abysmal ignorance. Perhaps it was merely an attempt by the general to explore the terrain.

We cite the following document:

173

Proceedings of the session of the Commanding Staff of the Ukrainian Revolutionary Insurgent (Makhnovist) Army, held at Vrem'evka, district of Mariupol', on July 9, 1920.

Paragraph 4. Message from General Wrangel.

Toward the end of the session, a messenger from General Wrangel was brought before the staff; he presented the following letter:

"To the Ataman of the insurrectionary troops, Makhno.

"The Russian Army makes war exclusively against the Communists in order to deliver the people from the Communes and Commissars and to guarantee the working peasants the fruits of the land which belonged to the State, to large landowners, and others. This measure has already been put into practice.

"The Russian soldiers and officers are fighting for the cause of the people and for their happiness. All those who are with the people should join us. This is why you must now exert all your forces against the Communists, attack their rearguard, destroy their means of transport, and give us your assistance in wiping out Trotsky's troops. Our high command will assist you with armaments, supplies and also specialists. Send your delegate to our Staff with information about your particular needs and to coordinate our military activities.

"(Signed)
Chief of Staff of the Command of the Armed Forces of Southern Russia, *Lt.-Gen. Shatilov;*
Quartermaster-General of the General Staff, *Major-General Konovalets.*

Melitopol', June 18, 1920."

The messenger, Ivan Mikhailov, 28 years old, said that he had received the letter from Slashchev's adjutant, with instructions to deliver it to Batko Makhno, and that in his camp everyone was convinced that Makhno was working together with Wrangel.

Popov:[1] "We have only today sent an appropriate answer to the Reds. We must now answer the White oppressors."

Makhno: "The only answer we can give to such vile offers is the following: any delegate sent from Wrangel, or from anyone on the right, should be executed on the spot, and no answer will be given."

It was unanimously decided to execute Wrangel's delegate and to have the Council publish the letter received as well as the answer.

Wrangel's messenger was immediately executed. This entire incident was reported in the Makhnovist press. All this was perfectly clear to the Bolsheviks. They nevertheless continued shamelessly to trumpet the alliance between Makhno and Wrangel. It was only after a military-political agreement had been concluded between the Makhnovists and the Soviet power that the Soviet Commissariat of War announced that there had never been an alliance between Makhno and Wrangel, that earlier Soviet assertions to this effect were an error caused by faulty information, and that, on the contrary, the Makhnovists had executed delegates sent by Wrangel, without entering into any negotiations with them. (See the declarations made by the Chief Commissar of War, entitled "Makhno and Wrangel," in *Proletar* and other Khar'kov newspapers, about October 20, 1920.) This announcement, in which the Soviet authorities admitted their own lies, was obviously not made because of the desire to tell the truth, but only because the Bolsheviks were obliged to admit the truth, having just concluded a military-political agreement with the Makhnovists.

* * *

In mid-summer, 1920, Wrangel began to gain the upper hand. He advanced slowly but systematically, and began to

[1] Secretary of the Council of Revolutionary Insurgents.

175

threaten the entire Donets Basin. In view of the events at the Polish front, Wrangel represented a serious threat to the entire revolution, and at one point this threat grew to enormous proportions.

The Makhnovists could not remain indifferent to Wrangel's advance. It was clear to them that they had to fight him without delay, without allowing him time to consolidate his struggle against the revolution. Everything done to destroy him would in the last analysis benefit the revolution. But what was to be done about the Communists? Their dictatorship was as evil and as hostile to the freedom of the workers as Wrangel's. However, the difference between the Communists and Wrangel was that the Communists had the support of the masses with faith in the revolution. It is true that these masses were cynically misled by the Communists, who exploited the revolutionary enthusiasm of the workers in the interests of Bolshevik power. Nevertheless the masses themselves, antagonistic to Wrangel, believed in the revolution, and this fact was very important. At a conference of the Council of Revolutionary Insurgents and the Army Staff, it was decided to concentrate on the struggle against Wrangel. It was then up to the mass of insurgents to make the final decision and settle the question.

According to the assembly, the destruction of Wrangel would have important consequences. First of all, it would eliminate a threat to the revolution. Secondly, all of Russia would be freed from the counter-revolutionary barrage from which it had suffered during all the revolutionary years. The mass of workers and peasants urgently needed an end to all these wars. This would make it possible for them to look about calmly, to evaluate the past, to draw deductions and conclusions, and to furnish new forces to the revolution. The assembly decided to propose to the Communists that hostilities between them and the Makhnovists be suspended in order that together they might wipe out Wrangel. In July and August, 1920, telegrams to this effect were sent to Moscow and Khar'kov in the name of the Council and the Commander of the Insurrectionary Army. There was no response. The Communists continued their war against the Makhnovists, and they also continued their previous campaign of lies and calumnies against them. But in September, when Ekaterinoslav was evacuated by the Communists, and when Wrangel occupied Berdyansk, Aleksandrovsk, Gulyai-Polye and Sinel'nikovo, a plenipotentiary delegation from the Central Committee of the Communist-Bolshevik Party, headed by the Communist Ivanov, came to Starobel'sk, where the Makhnovists were camped, to begin negotiations on the subject of combined action against Wrangel. These negotiations took place on the spot, in Starobel'sk, and it was there that a preliminary military-political agreement between the Makhnovists and the Soviet authorities was formulated. The clauses were to be sent to Khar'kov to be officially ratified. For this purpose, and also to maintain subsequent contact with the Bolshevik staff of the southern front, a Makhnovist military and political delegation headed by Kurilenko, Budanov and Popov left for Khar'kov.

Between October 10th and 15th, 1920, the clauses of the agreement were worked out and adopted by the two contracting parties in the following form:

PRELIMINARY
POLITICAL AND MILITARY AGREEMENT
BETWEEN THE SOVIET GOVERNMENT
OF THE UKRAINE
AND THE
UKRAINIAN REVOLUTIONARY
INSURRECTIONARY ARMY (MAKHNOVIST)

PART I — POLITICAL AGREEMENT

1. Immediate release of all Makhnovists and anarchists imprisoned or in exile in the territories of the Soviet Republic; cessation of all persecutions of Makhnovists or anarchists, except those who carry on armed conflict against the Soviet Government.

2. Complete freedom in all forms of public expression and propaganda for all Makhnovists and anarchists, for their principles and ideas, in speech and the press, with the exception of anything that might call for the violent overthrow of the Soviet Government, and on condition that the requirements of military censorship be respected. For all kinds of publications, the Makhnovists and anarchists, as revolutionary

organizations recognized by the Soviet Government, may make use of the technical apparatus of the Soviet State, while naturally submitting to the technical rules for publication.

3. Free participation in elections to the Soviets; and the right of Makhnovists and anarchists to be elected thereto. Free participation in the organization of the forthcoming Fifth Pan-Ukrainian Congress of Soviets, which will take place next December.

(Signed)
By mandate of the Soviet Government of the Ukrainian S.S.R., *Ya. Yakovlev.*
Plenipotentiaries of the Council, and Commanders of the Ukrainian Revolutionary Insurrectionary Army (Makhnovist): *Kurilenko. Popov.*

PART II – MILITARY AGREEMENT

1. The Ukrainian Revolutionary Insurrectionary Army (Makhnovist) will join the armed forces of the Republic as a partisan army, subordinate, in regard to operations, to the supreme command of the Red Army; it will retain its established internal structure, and does not have to adopt the bases and principles of the regular Red Army.

2. While crossing Soviet territory at the front, or going between fronts, the Insurrectionary Army will accept into its ranks neither detachments of, nor deserters from, the Red Army.[2]

Remarks:

a) The units of the Red Army as well as isolated Red soldiers who have met and joined the Revolutionary Insurrectionary Army behind the Wrangel front shall re-enter the ranks of the Red Army when they again make contact with it.

---

[2]The representatives of the Soviet Government insisted on this last point because of the frequent passage of Red Army units into the Makhnovist ranks—*P.A.*

b) The Makhnovist insurgents behind the Wrangel front, as well as all men at present in the Insurrectionary Army, will remain there, even if they were previously mobilized by the Red Army.

3. For the purpose of destroying the common enemy—the White Army—the Ukrainian Revolutionary Insurrectionary Army (Makhnovist) will inform the working masses that collaborate with it of the agreement that has been concluded; it will call upon the people to cease all military actions hostile to the Soviet power; for its part, the Soviet power will immediately publish the clauses of the agreement.

4. The families of the combatants of the Makhnovist Revolutionary Insurrectionary Army living in the territory of the Soviet Republic shall enjoy the same rights as those of soldiers of the Red Army, and for this purpose shall be supplied by the Soviet Government of the Ukraine with the necessary documents.

> (Signed)
> Commander of the Southern Front, *Frunze.*
> Members of the Revolutionary Council of the Southern Front: *Bela Kun, Gusev.*
> Plenipotentiary delegates of the Council, and Commanders of the Makhnovist Insurrectionary Army: *Kurilenko. Popov.*

In addition to the above-mentioned three clauses of the political agreement, the representatives of the Council and the commander of the Makhnovist Army submitted to the Soviet Government a fourth special clause of the political agreement:

FOURTH CLAUSE OF
THE POLITICAL AGREEMENT

Since one of the essential principles of the Makhnovist movement is the struggle for the self-management of the workers, the Insurrectionary Army

(Makhnovist) believes it should insist on the following fourth point of the political agreement: in the region where the Makhnovist Army is operating, the population of workers and peasants will create its own institutions of economic and political self-management; these institutions will be autonomous and joined in federation, by means of agreements, with the governmental organs of the Soviet Republic.

* * *

Under various pretexts, the Soviet authorities continually put off the publication of this agreement. The Makhnovists understood that this was not a good sign. The full meaning of this delay only became clear some time later, when the Soviet power unleashed a new and brutal assault against the Makhnovists. We will return to this later.

Aware of the lack of sincerity of the Soviet authorities, the Makhnovists declared firmly that as long as the agreement was not published, the Insurrectionary Army could not act according to its clauses. It was only after this direct pressure that the Soviet Government finally decided to publish the text of the agreement. But they did not publish the entire agreement. They first published Part II, the military agreement, and a week later they published the first part, the political agreement. The real meaning of the pact was thereby obscured, and consequently it was not accurately understood by most readers. As for the fourth clause of the political agreement, the Bolsheviks separated it from the rest of the agreement, claiming they had to confer with Moscow on this subject. The Makhnovist representatives agreed to treat this subject separately.

After this, between October 15th and 20th, the Makhnovist army set out to attack Wrangel. The battle front extended from Sinel'nikovo to Aleksandrovsk, Pologi, Berdyansk; the Makhnovists advanced in the direction of Perekop. In the first battles in the region between Pologi and

Orekhov a large group of Wrangel's troops, commanded by General Drozdov, was beaten, and more than 4000 soldiers were captured. Three weeks later, the region was liberated from Wrangel's troops. By November the Makhnovists together with the Red Army had already reached Perekop.

It is important to point out here that, as soon as it was known that the Makhnovists had joined with the Reds to oppose Wrangel, the population in the region regained its confidence and enthusiasm. Wrangel was irremediably doomed, and his complete defeat was expected from one day to the next.

The role of the Makhnovists in liberating the Crimea of Wrangel's troops was the following. While the Red Army blocked Perekop, some of the Makhnovist troops, following the orders of the staff, went 20 miles to the left of the Isthmus and set out over the ice of the Sivash Strait, which was frozen at this time. The Cavalry, commanded by Marchenko, an anarchist peasant originally from Gulyai-Polye, went first, followed by a machine-gun regiment commanded by Kozhin. The crossing was made under violent and continuous fire by the enemy, which cost many lives. The commander, Foma Kozhin, was seriously wounded several times. But the boldness and perseverance of the attackers caused Wrangel's troops to take flight. Then another Makhnovist army, the Crimean, under the command of Simon Karetnik, moved to the right toward Simferopol', which they took on November 13th or 14th. At the same time the Red Army occupied Perekop. It is incontestable that, having entered the Crimea across the Sivash, the Makhnovists contributed greatly to the taking of the Perekop Isthmus, hitherto considered impregnable, by forcing Wrangel to retreat into the interior of the peninsula in order to avoid being surrounded in the gorges of Perekop.

* * *

After a long period of incessant warfare, the agreement between the Makhnovists and the Soviet Government appeared to give the region some possibility of proceeding in tranquility with a certain amount of social construction. We said "some possibility" because, aside from the fact that in several places fierce warfare took place against Wrangel's troops (Gulyai-Polye, for example, changed hands several times during this period), the Soviet authorities, despite the agreement, maintained a partial blockade of the region and did all they could to paralyze the creative constructive activity of the workers. Nevertheless, the active core of the Makhnovists residing in Gulyai-Polye carried on energetic activity in the field of social construction. First of all they were concerned with the organization of free workers' soviets which were to be organs of local self-management by the workers and peasants. These councils were based on the principle of independence from any and all outside authority, and were to be responsible only to the local workers.

The first practical step in this direction was taken by the inhabitants of Gulyai-Polye. From November 1st to 25th, 1920, they met at least five to seven times in order to examine this question, and in order to move toward its solution gradually and carefully. The free soviet of Gulyai-Polye was established in the middle of November, 1920, but it was not a fully developed institution, since as a completely new practical step of the workers it needed time and experience. At this same time the Council of Revolutionary Insurgents drew up and published the "Fundamental Statutes of the Free Soviets" (Draft).

The workers of Gulyai-Polye also devoted a great deal of attention to the question of schooling. The repeated armed invasions had seriously disrupted educational activity throughout the region. The teachers, having received no remuneration for a long time, had dispersed to earn their living as best they could. School buildings were abandoned. After the agreement between the Makhnovists and the Soviet authorities, the masses directly confronted the problem of education. The Makhnovists felt that this question had to be resolved on the basis of self-management by the workers. Educational activity, they said, like all other activity which concerns the basic needs of the workers, is the task of the local working population. They themselves should supervise the process of teaching their children reading, writing and the sciences. But this was still not all. By taking charge of the instruction and education of the young people, the workers purify and elevate the very idea of schooling. In the hands of the people, school becomes more than a source of knowledge; it also becomes a means of developing conscious and free people such as there ought to be in the free workers' society. This is why, from the first moments of workers' self-management, the school should be separate not only from the Church, but also and to the same extent, from the State.

Inspired by this idea, the peasants and workers of Gulyai-Polye eagerly accepted the separation of schools from the State. In Gulyai-Polye there were several supporters and proponents of the principles of the free school as expressed by Francisco Ferrer, as well as theoretical and practical projects for a unified workers' school.

This new approach to education gave rise to a great deal of activity and enthusiasm among the inhabitants of Gulyai-Polye. The majority of peasants concerned with cultural work took part in this activity. Nestor Makhno, although at this time he had a serious wound in his leg, was actively interested in this work, attended all meetings of Gulyai-Polye inhabitants which dealt with this question, and urged competent people to prepare for him a course on the theory and practice of a unified workers' school.

In practice the undertakings of the Gulyai-Polye inhabitants in the field of education consisted of the following. The peasants and workers of the entire village undertook the maintenance of the teaching personnel needed by all the schools of the village (in Gulyai-Polye there were several primary schools and two high schools). A mixed commission composed of peasants, workers and teachers was created in order to take charge of providing for all the needs—economic as well as pedagogical—of the school system. Having accepted the principle of separation of schools from the State, the Gulyai-Polye inhabitants adopted a plan for free education very similar to that of Francisco Ferrer. The educational commission elaborated this plan in detail and prepared a major theoretical study on the principles and organization of the free school. (Unfortunately we do not have these documents.)

At the same time, special courses were organized for illiterate or semi-literate insurgents. People with many years of training and experience were found to teach literacy to adults.

Finally, courses in political theory were organized for insurgents who were in Gulyai-Polye at this time. Their goal was to furnish elementary notions of history, sociology and other subjects of this type, in order to supplement their combat weapons with weapons of knowledge and to prepare them for a more profound understanding of the goals and strategies of the revolution. These courses were taught by insurgent peasants and workers who had read a great deal. The program included: a) political economy; b) history; c) theory and practice of socialism and anarchism; d) history of the great French revolution (according to Kropotkin); e) history of the revolutionary insurrection at the heart of the Russian revolution, etc. Professorial abilities among the Makhnovists were extremely limited; in spite of this, due to the care and interest on the part of the lecturers as well as the listeners, the courses were from the very beginning lively and serious, and promised to play an important role in the further development of the movement.

The insurgents also devoted a great deal of attention to theater. Even before the agreement with the Bolsheviks, while the insurrectionary army was forced to fight daily against its numerous adversaries, the army always maintained a drama section composed of the insurgents themselves; this section presented plays for the insurgents and frequently for peasants from neighboring villages, whenever the military situation allowed.

There is a fairly large playhouse in Gulyai-Polye. But professional dramatic artists were always rare in the region. Generally amateurs recruited among the peasants, workers and intellectuals, especially teachers and students, served as actors. During the civil war, even though Gulyai-Polye suffered enormously, the inhabitants' interest in the theater did not diminish; on the contrary it grew. During the period of the agreement with the Bolsheviks, when the blockade of the region was lifted, the Gulyai-Polye playhouse filled daily with working people; peasants, insurgents, and their wives took part in the performances, not only as spectators and actors, but also as playwrights.[3] The cultural and educational section of the Makhnovist army took an active and direct part in the organization of drama in Gulyai-Polye and in the rest of the region.

* * *

No one among the Makhnovists believed in either the solidity or the permanence of the agreement with the Bolsheviks. On the basis of previous experience, everyone expected the Bolsheviks to find a pretext for a new attack on the Makhnovshchina. But the political conditions of the time led people to expect the agreement to last at least two or three

---

[3] I will mention a play written by a young Gulyai-Polye peasant who took an active part in different phases of the insurrectionary movement. This play was called "The Life of the Makhnovists" and consisted of several acts. The action begins in the summer of 1919, when Denikin's army occupied all of the Ukraine. The free villages at that time were inundated by police and military officers. After their arrival, the workers are once again subjected to the old oppression. The peasants suffer at every step; their goods are requisitioned; they are constantly searched. The peasants look for the Makhnovists. Old and young peasants are beaten and shot. The spirit of revolt burns in the peasants. They meet in groups to discuss their disastrous situation, prepare for a new insurrection and increasingly turn their glances toward Makhno, who three months earlier was forced to retreat under the pressure of the armies of Denikin and Trotsky.

But one day it is rumored that Makhno had defeated Denikin and was again marching across the Ukraine, approaching Gulyai-Polye. This news gives courage and energy to the Gulyai-Polye inhabitants. Hearing the cannons of the Makhnovists in the distance, the peasants rebel, initiating a fierce struggle against Denikin's troops and forcing them to leave Gulyai-Polye supported by Makhno's cavalry which at this moment enters the village.

The play is a powerful description of life in the Ukrainian countryside in the summer of 1919. In it the hardships of the people, their poignant emotion, their honesty, their revolutionary enthusiasm and heroism, are depicted with remarkable force. The powerful tension of the play is maintained until the end.

months. This period would have been extremely important for the dissemination of extensive propaganda in the region; the need for such activity was enormous, and the Makhnovists devoted a great deal of energy to it. The demands of their situation had forced the Makhnovists to abandon this type of activity almost completely. They hoped that on the basis of this agreement there would be ample opportunity to demonstrate to the workers the essence of the disagreement between the Bolsheviks and the Makhnovists, the reason for the violent opposition between them. This was in fact fully realized. The fourth clause of the political agreement—the clause in which the Makhnovists demanded that the Bolsheviks recognize the workers' and peasants' right to economic and social self-management—turned out to be completely unacceptable to the Soviet Government. The representatives of the Makhnovshchina demanded that the Soviet authorities choose between two possibilities: either sign the clause in question, or explain why they were against it. The Makhnovists submitted this clause to public evaluation by the masses. In Khar'kov, Makhnovists and anarchists discussed this theme at public meetings. At Gulyai-Polye and its surroundings, leaflets which dealt with this question were widely distributed. By the middle of November this fourth clause, which was stated in five or six lines, became the center of attention of the masses.

At about this time, Wrangel's expedition was completely destroyed. For the uninitiated, this circumstance would not appear to affect the agreement between the Makhnovists and the Soviet Government. But the Makhnovists saw in this circumstance the beginning of the end of the agreement. As soon as Simon Karetnik's dispatch—announcing that he was with the insurrectionary troops in the Crimea and marching on Simferopol'—arrived in Gulyai-Polye, Grigory Vasilevsky, Makhno's aide, exclaimed: "This is the end of the agreement! I wager that in a week the Bolsheviks will be on our backs." This was said on November 16, and on November 26th the Bolsheviks treacherously attacked the Makhnovist staff and troops in the Crimea and in Gulyai-Polye; they seized the Makhnovist representatives in Khar'kov, destroyed all the recently established anarchist organizations and imprisoned all the anarchists. They proceeded the same way all over the Ukraine.

The Soviet authorities were not slow to explain their treachery by means of their favorite argument: the Makhnovists and the anarchists were preparing an insurrection against the Soviet Government, and point 4 of the political agreement was the call for this insurrection; even the time and place of this insurrection had been determined. Furthermore, they accused Makhno of having refused to go to the Caucasian front and of having started to mobilize troops from among the peasants in order to form an army against the Soviet authorities; instead of fighting Wrangel in the Crimea, the Makhnovists had been sniping at the rearguard of the Red Army, etc.

It goes without saying that all of these explanations were complete fabrications. We fortunately possess all the documents needed to expose these lies and establish the truth.

First of all, on November 23, 1920, in Pologi and Gulyai-Polye, the Makhnovists arrested nine Bolshevik spies belonging to the 42nd Infantry Division of the Red Army, who confessed that they had been sent to Gulyai-Polye by the chief of the counter-espionage service to obtain information about the location of the houses of Makhno, the members of his staff, the commanders of the insurrectionary army and the members of the Council. After this, they were supposed to remain in Gulyai-Polye to wait for the arrival of the Red Army, and then point out where the persons in question were to be found. In case the unexpected arrival of the Red Army forced these persons to flee into hiding, the spies were supposed to shadow them and not lose sight of them. The spies declared that there was going to be an attack on Gulyai-Polye by November 24th or 25th.

On the basis of this, the Council of the revolutionary insurgents and the commander of the army sent to Rakovsky and to the Revolutionary Military Council of the Southern Front a detailed communication about this plot, demanding: 1) the immediate arrest and arraignment before the military tribunal of the Commander of the 42nd Division, the Chief of Staff of the Division, and other persons involved in the plot, and 2) the prohibition of Red units travelling through Gulyai-Polye, Pologi, Malaya Takmachka and Turkenovka, in

187

order to forestall any unpleasant incidents.

The response of the Soviet Government in Khar'kov was as follows: the so-called plot is nothing but a simple misunderstanding; nevertheless the Soviet authorities, desiring to clear up the matter, are putting it in the hands of a special commission and propose that the staff of the Makhnovist army delegate two members to take part in the work of this commission. This response was sent from Khar'kov by direct wire on November 25. The following morning, P. Rybin, secretary of the Council of revolutionary insurgents, again discussed this question with Khar'kov by direct wire; the Bolsheviks assured him that the affair of the 42nd Division would certainly be resolved to the complete satisfaction of the Makhnovists, and added that the 4th clause of the political agreement was also about to be settled in a satisfactory manner. This discussion took place on November 26th at 9 a.m. However, six hours earlier, at 3 a.m., the Makhnovist representatives at Khar'kov had been seized, and all the anarchists in Khar'kov and in the rest of the Ukraine were arrested. Exactly two hours after Rybin's conversation by direct wire, Gulyai-Polye was surrounded on all sides by Red troops and subjected to furious bombardment. On the same day and at the same hour, the Makhnovist army in the Crimea was attacked; by means of a ruse the Bolsheviks succeeded in capturing all members of the Makhnovist staff as well as its commander, Simon Karetnik, and executed every single one of them.

It is obvious that this vast operation had been carefully prepared and that its elaboration must have taken at least ten or fifteen days.

We see here not only a treacherous attack of the Soviet Government against the Makhnovists, but also the meticulousness with which they organized this plot and the efforts with which they dulled the vigilance of the Makhnovists by verbal assurances of their security in order to surround and destroy their forces.

Secondly, on November 27, the day after the attack on Gulyai-Polye, the Makhnovists found on the Red Army prisoners whom they captured undated proclamations entitled "Forward against Makhno!" "Death to Makhnovism! " published by the political section of the 4th Army. The prisoners said they had received these proclamations on November 15th and 16th; they contained a call to action against Makhno, who was accused of having violated the clauses of the political and military agreement, of having refused to go to the Caucasian front, of having planned an uprising against the Soviet power, etc. This proves that all these accusations were fabricated and sent to the press even while the insurrectionary army was still in the process of beating a path across the Crimea and occupying Simferopol', and while the Makhnovist representatives were peacefully working with the Soviet authorities at Khar'kov.

Thirdly, during the months of October and November, 1920, namely while the military and political agreement between the Makhnovists and Bolsheviks was being negotiated and after it had just been concluded, two Bolshevik plots to assassinate Makhno at Gulyai-Polye were uncovered.

We should add that the central staff of the Makhnovist army in Gulyai-Polye did not receive a single order to report to the Caucasian front. At this time Makhno was suffering from a serious leg wound and did not concern himself at all with paper work, which was handled by the chief of staff, Belash, and by the Council secretary, P. Rybin, who made daily reports to the Council on all the documents received by the staff.

We should remember the manner in which the Bolsheviks delayed the publication of the text of the military-political agreement, which we described earlier. It now becomes clear why they stubbornly kept postponing the publication of this text. For the Bolsheviks this agreement was nothing more than a military and strategic step calculated to last at most a month or two—the time needed to defeat Wrangel. Once this was accomplished, they were determined to resume slandering the Makhnovists as bandits and counter-revolutionaries, and under this pretext to make war on them. This is why it was not in their interest to publish the political agreement with the Makhnovists and to present it to the judgment of the masses. They would in fact have preferred to hide the very existence of this agreement from the masses in order to continue the war against the Makhnovists under the pretext of a struggle against banditry and counter-revolution, on the very day after Wrangel's defeat, and as if nothing had happened between the Bolsheviks and the Makhnovists.

Such are the facts concerning the breaking of the military-political pact between the Makhnovists and the Soviet power.

It is necessary to examine closely the text of this agreement. It clearly distinguishes the two opposed tendencies: the statist tendency which defends the usual privileges and prerogatives of authority; and the popular and revolutionary tendency which defends the demands of the subjugated masses against the wielders of power. It is extremely significant that the first part of the agreement, concerning the political rights of the workers, contains only Makhnovist theses. In this matter, the Soviet authorities had the classic attitude of all tyrannies: they sought to limit the demands formulated by the Makhnovists, bargained on all points, and did everything possible to reduce the rights of the working people—rights which were inalienable from and indispensable to their real freedom

We should also point out that the Makhnovists, because of their anarchist conception of struggle, were always opposed to political conspiracies. They engaged in revolutionary struggle openly, in the midst of the broad working masses, convinced that only a struggle of the revolutionary masses could lead the workers to victory; whereas conspiracies could only lead to a change of authority—an event which contradicted the very nature of the Makhnovshchina.

Thus the agreement between the Makhnovists and the Bolsheviks was doomed from the very beginning and could not have lasted after the defeat of Wrangel.

This is also clear from certain documents of the Soviet authorities themselves, for example, the order issued by Frunze, who was at the time commander of the southern front, a document which clearly exposes the treachery of the Bolshevik attack against the Makhnovists and reduces to nothing all their fabrications about the anarchists and the Makhnovists.

ORDER TO COMRADE MAKHNO, COMMANDER OF THE INSURREC-TIONARY ARMY.
COPIES TO THE COMMANDERS OF THE ARMIES ON THE SOUTHERN FRONT. NO. 00149.
ISSUED AT GENERAL HEAD-QUARTERS, MELITOPOL'. NOVEMBER 23, 1920.

By reason of the cessation of hostilities against Wrangel, and in view of his complete defeat, the Revolutionary Military Council of the Southern Front considers that the task of the partisan army is completed. It therefore proposes to the Revolutionary Military Council of the Insurrectionary Army that it immediately begin transforming the insurrectionary partisan units into regular military units of the Red Army.

There is no longer any reason for the Insurrectionary Army to continue to exist as such. On the contrary, the existence, alongside of the Red Army, of these units with a special organization, pursuing special tasks, produces absolutely unacceptable results...[4]

That is why the Revolutionary Military Council of the Southern Front orders the Revolutionary Military Council of the Insurrectionary Army to do the following: 1) All units of the Insurrectionary Army forma-

---

[4]Frunze mentions several cases where soldiers of the Red Army were disarmed and killed by the Makhnovists. But all the cases he refers to were closely examined by himself, Rakovsky and the representatives of the Makhnovists at Khar'kov, and it was conclusively established: 1) that the Makhnovist Army had nothing to do with these misdeeds; 2) that if hostile acts toward the army were committed by certain military detachments which did not belong to the Makhnovist Army, this was primarily due to the fact that the Soviet authorities had neglected to publish, at an opportune time and intelligibly, their agreement with the insurgents. In fact it was known that numerous isolated military units, not incorporated into the Makhnovist Army, operated here and there in the Ukraine. The majority of these units, while acting on their own, nevertheless respected the opinion and the attitude of the insurrectionary army; they would certainly have ceased all hostility toward the Soviet authorities and armies if they had known about the agreement concluded with the Makhnovists.

tions, at present in the Crimea, should be immediately incorporated into the Fourth Army; the Revolutionary Military Council should take charge of this transfer. 2) The military formations at Gulyai-Polye should be liquidated. The combatants will be distributed among the reserve detachments, according to the instructions of the commander of that part of the Army. 3) The Revolutionary Military Council of the Insurrectionary Army shall take all necessary measures to explain to the combatants the need for these measures.

(Signed)
M. Frunze, Commander in Chief of the Southern Front;
Smil'ga, member of the Revolutionary Military Council;
Karatygin, Chief of Staff.

The reader should recall the history of the agreement between the Soviet Government and the Makhnovists.

As was said earlier, the conclusion of the agreement was preceded by negotiations between the Makhnovist plenipotentiaries and the Bolshevik delegation headed by the Communist Ivanov, which came to the Makhnovist camp at Starobel'sk especially for this purpose. These negotiations were continued at Khar'kov, where the Makhnovist representatives worked for three weeks with the Bolsheviks to conclude the pact satisfactorily. Each article was carefully examined and debated by the two parties.

The final version of this agreement was approved by the two parties, i.e., by the *Soviet Government and the Revolutionary Insurgent Region* represented by the Council of Ukrainian Revolutionary Insurgents, and was signed by the respective plenipotentiaries of these two sides.

According to the very nature of this agreement, none of the articles could be suspended or modified without prior agreement of the Soviet Government and the Council of Ukrainian Revolutionary Insurgents if the agreement had not been broken either by one side or by the other.

Article 1 of Part II of the agreement reads: ''The

Ukrainian Revolutionary Insurrectionary Army (Makhnovist) will join the armed forces of the Republic as a partisan army, subordinate, in regard to operations, to the supreme command of the Red Army; it will retain its established internal structure, and does not have to adopt the bases and principles of the regular Red Army.''

Frunze's Order No. 00149 of November 23, 1920, demands that the army of the Makhnovist insurgents be liquidated, that the combatants be incorporated into the Red Army, and that ''by reason of the cessation of hostilities against Wrangel and in view of his complete defeat'' the Soviet power ''considers that the task of the partisan army is completed.''

This order annihilates not only the above-cited first article of the military agreement, but the entire military-political agreement.

The fact that, instead of proposing a revision of, or an amendment to, the existing agreement, the Bolsheviks proceeded by way of an urgent military order enforced by arms, clearly shows that they considered the agreement to be nothing more than a trap designed to mislead the Makhnovists.

At the same time that the Makhnovists received Order No. 00149, the Fourth Red Army in the Crimea received an order to act against the Makhnovists with all the means at its disposal and to use all its military forces in case the insurgents refused to obey.

Frunze's order is so clear that no commentary is needed in order to depict the true situation. Frunze orders the Makhnovists to liquidate their army, to become a regular division of the Red Army: he thus orders the Makhnovshchina to commit suicide. Such naiveté would be surprising, if it had only been naiveté.

In actual fact, behind this naiveté there was a carefully worked-out plan, calculated to completely destroy the Makhnovshchina. Wrangel had been beaten. The Makhnovists had been put to good use. The time had come to wipe them out. Consequently, the Bolsheviks had to put an end to their existence. This is the meaning of the order.

But in spite of its brutal straightforwardness, Frunze's order was also deceitful. Neither the staff of the insurrectionary army, stationed at Gulyai-Polye, nor the Makhnovist delegation in Khar'kov, in fact received Frunze's order. The Makhnovists only learned about it three or four weeks after the Bolshevik attack, through some newspapers which fell into their hands. The explanation for this is simple. The Bolsheviks, who were preparing secretly for a surprise attack on the Makhnovists, could not afford to put them on their guard by sending them this order in advance, since the planned attack would then have been repulsed. This is why they kept the secret until the last moment. Frunze's order was published in the papers only after the attack, after the break had become an accomplished fact. It appeared for the first time on December 15, 1920, in the Khar'kov newspaper *Kommunist,* and was given the date November 23. All these machinations had the objective of surprising the Makhnovists, of destroying them, and of explaining this action afterwards by means of "legal evidence."

The assault on the Makhnovists was accompanied by mass arrests of anarchists. The purpose of these arrests was not only the total destruction of all anarchist thought and activity, but also the stifling of any possibility of protest, of any attempt to explain to the people the real meaning of what was happening. Not only anarchists, but also their friends and acquaintances, and those who were interested in anarchist literature, were arrested. At Elisavetgrad fifteen youths between 15 and 18 years old were arrested. Although the district authorities in Nikolaev were dissatisfied with this capture, saying that they wanted "real" anarchists and not children, none of these children were released.

In Khar'kov the pursuit of anarchists assumed proportions unheard of in Russia in past years. Snares and ambushes were organized at the homes of all local anarchists. A trap of this kind was set up in the "Vol'noe bratstvo" ("Free Brotherhood") bookshop. Anyone who came to buy a book was seized and sent to the *Cheka.* They even imprisoned people who stopped to read the newspaper *Nabat* which had appeared legally and was posted on the wall of the bookshop. When one of the Khar'kov anarchists, Grigory Tsesnik, escaped arrest, the Bolsheviks threw his wife, who had no political interests of any kind, into prison. She started a hunger strike, demanding her immediate release. The Bolsheviks then told her that if Tsesnik wanted to obtain her release, he had only to give himself up to the *Cheka*. Tsesnik, though ill with tuberculosis, gave himself up and was imprisoned.

We have already mentioned that the staff of the Makhnovist army in the Crimea had been treacherously seized. The commander of the cavalry, Marchenko, although surrounded and fiercely attacked by numerous units of the Bolshevik 4th Army, managed to escape and break a passage through the natural obstacles and barricades of the fortified Perekop Isthmus. Leading his men, or rather the remnants of his men, by forced marches during the day and night, he succeeded in rejoining Makhno in the little village of Kermenchik, inhabited by Greeks. On December 7th, a horseman arrived to announce that Marchenko's troops would be there in a few hours. The Makhnovists at Kermenchik came out excitedly to meet the heroes. Their anguish can be imagined when they finally saw the small group of horsemen; instead of the powerful cavalry of 1500 men, a small detachment of 250 men returned. At their head were Marchenko and Taranovski.

"I have the honor of announcing to you—the return of the Crimean army," said Marchenko with bitter irony. Everyone smiled sadly. "Yes, brothers," continued Marchenko. "Now we know what the Communists are." Makhno was somber. The sight of the broken and nearly destroyed famous cavalry shocked him. He was silent, seeking to control his emotions. A general assembly took place on the spot. The story of the events in the Crimea was retold: how the commander of the army, Karetnik, sent by the Bolshevik staff to Gulyai-Polye, ostensibly to attend a military council, was treacherously arrested on the way; how Gavrilenko, chief of staff of the Crimean army, as well as all his aides and several of the unit commanders, were deceived with a similar pretext. All those who were caught were shot immediately. The cultural-educational section, at Simferopol', was arrested without recourse to any military ruse.

* * *

195

On November 26, when Gulyai-Polye was surrounded by Red troops, only a special group of 150 to 200 Makhnovist horsemen were there. With this handful of men, Makhno routed the cavalry regiment of the Red Army, which was advancing on Gulyai-Polye from Uspenovka, and thus escaped from the enemy's grip. During the subsequent week he organized the units of insurgents that flocked to him from all sides, as well as some Red Army units who left the Bolsheviks and came to join him. He succeeded in forming a unit of 1000 horsemen and 1500 infantrymen, with whom he attempted a counter-attack. Exactly a week later he occupied Gulyai-Polye, having routed the 42nd Division of the Red Army and taken nearly 6000 prisoners. Of these, about 2000 men declared themselves willing to join the insurrectionary army; the rest were set free on the same day, after having attended a large public meeting. Three days later Makhno inflicted another serious defeat on the Bolsheviks near Andreevka. During the whole night and the following day, he fought two divisions of the Red Army, and ended by defeating them, again taking from 8000 to 10,000 prisoners. As in Gulyai-Polye, these prisoners were set free; volunteers remained with the insurrectionary army. Makhno then struck three further consecutive blows at the Red Army: near Komar', Tsare-Konstantinovka and Berdyansk. The Bolshevik infantry fought reluctantly, and took advantage of every opportunity to surrender.[5]

[5]As soon as they were taken prisoner, the soldiers of the Red Army were set free. They were advised to return to their homes and no longer serve as instruments of power to subjugate the people. But in view of the fact that the Makhnovists were forced to move on immediately, the freed prisoners were reinstated in their respective units a few days later. The Soviet authorities organized special commissions to recapture the soldiers of the Red Army who were set free by the Makhnovists. Thus the Makhnovists were caught in a vicious circle from which they could not escape. As for the Bolsheviks, their procedure was much simpler. Following the orders of the "Special Commission for the Struggle against the Makhnovshchina," all the Makhnovist prisoners were shot on the spot.

We truly regret that we cannot cite verbatim an important Soviet document which was lost in the conditions of war of 1920. This document is an order to the Bogucharski Brigade of the Red Army (the

For some time the Makhnovists were encouraged by the thought that victory would be on their side. It appeared to them that it was only necessary to defeat two or three Bolshevik divisions for an important part of the Red Army to join them, and the rest to retreat toward the north. But soon the peasants of various districts brought news that the Bolsheviks were installing whole regiments, primarily of cavalry, in all the villages, and were concentrating enormous military forces in various places. In fact, Makhno was soon surrounded at Fedorovka, to the south of Gulyai-Polye, by several divisions of infantry and cavalry. The battle raged continuously from 2 a.m. to 4 p.m. Breaking through the enemy ranks, Makhno managed to escape to the northeast. But three days later he had to fight another battle, near the village of Konstantin (inhabited by Greek peasants), against a very large cavalry force and a vigorous artillery. From several officers who were captured, Makhno learned that there were four Bolshevik armies—two cavalry and two mixed—and that the Red commander hoped to surround him with the assistance of several additional divisions. This information agreed perfectly with that furnished by the peasants, as well as with the observations and conclusions of Makhno himself. It became increasingly clear that the defeat of two or three Red units was of no importance, in view of the enormous mass of troops which was being sent against the Makhnovists. It was no longer a question of achieving victory over the Bolshevik armies, but of avoiding the complete destruction of the insurrectionary army. This army, reduced to some 3000 soldiers, was obliged to fight *daily,* each time against an enemy of 10,000 to 15,000 men. In these conditions, catastrophe was no longer in doubt. The Council of Revolutionary Insurgents then decided to abandon the southern region

---

41st, if I am not mistaken), which was defeated by the Makhnovists in December, 1920, near the Greek village of Konstantin. The order stated (almost verbatim): In accordance with the regulations of the "Special Commission for the Struggle against the Makhnovshchina," "in order to discourage a soft attitude among the soldiers" (i.e. conciliatory sentiments—*P.A.*) "and to prevent the Makhnovists from contaminating the Red soldiers—*all* the Makhnovist prisoners are to be shot on the spot."

provisionally, leaving Makhno full freedom as to the direction of the general retreat.

Makhno's genius was about to be submitted to a supreme test. It appeared absolutely impossible to escape from the monstrous network of troops advancing from all sides toward the small group of insurgents. Three thousand revolutionary fighters were surrounded by an army of at least 150,000 men. But Makhno did not for an instant lose courage or presence of mind. He embarked on a heroic duel against this mass of troops. Surrounded on all sides by Red divisions, he marched like a legendary Titan, fighting battle after battle, to the right, to the left, in the front and to the rear. After routing several units of the Red Army and taking more than 20,000 prisoners, Makhno, as if he were striking out blindly, set out first toward the east toward Yuzovka, although the workers of this mining region had warned him that he was awaited by a solid military barrier; he then turned sharply west, following fantastic routes which only he knew. From this moment, the ordinary roads were completely abandoned. The movement of the army continued for hundreds of miles, across snow-covered fields, guided by a prodigious sense of direction and orientation in this icy desert.[6] This maneuver permitted the Makhnovist army to avoid hundreds of enemy cannon and machine guns, and allowed it to defeat two brigades of the 1st Bolshevik cavalry at Petrovo in the government of Kherson which, believing Makhno to be a hundred miles away, were taken completely by surprise.

The struggle lasted for several months, with incessant battles day and night.

Arriving in the government of Kiev, the Makhnovist army found itself, in the coldest part of the winter, in a hilly, rocky country, which made it necessary to abandon all the

[6]No map, no compass could be of any use in such movements. Maps and instruments could indicate the direction, but could not prevent falling into a ravine or a torrent, which did not once happen to the Makhnovist army. Such a march across the hilly and roadless Steppes was possible because the troops knew the configuration of the Ukrainian Steppes perfectly.

artillery, supplies, and almost all munitions, and even most of the wagons. At the same time, two enemy cavalry divisions, called Red Cossacks, came from the western frontier to join the mass of armies sent by the Bolsheviks against Makhno. All the routes were cut off. The place contained as few resources as a graveyard: there were only cliffs and steep ravines, all covered with ice, over which one could only advance slowly. On all sides there was an incessant barrage of cannon and machine-gun fire. None of the Makhnovists expected to get out to safety again. But none thought of dispersing in shameful flight. They decided to die together.

It was unspeakably sad to see this handful of men, alone among the cliffs, the sky, and the enemy fire, ready to fight to the end, and already seemingly condemned to death. Grief, despair and sorrow took hold of them. They wanted to shout to the whole world that a dreadful crime was about to be committed; what was greatest in the hearts of the people, what the people create in their most heroic epochs, was about to be destroyed, was about to perish forever.

Makhno honorably met the test that fate had imposed on him. He advanced to the borders of Galicia, went back to Kiev, re-crossed the Dnieper near Kiev, went down into the departments of Poltava and Khar'kov, turned north again toward Kursk, and, following the railway tracks between Kursk and Belograd, got out of the enemy circle into a much more favorable situation, and left far behind him the many Bolshevik divisions sent to pursue him.

* * *

The heroic duel between a handful of Makhnovists and the State army of the Bolsheviks was not yet over. The Bolshevik command did everything possible to capture the central nucleus of the Makhnovshchina and to destroy it. From all parts of the Ukraine, infantry and cavalry divisions were sent to blockade Makhno. The vise of iron and fire again tightened around the revolutionary heroes and the deadly struggle began again.

In a letter to his comrade, Makhno himself depicted

the end of this heroic and moving episode in the history of the Makhnovshchina.

He wrote:[7]

Two days after your departure, my dear friend, I took the village of Korocha (in the government of Kursk), where I distributed several thousand copies of the "Statutes of the Free Soviets." Then I set out through Varpnyarka and the Don region toward Ekaterinoslav and Tauride. I had to fight fierce battles every day—on one side against the Bolshevik-Communist infantry which followed us step by step, and on the other side against the Second Cavalry army, which was sent against us by the Bolshevik command. You know our horsemen. The Red Cavalry could never hold them if it was not supported by infantry and armored cars. That is why I managed, though not without serious losses, to break through without changing my direction. Our army demonstrated every day that it was really a popular and revolutionary army. In the material conditions which it endured, it should have melted away immediately, but, on the contrary, it never ceased to grow in manpower and resources.

In one of the serious battles which we had to fight, our special detachment of cavalry lost more than 30 men, half of whom were commanders. Among others, our dear and good friend, young in years but old in military exploits, the chief of the detachment, Gavrvusha Troyan, was killed instantly by a bullet. At his side also fell Apollon and several other brave and devoted comrades.

At some distance from Gulyai-Polye, we were joined by our new troops, fresh and full of spirit, who were commanded by Brova and Parkhomenko. A little later, the first brigade of Budenny's Fourth Cavalry Division, with its commander Maslak, came over to our side. The struggle against the authority and despotism of the Bolsheviks became even more fierce.

At the beginning of March, 1921, I asked Brova and Maslak to form a special unit from among the troops

[7]This letter was written after N. Makhno had left Russia.

who were with me, and to proceed toward the Don and the Kuban. Another group was formed under the command of Parkhomenko and sent to the Voronezh region. (Parkhomenko was killed, and an anarchist from Chuguev replaced him.) A third group, composed of 600 horsemen and Ivanyuk's regiment was sent toward Khar'kov.

About the same time, our best comrade and revolutionary Vdovichenko was wounded in the fighting, and had to be taken to Novospasovka for treatment, accompanied by a small detachment. An expeditionary force of Bolsheviks discovered his hiding place; Vdovichenko and his comrade Matrosenko,[8] while defending themselves against the enemy and seeing that they were about to be captured, shot themselves. Matrosenko died instantly, but Vdovichenko's bullet was embedded under his skull above the neck. When the Communists found out who he was, they gave him first aid and saved him from death. Soon after this I had news about him. He was in the hospital at Aleksandrovsk and begged his comrades to find a way of rescuing him. He was tortured atrociously. They tried to make him renounce the Makhnovshchina and sign a paper to that effect. He scornfully repulsed their offers, although he was so weak that he could hardly talk. Because of this refusal, he might have been shot at any moment—but I did not find out whether or not he was shot.

During this time I myself made a raid across the Dnieper toward Nikolaev; then I re-crossed the Dnieper above Perekop and went toward our region, where I hoped to meet some of our detachments. But the Communist command had prepared an ambush for me near Melitopol'. It was impossible either to advance or to re-cross the Dnieper, since the snow had begun to melt and the river was covered with floating ice. We had to fight, which meant that I had to get back into the saddle[9] and direct operations myself. A

[8]Matrosenko was a Ukrainian insurgent and peasant poet—*P.A.*

[9]Makhno had been wounded by a bullet which fractured all the bones in his ankle. This is why he mounted a horse only in cases of extreme necessity.—*P.A.*

section of the enemy troops was skillfully eluded by our troops, while I forced the others to keep on the alert for a whole 24 hours, harassing them with our patrols. During this time I managed to make a forced march of 40 miles, to overcome (at dawn on March 8) a third Bolshevik army, camped on the shore of Molochni Lake, and to get to the open space of the Verkhni Tokmak region over the narrow promontory between Molochni Lake and the Sea of Azov. From there I sent Kurilenko into the Berdyansk-Mariupol' region to direct the insurrectionary movement there. I myself went through the Gulyai-Polye region toward Chernigov, since peasant delegations had come from several of its districts to ask me to visit their region.

In the course of this journey, my troops—1500 horsemen under Petrenko and two infantry regiments—were halted and encircled by strong Bolshevik divisions. Again I had to direct the counter-attack myself. Our efforts were successful. We beat the enemy thoroughly, and took many prisoners, as well as arms, guns, amunition and horses. But two days later, we were attacked by fresh and powerful enemy units. I must tell you that these daily combats had accustomed our men to placing so little value on their lives that exploits of extraordinary heroism had become daily events. With a cry of "Live free or die fighting," the men would throw themselves into the midst of no-matter what unit, overturning enemies much stronger than themselves and forcing them to flee. During one counter-attack, which was bold to the point of folly, I was struck with a bullet that entered my thigh and come out through the stomach, near the appendix. I fell off my horse. This forced us to retreat, because someone who had no experience cried out: "Batko was killed!"

They carried me for a dozen versts in a cart before dressing my wound, and I lost a great deal of blood. I remained unconscious, under the guard of Lev Zin'kovsky. This was March 14. During the night of the 15th, I regained consciousness. All the commanders of our army and the members of the staff, with Belash at their head, assembled at my bedside, asking me to sign an order to send detachments of 100 to 200 men to Kurilenko, Kozhin and others who were directing the insurrectionary movement in various regions. They wanted me to retire with one regiment to a relatively quiet place until I could get back in the saddle. I signed the order, and I permitted Zabud'ko to form a light combat unit to act on its own in our region, without losing touch with me. By the morning of March 16, all these detachments had already left except for a small, special unit that remained with me. And at this moment the 9th Red Cavalry Division fell upon us and forced us to break camp; they pursued us for 13 hours and over 180 versts. Finally, upon leaving Sloboda on the shore of the Sea of Azov, we were able to change horses and halt for five hours.

At dawn on March 17, we resumed the march toward Novospasovka, but after 17 versts on the road we met a new and quite fresh force of Bolsheviks. They had been sent after Kurilenko, but having lost sight of him, they fell on us. After pursuing us for 25 versts (we were completely exhausted and really incapable of fighting), these horsemen threw themselves on us. What were we to do? I was not only incapable of getting into the saddle; I could not even sit up. I was lying in the bottom of the cart, and saw a terrible hand-to-hand battle—an unbelievable hacking—take place about a hundred yards away from me. Our men died only for my sake, only because they would not abandon me. But in the last resort, there was no way to safety, either for them or for me. The enemy was five or six times as strong, for fresh reserves were constantly arriving. All at once, near my cart, I saw the "Lewisists"[10] who had been with me in your time. There were five men under the command of Misha from the village of Chernigovka near Berdyansk. They took leave of me, saying: "Batko, you are indispensable to the cause of our peasant organization. That cause is dear to us. We are going to die soon, but our death will save you and those who will take faithful care of you. Don't forget to repeat our words to our parents." One of them embraced me; then I could no longer see any of them near me. A moment

---

[10]The "Lewisists" were a unit of machine-gunners armed with Lewis machine-guns—P.A.

later Lev Zin'kovsky carried me in his arms to the cart of a peasant who passed nearby. I heard the machine-guns rattle and the bombs explode in the distance. It was our gunners who were keeping the Bolsheviks from passing. We had time to travel three or four versts and cross a river. I was saved, but all the "Lewis-ists" died there.

Sometime later we passed the place again and the peasants of the village of Starodubovka, dist. of Mari-upol', showed us the grave where they had buried our "Lewisists." I still cannot keep back my tears when I think of those brave fighters, simple and honest peas-ants. Moreover I must tell you, my dear friend, that this episode seemed to cure me. On the evening of the same day I got back into the saddle and left the region.

During April I re-established contact with all the units of our troops, and sent those who were nearby to the Poltava region. During May, Kozhin's and Kuri-lenko's units joined us and formed a body of 2000 horsemen and several infantry regiments. It was de-cided to march on Khar'kov and to chase out the big bosses of the Bolshevik-Communist Party. But they were not asleep. They sent more than 60 armored cars, several divisions of cavalry, and a swarm of infantry against me. The fight with these troops lasted for several weeks.

A month later, comrade Shchus' was killed in battle in the Poltava region. He was then chief of staff for Zabud'ko's group. He had worked honorably and valiantly.

A month later Kurilenko was killed. He covered the march of our troops along the railway tracks, took personal charge of stationing the units, and was always in the leading squad. One day he was surprised by Budenny's cavalry and perished in the fight.

On May 18, 1921, Budenny's horsemen were on the march from the Ekaterinoslav region toward the Don, to put down a peasant insurrection led by our comrades Brova and Maslak (who had been chief of Budenny's 1st Brigade and had joined us with all his men).

Our group was formed of several detachments united under the command of Petrenko-Platonov; the main staff and I formed part of the group. The group was 15 to 20 versts from the road along which Budenny's army moved. Knowing, among other things, that I was always near this group, Budenny was tempted by the short distance that separated us from him. He ordered the chief of the 21st armored car unit, which was supposed to suppress the uprising of the peasants in the Don, to send out 16 cars and blockade the village of Novo-Grigor'evka (Stremennoe). Budenny himself marched across the fields at the head of a part of the 19th Cavalry Division (formerly the "Internal Service" Division), in the direction of Novo-Grigor'evka. He arrived there before the armored cars, which were forced to avoid ravines, seek out fords and post sentries. The vigilance of our scouts put us in touch with all these movements, and allowed us to take precautions. At the moment when Budenny came in sight of our camp, we threw ourselves upon him.

Budenny, who was proudly galloping in the first rank, immediately turned tail. The disgraceful coward fled, abandoning his comrades.

A nightmarish combat unfolded in front of us. The soldiers of the Red Army who were sent against us belonged to the troops who had, until then, been in Central Russia, where they had ensured internal order. They did not know us; they had been told that we were common "bandits," and made it a point of honor not to retreat before bandits.

Our insurgent comrades felt in the right and were firmly resolved to conquer and disarm the enemy.

This combat was the fiercest of all we had to fight, either before or after. It ended in complete defeat for Budenny's troops, which led to the disintegration of his army and the desertion of many of his soldiers.

Then I formed a unit of former Siberians, and sent them, armed and equipped with necessities, to Siberia, under the command of comrade Glazunov.

At the beginning of August 1921, we learned from Bolshevik newspapers that this unit had made its appearance in the government of Samara. Then no more was said about it.

During the whole summer of 1921 we did not cease fighting.

The extreme drought of that season and the consequent bad harvests in the governments of Ekaterinoslav, Tauride and parts of Kherson and Poltava, as well as the Don region, forced us to move in one direction toward Kuban and below Tsaritsyn and Saratov, and in the other direction toward Kiev and Chernigov. In the latter place the struggle was led by comrade Kozhin. When we met again, he gave me a bundle of resolutions taken by the peasants of Chernigov, declaring that they wanted to support us completely in our struggle for a free system of councils.

I made a raid across the Volga with the units of comrades Zabud'ko and Petrenko; then I withdrew across the Don, meeting on the way several of our units, which I combined and to which I added Vdovichenko's old group from Azov.

At the beginning of August, 1921, it was decided that in view of the severity of my wounds I would leave with some of our commanders to get medical treatment abroad.

About this time our best commanders—Kozhin, Petrenko and Zabud'ko—were seriously wounded.

On August 13, 1921, accompanied by 100 horsemen, I set out toward the Dnieper, and on the morning of the 16th we crossed the river between Orlik and Kremenchug with the help of 17 peasant fishing boats. On this day I was wounded six times, but not seriously.

On the way we met several of our units, and explained to them the reasons for our departure for abroad. They all said the same thing: "Go and get well, Batko, and then come back and help us. . ." On August 19 we came upon the 7th Cavalry Division of the Red Army, camped along the Ingulets River, 12 versts from Bobrinets. To go back meant trouble, since we had been seen by a cavalry regiment on our right which was advancing to cut off our retreat. I therefore asked Zin'kovsky to put me on horseback. In an instant, with drawn sabres and loud cheers, we hurled ourselves on the division's machine guns, which were massed in a village. We managed to capture 13 "Maxim" and three "Lewis" guns. Then we prepared to continue our journey.

But as soon as we had captured the machine guns, the entire cavalry division stationed in the village of Nikolaev and in neighboring villages was alerted and attacked us. We were caught in a trap. But, without losing courage, we attacked and beat the 38th Regiment of the 7th Cavalry Division, and we then rode 110 versts without stopping. Defending ourselves continuously from the furious attacks of all these troops, we finally escaped, but only after having lost 17 of our best comrades.

On August 22, they had to take care of me again; a bullet struck me in the neck and came out of the right cheek. Once again I was lying in the bottom of a cart. On the 26th we were obliged to fight a new battle with the Reds. We lost our best comrades and fighters: Petrenko-Platonov and Ivanyuk. I was forced to change our route for the last time, and on August 28, 1921, I crossed the Dniester. I am now abroad. . .

* * *

The third campaign of the Bolsheviks against the Makhnovists was at the same time a campaign against the Ukrainian peasantry. The general aim of this campaign was not merely to destroy the Makhnovist army, but to subjugate the dissatisfied peasants and to remove from them all possibility of organizing any type of revolutionary-guerrilla movement. The enormous Red Army, freed from the war against Wrangel, made it fully possible for the Bolsheviks to carry out this plan. The Red Divisions travelled through all the rebel villages in the insurgent region and exterminated masses of peasants on the basis of information provided by local *kulaks*. When, a week after the treacherous Bolshevik attack on Gulyai-Polye, Makhno returned there, the peasants of the village thronged around the Makhnovists and sadly told how the Communists had shot more than three hundred inhabitants the night before. The population of Gulyai-Polye had daily anticipated the arrival of the Makhnovists, hoping that they would save these unfortunate peasants. A few days later the Makhnovists arrived in Novospasovka, and there learned that a similar execution had just taken place. The cultural-educational section of the Makhnovist Army, as well as the insurgent Council, learned that in Novospasovka, the *Chek-*

ists, thirsting for murder, forced mothers to hold their babies in their arms so as to kill both with one blow. This was done to the wife and newborn child of an insurgent from Novospasovka, Martyn. The child was killed, but the wounded mother survived due to the carelessness of the *Chekists.* Such cases were quite frequent. One day history will narrate them. The Bolsheviks also carried out mass shootings of peasants in the villages of Malaya Tokmachka, Uspenovka, Pologi and elsewhere.

This entire repressive campaign was directed by the Commander of the Army of the Southern Front, Frunze.

"We have to finish off the Makhnovshchina by the count of two," he wrote in an order to the Army of the Southern Front before setting out on this expedition. And like a brave soldier, full of desire to distinguish himself in the eyes of his superiors, he set out on the Ukrainian campaign with his sabre flashing, sowing death and desolation around him.[11]

[11]We cite two characteristic examples of Bolshevik executions:
Sereda—peasant, Makhnovist insurgent, native of the government of Ekaterinoslav, belonging to no party. He took care of the finances of the army and was paymaster. Sometimes he replaced Makhno, whom he loved and over whom he watched with extraordinary devotion. In October, 1920, at the time of the agreement between the Bolsheviks and the Makhnovists, a bullet went through his chest and another remained inside during a battle against Wrangel. Needing an operation, he went to Khar'kov, certain that the Soviet authorities would help him in view of his serious condition. In Khar'kov he was placed in a hospital, but a week later, when the Bolsheviks attacked the Makhnovists and anarchists, he was imprisoned and shot, in March, 1921. Let us recall the following facts: when the Makhnovists occupied Ekaterinoslav in October, 1919, they did not in any way disturb the soldiers and officers of Denikin's army who were undergoing treatment in hospitals, believing that the murder of a disarmed enemy was not worthy of the honor of a revolutionary. General Slashchev, at that time under Denikin's orders (today under the Bolsheviks), who took Ekaterinoslav a month later, put to death all the sick and wounded Makhnovists who were in the hospitals. The Communist authorities went even further than Slashchev by shooting a man who, having fought on the same front with them, and having been wounded there, came to them for help, believing that his life was safe because of the agreement signed by them.
Bogush—anarchist who had just returned from America with

Chapter 10

The Meaning of the National Problem in the Makhnovshchina. The Jewish Question.

All that has just been said about the Makhnovshchina shows that it was a true popular movement of peasants and workers, and that its essential goal was to establish the freedom of workers by means of revolutionary self-activity on the part of the masses.

From its beginnings, the movement included poor peasants of all nationalities who lived in the region. The majority naturally consisted of Ukrainian peasants. Six to eight percent were peasants from Great Russia. Then there were Greeks, Jews, Caucasians and other poor people of various nationalities. The Greek and Jewish settlements scattered in the region of the Sea of Azov maintained constant links with the movement. Several of the best commanders of the revolutionary army were of Greek origin, and until the very end the army included several special detachments of Greeks.

---

other anarchists expelled from the United States. At the time of the agreement between the Makhnovists and the Bolsheviks, he was at Khar'kov, and having heard about the legendary Gulyai-Polye, he wanted to go there to become acquainted with the Makhnovshchina. At this time, the Bolsheviks facilitated such journeys by putting at the disposal of the Makhnovists in Khar'kov a locomotive and a railway car to transport militants working in the cultural domain to Gulyai-Polye. However, Bogush was able to see free Gulyai-Polye only for a few days, and in view of the rupture between the Bolsheviks and the Makhnovists and the beginning of hostilities between them, he returned to Khar'kov, where he was arrested by the Bolsheviks and shot by order of the *Cheka* in March, 1921.

This event can have only one explanation: the Bolsheviks did not want to leave alive a single person who knew the truth about their aggression against the Makhnovists and who could have narrated it.

Composed of the poorest peasants, who were united by the fact that they all worked with their own hands, the Makhnovist movement was founded on the deep feeling of fraternity which characterizes only the most oppressed. During its entire history it did not for an instant appeal to national sentiments. The whole struggle of the Makhnovists against the Bolsheviks was conducted solely in the name of the rights and interests of the workers. Denikin's troops, the Austro-Germans, Petliura, the French troops in Berdyansk, Wrangel—were all treated by the Makhnovists as enemies of the workers. Each one of these invasions represented for them essentially a threat to the workers, and the Makhnovists had no interest in the national flag under which they marched.

In the "Declaration" published by the Revolutionary Military Council of the army in October, 1919, in the section dealing with the national question, the Makhnovists stated:

When speaking of Ukrainian independence, we do not mean national independence in Petliura's sense, but the social independence of workers and peasants. We declare that Ukrainian, and all other, working people have the right to self-determination not as an "independent nation," but as "independent workers."

On the question of the language to be taught in schools, the Makhnovists wrote the following:

The cultural-educational section of the Makhnovist army constantly receives questions from school teachers asking about the language in which instruction should be given in the schools, now that Denikin's troops have been expelled.

The revolutionary insurgents, holding to the principles of true socialism, cannot in any field or by any measure do violence to the natural desires and needs of the Ukrainian people. This is why the question of the language to be taught in the schools cannot be solved by our army, but can only be decided by the people themselves, by parents, teachers and students.

It goes without saying that all the orders of Denikin's so-called "Special Bureau," as well as General Mai-Maevsky's order No. 22, which forbids the use of the mother tongue in the schools, are null and void, having been forcibly imposed on the schools.

In the interest of the greatest intellectual development of the people, the language of instruction should be that toward which the local population naturally tends, and this is why the population, the students, the teachers and the parents, and not authorities or the army, should freely and independently resolve this question.

(Signed)
Cultural-Educational Section of the Makhnovist Insurgent Army
(*Put' k Svobode* No. 10, October 18, 1919.)

Thus we see that national prejudices had no place in the Makhnovshchina. There was also no place in the movement for religious prejudices. As a revolutionary movement of the poorest classes of the city and the country, the Makhnovshchina was a principled adversary of all religion and of every god. Among modern social movements, the Makhnovshchina was one of the few in which an individual had absolutely no interest in his own or his neighbor's religion or nationality, in which he respected only the labor and the freedom of the worker.

This did not keep the movement's opponents from seeking to discredit it in this field. In the Russian press as well as abroad, the Makhnovshchina was often pictured as a very restricted guerrilla movement, foreign to ideas of brotherhood and international solidarity, and even tainted with anti-Semitism. Nothing could be more criminal than such slanders. In order to shed light on this question, we will cite here certain documented facts which relate to this subject.

An important role was played in the Makhnovist army by revolutionaries of Jewish origin, many of whom had been sentenced to forced labor for participation in the 1905 revolution, or else had been obliged to emigrate to Western Europe or America. Among others, we can mention:

Kogan—vice-president of the central organ of the movement, the Regional Revolutionary Military Council of

211

Gulyai-Polye. Kogan was a worker who, for reasons of principle, had left his factory well before the revolution of 1917, and had gone to do agricultural work in a poor Jewish agricultural colony. Wounded at the battle of Peregonovka, near Uman, against the Denikinists, he was seized by them at the hospital at Uman where he was being treated, and, according to witnesses, the Denikinists killed him with sabres.

L. Zin'kovsky (Zadov)—head of the army's counter-espionage section, and later commander of a special cavalry regiment. A worker who before the 1917 revolution was condemned to ten years of forced labor for political activities. One of the most active militants of the revolutionary insurrection.

Elena Keller—secretary of the army's cultural and educational section. A worker who took part in the syndicalist movement in America. One of the organizers of the "Nabat" Confederation.

Iosif Emigrant (Gotman)—Member of the army's cultural and educational section. A worker who took an active part in the Ukrainian anarchist movement. One of the organizers of the "Nabat" Confederation, and later a member of its secretariat.

Ya. Alyi (Sukhovol'sky)—worker, and member of the army's cultural and educational section. In the Tsarist period he was condemned to forced labor for political activity. One of the organizers of the "Nabat" Confederation and a member of its secretariat.

We could add many more names to the long list of Jewish revolutionaries who took part in different areas of the Makhnovist movement, but we will not do this, because it would endanger their security.

At the heart of the revolutionary insurrection, the Jewish working population was among brothers. The Jewish agricultural colonies scattered throughout the districts of Mariupol', Berdyansk, Aleksandrovsk and elsewhere, actively participated in the regional assemblies of peasants, workers and insurgents; they sent delegates there, and also to the regional Revolutionary Military Council.

Following certain anti-Semitic incidents which occurred in the region in February, 1919, Makhno proposed to all the Jewish colonies that they organize their self-defense

212

and he furnished the necessary guns and ammunition to all these colonies. At the same time Makhno organized a series of meetings in the region where he appealed to the masses to struggle against anti-Semitism.

The Jewish working population, in turn, expressed profound solidarity and revolutionary brotherhood toward the revolutionary insurrection. In answer to the call made by the Revolutionary Military Council to furnish voluntary combatants to the Makhnovist insurgent army, the Jewish colonies sent from their midst a large number of volunteers.

In the army of the Makhnovist insurgents there was an exclusively Jewish artillery battery which was covered by an infantry detachment, also made up of Jews. This battery, commanded by the Jewish insurgent Shneider, heroically defended Gulyai-Polye from Denikin's troops in June, 1919, and the entire battery perished there, down to the last man and the last shell.

In the extremely rapid succession of events after the uprising of 1918-19, there were obviously individuals who were hostile to Jews, but these individuals were not the products of the insurrection; they were products of Russian life. These individuals did not have any importance in the movement as a whole. If people of this type took part in acts directed against Jews, they were quickly and severely punished by the revolutionary insurgents.

We described earlier the speed and determination with which the Makhnovists executed Grigor'ev and his staff, and we mentioned that one of the main reasons for this execution was their participation in pogroms of Jews.

We can mention other events of this nature with which we are familiar.

On May 12, 1919, several Jewish families—20 people in all—were killed in the Jewish agricultural colony of Gor'kaya, near Aleksandrovsk. The Makhnovist staff immediately set up a special commission to investigate this event. This commission discovered that the murders had been committed by seven peasants of the neighboring village of Uspenovka. These peasants were not part of the insurrectionary army. However, the Makhnovists felt it was impossible to leave this crime unpunished, and they shot the murderers. It was later established that this event and other attempts of this nature had been carried out at the instigation of Denikin's agents, who had managed to infiltrate the region and had sought by these means to prepare an atmosphere favorable for the entry of Denikin's troops into the Ukraine.

On May 4th or 5th, 1919, Makhno and a few commanders hurriedly left the front and went to Gulyai-Polye, where they were awaited by the Extraordinary Plenipotentiary of the Republic, L. Kamenev, who had arrived from Khar'kov with other representatives of the Soviet government. At the Verkhnii Tokmak station, Makhno saw a poster with the words: "Death to Jews, Save the Revolution, Long Live Batko Makhno."

"Who put up that poster?" Makhno asked.

He learned that the poster had been put up by an insurgent whom Makhno knew personally, a soldier who had taken part in the battle against Denikin's troops, a person who was in general decent. He presented himself immediately and was shot on the spot.

Makhno continued the journey to Gulyai-Polye. During the rest of the day and during his negotiations with the Plenipotentiary of the Republic, he could not free himself from the influence of this event. He realized that the insurgent had been cruelly dealt with, but he also knew that in conditions of war and in view of Denikin's advance, such posters could represent an enormous danger for the Jewish population and for the entire revolution if one did not oppose them quickly and resolutely.

When the insurrectionary army retreated toward Uman in the summer of 1919, there were several cases when insurgents plundered Jewish homes. When the insurrectionary army examined these cases, it was learned that one group of four or five men was involved in all these incidents—men who had earlier belonged to Grigor'ev's detachments and who had been incorporated into the Makhnovist army after Grigor'ev was shot. This group was disarmed and discharged immediately. Following this, all the combatants who had served under Grigor'ev were discharged from the Makhnovist army as an unreliable element whose re-education was not possible in view of the unfavorable conditions and the lack of time. Thus we see how the Makhnovists viewed anti-Semitism. Outbursts of anti-Semitism in various parts of the Ukraine had no relation to the Makhnovshchina.

Wherever the Jewish population was in contact with the Makhnovists, it found in them its best protectors against anti-Semitic incidents. The Jewish population of Gulyai-Polye, Aleksandrovsk, Berdyansk, Mariupol', as well as all the Jewish agricultural colonies scattered throughout the Donets region, can themselves corroborate the fact that they always found the Makhnovists to be true revolutionary friends, and that due to the severe and decisive measures of the Makhnovists, the anti-Semitic leanings of the counter-revolutionary forces in this region were promptly squashed.

Anti-Semitism exists in Russia as well as in many other countries. In Russia, and to some extent in the Ukraine, it is not a result of the revolutionary epoch or of the insurrectionary movement, but is on the contrary a vestige of the past. The Makhnovists always fought it resolutely in words as well as deeds. During the entire period of the movement, they issued numerous publications calling on the masses to struggle against this evil. It can firmly be stated that in the struggle against anti-Semitism in the Ukraine and beyond its borders, their accomplishment was enormous. We have at hand an appeal published by Makhnovists together with anarchists referring to an anti-Semitic incident which took place in the spring of 1919—an incident which was undoubtedly linked to the beginning of Denikin's general offensive against the revolution. Here is an abridged version of the text:

WORKERS, PEASANTS AND INSURGENTS.
FOR THE OPPRESSED,
AGAINST THE OPPRESSORS—ALWAYS!

During the painful days of reaction, when the situation of the Ukrainian peasants was especially difficult and seemed hopeless, you were the first to rise as fearless and unconquerable fighters for the great cause of the liberation of the working masses. . . This was the most beautiful and joyful moment in the history of our revolution. You marched against the enemy with weapons in your hands as conscious revolutionaries, guided by the great idea of freedom and

215

equality. . . But harmful and criminal elements succeeded in insinuating themselves into your ranks. And the revolutionary songs, songs of brotherhood and of the approaching liberation of the workers, began to be disrupted by the harrowing cries of poor Jews who were being tormented to death. . . On the clear and splendid foundation of the revolution appeared indelible dark blots caused by the parched blood of poor Jewish martyrs who now, as before, continue to be innocent victims of the criminal reaction, of the class struggle. . . . Shameful acts are being carried out. Anti-Semitic pogroms are taking place.

Peasants, workers and insurgents! You know that the workers of all nationalities—Russians, Jews, Poles, Germans, Armenians, etc.—are equally imprisoned in the abyss of poverty. You know that thousands of Jewish girls, daughters of the people, are sold and dishonored by capital, the same as women of other nationalities. You know how many honest and valiant revolutionary Jewish fighters have given their lives for freedom in Russia during our whole liberation movement. . . The revolution and the honor of workers obliges all of us to declare as loudly as possible that we make war on the same enemies: on capital and authority, which oppress all workers equally, whether they be Russian, Polish, Jewish, etc. We must proclaim everywhere that our enemies are exploiters and oppressors of various nationalities: the Russian manufacturer, the German iron magnate, the Jewish banker, the Polish aristocrat. . . The bourgeoisie of all countries and all nationalities is united in a bitter struggle against the revolution, against the laboring masses of the whole world and of all nationalities.

Peasants, workers and insurgents! At this moment, when the international enemy—the bourgeoisie of all countries—hurries to the Russian revolution to create nationalist hatred among the mass of workers in order to distort the revolution and to shake the very foundation of our class struggle—the solidarity and unity of all workers—you must move against conscious and unconscious counter-revolutionaries who endanger the emancipation of the working people from capital and authority. Your revolutionary duty is to stifle all nationalist persecution by dealing ruthlessly with all instigators of anti-Semitic pogroms.

The path toward the emancipation of the workers can be reached by the union of all the workers of the world.

Long live the workers' international!

Long live the free and stateless anarchist commune!

> (signed)
> Executive Committee of the Revolutionary Military Council of the Gulyai-Polye region.
> "Nabat" Anarchist Group in Gulyai-Polye.
> Commander of the Makhnovist Insurrectionary Army, *Batko Makhno.*
> Chief of Staff of the Makhnovist Insurrectionary Army, *B. Veretel'nikov.*

> Village of Gulyai-Polye
> May 1919.

Appendix to Chapter 10

Order No. 1.[1]

From the Commander of the Ukrainian Revolutionary Insurrectionary Army, Batko Makhno.

To all the commanders of the infantry: corps, brigades, regiments, batallions, companies, platoons, and sections; cavalry: brigades, regiments, squadrons, and platoons; artillery: divisions, batteries. To all heads of staffs, garrisons. To all revolutionary insurgents without exception.

1. The goal of our revolutionary army, and of every insurgent participating in it, is an honorable struggle

---

[1] This order was published at the time of the unification and organization of all the insurrectionary forces into a single army; when, after the forced retreat from the region of Gulyai-Polye, the detachments who had served under Grigor'ev and the Red Army troops who had come from Novy Bug to join the Makhnovists were incorporated into the insurrectionary army in the region of Elisavetgrad-Pomoshchnaya.

for the full liberation of the Ukrainian workers from all oppression. This is why every insurgent should constantly keep in mind that there is no place among us for those who, under the cover of the revolutionary insurrection, seek to satisfy their desires for personal profit, violence and plunder at the expense of the peaceful Jewish population.

2. Every revolutionary insurgent should remember that his personal enemies as well as the enemies of all the people are the rich bourgeoisie, regardless of whether they be Russian, or Jewish, or Ukrainian. The enemies of the working people are also those who protect the unjust bourgeois regime, i.e., the Soviet Commissars, the members of repressive expeditionary corps, the Extraordinary Commissions which go through the cities and villages torturing the working people who refuse to submit to their arbitrary dictatorship. Every insurgent should arrest and send to the army staff all representatives of such expeditionary corps, Extraordinary Commissions and other institutions which oppress and subjugate the people; if they resist, they should be shot on the spot. As for any violence done to peaceful workers of whatever nationality—such acts are unworthy of any revolutionary insurgent, and the perpetrator of such acts will be punished by death.

3. All acts of individual requisition or confiscation as well as any exchange of horses or vehicles with the peasants without written authorization from the supply commander will be severely punished. Every insurgent should realize that requisitions of this type would only attract to the ranks of the insurrectionary army hooligans of the worst type, individuals thirsting for wealth and eager to carry out shameful acts which distort our liberatory revolutionary movement under the very cover of the revolutionary insurrection.

I appeal to all insurgent militants to take it upon themselves to protect the honor of our truly revolutionary insurrectionary army by opposing every unjust act either among ourselves or among the working people whom we are defending.[2] We cannot practice

---

[2] *i.e.* to struggle against injustice in the insurgents' own environment and in the insurgents' relations to the environment of the working people—*P.A.*

injustice among ourselves. We cannot mistreat even one son or daughter of the working people for whom we are fighting. And every insurgent who takes part in such an act covers himself with shame and brings upon himself the punishment of the popular revolutionary army.

4. In the interests of the revolution and of a just struggle for our ideals it is necessary to maintain the most rigorous fraternal discipline in our ranks. The greatest respect and obedience in military matters toward your chosen commanders are absolutely indispensable. This is required by the importance of the cause which has fallen to us to defend, which we will honorably carry to its conclusion, but which we will lose if we do not maintain discipline among ourselves. This is why I require the commanders and the insurgents to maintain strict discipline among themselves and in all their actions.

5. Drunkenness is to be considered a crime. It is a still greater crime for a revolutionary insurgent to show himself drunk in the street.

6. Every insurgent travelling from one village to another should be ready for combat. The relations with the peaceful population in the villages and on the roads should be above all amicable and comradely. Remember, comrade commanders and insurgents, that we are the sons of the great working people, that all the workers are our brothers and our sisters. The cause for which we fight is a great one, which demands that we be untiring, generous, full of brotherly love and revolutionary honor. That is why I call on all revolutionary insurgents to be real friends of the people and true sons of the revolution. This is the source of our power and the guarantee of our victory.

(signed)
Commander of the Ukrainian Revolutionary Insurrectionary Army, *Batko Makhno.*

Hamlet of Dobrovelichkovka, government of Kherson.
August 5, 1919.

Gulyai-Polye Insurgents.

Chapter 11

Makhno's Personality.

Biographical Notes on
Some Members of the Movement.

The Makhnovshchina is a revolutionary mass movement created by the historical living conditions of the poorest sectors of the Russian peasantry. Whether or not Makhno had existed, this movement would inevitably have risen from the depths and would have expressed itself in original forms. From the very first days of the revolution, it rose out of the depths of the people in various parts of Russia. If it had not appeared in the Ukraine, it could just as well have appeared elsewhere. Its seeds were carried by the Russian revolution. The conditions in the Ukraine in 1918 helped the movement to break through in a torrent and to consolidate its position to some extent. From its very beginnings, this movement, stemming from the lowest depths of society, thrust forward an impressive array of personalities who were until then unknown, but who possessed an indomitable spirit, a remarkable revolutionary instinct, and enormous abilities in the field of military strategy. Such individuals at the beginning of the movement included: Kalashnikov, the Karetnik brothers, Vasilevsky, Marchenko, Vdovichenko, Kurilenko, Gavrilenko, Petrenko, Belash, Shchus', Ivan and Aleksandr Lepetchenko, Isidor Lyutyi, Veretel'nikov, Chubenko, Tykhenko, the Danilov brothers, L. Zinkovsky, Krat, Seregin, Taranovsky, Puzanov, Troyan, and many others, less well-known. All of them were pioneers of the Makhnovist movement, its standard-bearers and admirable guides. The movement also found a general leader worthy of holding this post in the person of Nestor Makhno.

We knew Makhno during the three stages of his development.

Nestor Makhno.

222

The first stage begins when he was condemned to forced labor as a young revolutionary. In prison he did not distinguish himself from the others—he led the same life as the other prisoners, he was in irons, he sat in the dungeons, he responded to the roll call. His only characteristic that attracted attention was his tireless energy. He was constantly engaged in discussions and controversies, and flooded the prison with his writings. He had a passion for writing on revolutionary and political themes. While in prison, he loved to make up verses, and he was more successful at poetry than at prose. At this time he was very proud of being called an anarchist, believing that nothing was more sublime and beautiful than the world of anarchist ideas. During the imperialist war he was absolutely a stranger to the patriotic fever which took hold of at least half of the political prisoners. Kropotkin's calls to support one of the two warring sides profoundly distressed him, but did not in any way convince him.

The second stage of Makhno's development extends from March 1, 1917, to the summer of 1918. During this time he undertook feverish revolutionary activity in the region of Gulyai-Polye. Unions of workers and peasant associations in Gulyai-Polye, the first soviet of workers and peasants which met there, were the results of Makhno's untiring activity in 1917. He became extremely popular among the peasants of the region, but since the revolution brought forward numerous energetic individuals, he was not particularly distinguishable. But one trait was unique to him: when he was among comrades, he would often retreat into himself, and would unexpectedly make decisions which affected his whole life.

And finally, the third stage includes his activity in the ranks of the revolutionary insurrection from the time of the Hetman until today.

It is unquestionable that the insurrection of the peasant masses, the field of revolutionary and military activity, was the context in which his personality was able to develop fully.

In the spring of 1919, when we saw him for the first time in this new environment, as a leader of the revolutionary insurrection, he was already a completely new and *transformed* individual.

Outwardly he had not changed, but internally he was a different person. He was completely consumed by his activity. His every movement expressed the strength of his will and his shrewdness. At this time he was completely occupied with the struggle against Denikin on the southern front. The energy with which he engaged in this activity was colossal. He spent weeks and entire months at the front, standing guard and fighting in the ranks with the other insurgents. And when he came to Gulyai-Polye, he spent all his time working with the staff. This work continued late into the night. Only after everything was done did Makhno go to sleep. At five or six o'clock of the following morning, he was already waking the other members of the staff. He also took an active part in daily meetings and assemblies which were held in Gulyai-Polye itself or in neighboring villages. Nevertheless, he always found time to spend one or two hours at a peasant wedding to which the young bride-groom had invited him two or three weeks earlier. He related to the peasants as one of their own, remained vitally interested in their lives, and in general he lived the same life they lived.

A multitude of legends about Makhno are spread by the peasants and workers of the Ukraine; they represent Makhno as exceptionally brave, extremely shrewd and invincible. In fact, when one knew him personally and watched him at work, one became convinced that he was more remarkable than all the legends about him.

Makhno is a man of historic *action.* The three years of his revolutionary struggle are filled with incessant deeds, one more remarkable than the other.

The central characteristic of Makhno's personality is his enormous willpower. It seems as if this man of small stature was made of a particularly hard material. He never backed away from an obstacle once he had resolved to surmount it. During the most difficult moments of his life, when catastrophes took place at the front, or when his best friends perished before his eyes, he outwardly remained completely calm, almost as if this did not concern him. Yet, even if he did not externally show his pain, he suffered more than others from these incidents. When, after the rupture of the military and political agreement in November and

December, 1920, the Bolsheviks, knowing who their adversary was and hoping to avoid their errors of the preceding summer, threw against Makhno four armies, Makhno faced a catastrophic situation. But he did not lose his psychological equilibrium. His calm was in fact amazing: he paid no attention to the thousands of shells which decimated the insurgent troops nor to the imminent danger of being crushed at any instant by the enormous Red Army. To an external observer this composure of Makhno might have appeared like the composure of a mentally deranged individual. But only an outsider could have gotten such an impression. Those who knew Makhno saw that this calm represented an extraordinary effort of the will to victory over the enemy.

Makhno has the determination of a real hero, as opposed to the determination of those who act behind people's backs and at their expense. In all important situations Makhno marched in the front lines, and was the first to risk his life. Whether he rushed into battle with a detachment, or the entire army set out on a march of ten or fifteen miles, Makhno was always in the front lines, in the saddle if he was well, in a wagon if he was wounded. This is a rule without exceptions.

Makhno is undoubtedly gifted with great military talent. What difficulties he and his army met in the Ukraine! He always emerged from them with honor. The defeat which he inflicted on Denikin's divisions at Uman—divisions commanded by experienced generals educated at the military academy—and the way he disrupted the rearguard of the Denikinist army, are historical monuments to Makhno's military abilities. These are not the only monuments.

In terms of his revolutionary and social conceptions, Makhno is an anarchist-communist. He is fanatically devoted to his class—the poor, oppressed peasantry which is denied all rights.

Makhno is intelligent and shrewd. This trait, which he inherited from the people and which was nurtured by his peasant surroundings, is evident in everything he does. He fully deserves the devotion and affection of his army and of the peasantry. In these surroundings he is considered their own, unique and outstanding. "Batko is one of us," say the insurgents. "He is happy to drink with us, talk with us, and fight shoulder to shoulder with us." These words give the best possible characterization of Makhno as a son of the people. His links with the people were planted in rich black soil. There was hardly anyone in Russia who enjoyed the popularity and affection of the masses as much as Makhno. The peasants are profoundly proud of him. But he has never sought to profit from this affection, to use his position; on the contrary, he frequently ridiculed his position with a typically Ukrainian sense of humor.

Makhno was able to employ the firm and forceful hand of a leader. He was in no way inherently authoritarian, but in the midst of action he always found the necessary firmness, without introducing an authoritarian tendency into the movement, but at the same time not compromising it for lack of cohesion.

It is well known how much significance the Bolsheviks attached to the fact that the peasants called Makhno "Batko." In Chapter 3 we described how and in what circumstances he was given this name. After 1920 he was usually called "Malyi" ("Shorty"), a nickname referring to his short stature, which was introduced by chance by one of the insurgents.[1]

Makhno's personality contained many superior characteristics—spirit, will, courage, energy and activeness. Taken together, these traits created an imposing impression, and made him remarkable even among revolutionaries.

However, Makhno lacked the theoretical knowledge needed to understand politics and history. Because of this he frequently could not formulate broad revolutionary generalizations and conclusions, or simply refused even to consider them.

The vast movement of the revolutionary insurrection

[1] After 1920, the Bolsheviks wrote a great deal about the personal defects of Makhno, basing their information on the diary of his so-called wife, a certain Fedora Gaenko, who had been captured during a battle. But Makhno's wife is Galina Andreevna Kuz'menko. She has lived with him since 1918. She *never* kept, and therefore never lost, a diary. Thus the documentation of the Soviet authorities is based on a fabrication, and the picture these authorities draw from such a diary is an ordinary lie.

demanded that new social and revolutionary formulas be found that would be adequate to its nature. By reason of his inadequate theoretical knowledge, Makhno was not always equal to this task, and in view of the position which he occupied in the revolutionary insurrection, this defect had repercussions on the whole movement.

We believe that if Makhno had possessed more extensive knowledge in the fields of history and political and social sciences, the revolutionary insurrection would have recorded, instead of inevitable defeats, a series of victories which would have played a colossal and perhaps decisive role in the development of the Russian revolution.

In addition, Makhno possessed one characteristic that sometimes diminished his dominant qualities: at times he exhibited a certain carelessness. Though full of energy and will, he occasionally showed, in times of exceptionally serious crisis, a frivolity that was incompatible with the seriousness demanded by the gravity of the situation.

To give one example, the results of the victory over Denikin's counter-revolution in the fall of 1919 were not sufficiently exploited in the direction of developing a pan-Ukrainian insurrection, although the moment was particularly favorable for such a task. The reason for this was a certain intoxication with victory, as well as a powerful and erroneous sense of security and a measure of inattentiveness; the leaders of the insurrection, with Makhno at their head, installed themselves in the liberated region without giving sufficient attention to the persistence of the White danger or the peril of Bolshevism, which was descending from the north.

But Makhno grew and developed together with the growth and development of the Russian Revolution. Every year he became more intense. In 1921 he was much more profound than he had been in 1918-1919.

In studying Makhno's personality, one should not forget the unfavorable conditions in which Makhno had lived from his infancy: the almost complete lack of education among those who surrounded him and the complete absence of experienced and enlightened help in his social and revolutionary struggle. In spite of this, Makhno has brought about immortal achievements in the Russian revolution, and history will rightfully list him among the most remarkable individuals of this revolution.

To our great surprise, the majority of contemporary Russian anarchists, pretending to play a leading role in the field of anarchist thought, were not able to recognize the salient qualities of Makhno's personality. Many of them saw and judged him from a Bolshevik perspective, getting their materials from the hands of State agents, or else limited themselves to trifles. In this context, P. A. Kropotkin was a striking exception.

"Tell Comrade Makhno from me to take care of himself, for there are not many people like him in Russia."

These words were spoken by Kropotkin in June, 1919, i.e., when there was no information on Makhno in Central Russia other than the official distortions.

At an enormous distance, and on the basis of a few isolated facts, Kropotkin's penetrating insight recognized in Makhno an important historical figure.

Biographical Notes on Some Members of the Movement.

We conclude this chapter with brief notes on some of the principal participants in the movement. The biographical materials which we had collected about them were lost at the beginning of 1921, and consequently we are obliged to limit ourselves to extremely summary notes.

Simon Karetnik was a peasant from Gulyai-Polye—one of the poorest of the village. He worked as a farm laborer, and only attended school for one year. He participated in the movement from its first days, and was an anarchist-communist from 1907. He showed a remarkable military talent. He was wounded many times in the fighting against Denikin. After 1920 he often replaced Makhno as supreme commander of the army; he commanded the corps which was sent to the Crimea against Wrangel. He was a member of the Council of Revolutionary Insurgents of the Ukraine. After Wrangel's defeat, the Bolsheviks sent him to Gulyai-Polye, ostensibly to attend a military conference, but he was treacherously seized on route, and was shot at Melitopol'. He left a widow and several children.

Marchenko was the son of a family of poor peasants from Gulyai-Polye. His education was incomplete. An anarchist-communist since 1907, he was one of the first insurgents of the Gulyai-Polye region. He was imprisoned and wounded several times in the combats against Denikin's troops. During the last two years of the insurrection, he commanded the Makhnovist cavalry and was a member of the Council of Revolutionary Insurgents. He was killed in January, 1921, near Poltava, during a battle against the Reds. He left a widow.

Grigory Vasilevsky was the son of poor peasants of Gulyai-Polye. He received an elementary education. An anarchist before 1917, he participated in the Makhnovist movement from its beginnings. A personal friend of Makhno, he replaced him several times at the head of the army. He was killed in December, 1920, in the course of a battle against the Red Cossacks in the government of Kiev. He left a widow and some children.

B. Veretel'nikov was a peasant of Gulyai-Polye. Later he worked in a local foundry, and afterwards in the Putilov factory in Petrograd. First a Socialist-Revolutionary, he became an anarchist in 1918. A very gifted orator and organizer, he actively participated in all the phases of the Russian Revolution. In 1918 he returned to Gulyai-Polye, devoted himself mostly to propaganda and became very popular in the region. For some time he performed the functions of chief of staff of the army. In June, 1919, he marched at the head of a hastily formed unit to try to defend Gulyai-Polye against the forces of Denikin; about 10 miles from Gulyai-Polye, near Svyatodukhovka (dist. of Aleksandrovsk), he was surrounded by the enemy and perished with his entire detachment, continuing to fight until the very end. He left a widow and children.

Peter Gavrilenko was a peasant from Gulyai-Polye, an anarchist since the 1905 revolution, and one of the most active militants of the Makhnovist movement. He played an important role as commander of the Third Corps of Makhnovist Insurgents in the defeat of Denikin's troops in the fall of 1919. During all of 1920 he was a prisoner of the Bolsheviks in Khar'kov. On the basis of the military-political agreement between the Makhnovists and the Soviet authority, he was freed and immediately went to the Crimea to take part in the struggle against Wrangel, where he served as chief of the field staff of the Makhnovist army. After the destruction of Wrangel, he was treacherously seized by the Bolsheviks in the Crimea, and as far as we know, he was shot at Melitopol'. He was a military leader and a prominent revolutionary.

Vasily Kurilenko was a peasant from the village of Novospasovka who received a summary education. He was an anarchist. He commanded a cavalry regiment and was a member of the Council of Revolutionary Insurgents. As a skilled horseman, in 1919 he was invited by the Bolsheviks to the post of commander of a Red cavalry unit after the Makhnovists had been declared outlaws. After conferring with Makhno and other comrades, he accepted the post and held back Denikin's advance in the region of Ekaterinoslav. At the time of the military and political agreement, he was delegated by the Makhnovists to negotiate with the Bolsheviks. In 1920 he was wounded several times in battles against the Whites and the Reds. He was a popular speaker in large public meetings. He was killed in a skirmish with the Reds in the summer of 1921, and left a widow.

Viktor Belash was a peasant from Novospasovka who received an elementary education. He was an anarchist. From 1919 he commanded a Makhnovist regiment and took part in the attack on Taganrog. He was later chief of staff of the army. To revenge his participation in the Makhnovist movement, Denikin's troops killed his father, his grandfather and his two brothers, and burned all that belonged to them. He was a member of the Council of Revolutionary Insurgents, and a skillful military strategist. He elaborated all the plans concerning troop movements and assumed responsibility for them. He was captured by the Bolsheviks in 1921, and was under the threat of being shot. His fate is unknown.

Vdovichenko was a peasant from Novospasovka who received an elementary education. He was an anarchist. He commanded a special detachment of insurgent troops and was one of the most active participants in the revolutionary insurrection. He was extremely popular and greatly loved among the peasants of the Sea of Azov region and among the insurgents. He played a considerable part in the defeat of Denikin's forces in the fall of 1919. In 1921 he was seriously wounded and imprisoned by the Bolsheviks. Though threatened with death, he disdainfully turned down their proposal to transfer to their service. His fate is unknown.

Peter Rybin (Zonov) was a metal-worker, from the government of Orel. At the time of the Tsarist reaction he emigrated to America, where he immediately took part in the revolutionary syndicalist movement, and played a significant role as member of the Union of Russian Workers of the United States and Canada. At the beginning of the 1917 revolution he returned to Russia by way of Japan and Vladivostok, and arrived at Ekaterinoslav. There he took an active part in the syndicalist movement and became popular among the workers. Toward the end of 1917, Ekaterinoslav workers delegated him to the pan-Ukrainian conference of representatives of trade unions and factory committees. The conference adopted the *Rybin Plan,* which called for the unification of industry and the reconstruction of transportation. Following this, on the suggestion of the Bolsheviks, Rybin lived in Khar'kov, where he worked in the union of metal-workers and in other key sectors of industry and transportation. During the summer of 1920 he came to the conclusion that it was absolutely impossible to work with the Bolsheviks, since they directed all their efforts against the interests of the workers and peasants. It should be noted that Rybin had worked with the Bolsheviks as an assiduous and painstaking trade union worker, and did not dream of making his anarchist leanings known to the Soviet authorities. Even though limiting himself to this role, he found it impossible to serve the interests of the working class under the Communist dictatorship. In the fall of 1920 his thoughts turned toward the Makhnovists, and he went to the camp of the insurgents, where he worked with great energy in the cultural section of the movement. Shortly after his arrival, he was elected member of the Council of Revolutionary Insurgents, and served as secretary. Rybin had enormous energy, and was very well organized and cultured in his work habits. In January, 1921, he left the Makhnovist camp for a time and returned to Khar'kov. He intended to call Rakovsky by telephone and give his frank opinion about Rakovsky and the

231

Peter Rybin (Zonov).

other authors of the treacherous attack against the Makhno-vists and the anarchists. It is very probable that he carried out his plan and that this was the cause of his death. Five days after his arrival in Khar'kov, he was arrested by order of the *Cheka,* and was shot a month later. He was shot by the Bolsheviks, who had so recently predicted a brilliant career for him, calling him an outstanding organizer and theoreti-cian of the workers' movement.

Kalashnikov was a very young insurgent who had attended the municipal school. He was the son of a worker, and was a 2nd lieutenant in the Tsarist army before the revolution. In 1917 he became secretary of the anarchist-communist organization in Gulyai-Polye. He was an excep-tionally brave and talented commander. He was principal organizer of the uprising of Red troops at Novi Bug in the summer of 1919. At first he commanded the 1st brigade of the insurrectionary army, and then the 1st Donets corps of the Makhnovist army. He was killed by a shell in the summer of 1920 in a battle against the Red Army. He left a widow and a child.

Mikhalev-Pavlenko was the son of peasants of Great Russia. He was a member of an anarchist group in Petrograd, and arrived in Gulyai-Polye at the beginning of 1919. He organized and commanded the engineering corps of the Makhnovist army. He had the particularly pure and delicate spirit of a young idealist. On June 11th or 12th, 1919, while serving on an armored train which was engaged in the fight against Denikin's troops, he was treacherously seized with his comrade Burbyga, by order of Voroshilov, commander of the 14th Army, and was executed on June 17, 1919, at Khar'kov.

Makeev was a worker of Ivanovo-Voznesensk, and a member of the anarchist organization in that city. At the end of April, 1919, he arrived in Gulyai-Polye with 36 comrades who belonged to the same organization. He first devoted himself to propaganda. Later he was elected to the staff of the Makhnovist army. At the end of November, 1919, while commanding an insurrectionary detachment in the region of the Zaporozh'e Station, he was killed in a battle against the troops of General Slashchev.

Vasily Danilov was the son of a poor Gulyai-Polye

Fedor Shchus'.

family, and a blacksmith by trade. He was a soldier in the artillery, and took part in the revolutionary insurrection from its very first days. In the Makhnovist army he held the responsible post of chief of artillery supplies.

Chernoknizhnyi was an elementary school teacher in the village of Novo Pavlovka, district of Pavlograd. At the second congress of peasants, workers and insurgents held at Gulyai-Polye, he was elected president of the Revolutionary Military Council of the Gulyai-Polye region, and continued to carry out this function until the insurgent region was defeated by the Bolsheviks and Denikinists in June, 1919. For his participation in the insurrectionary movement, the Soviet authority declared him an outlaw.

Shchus' was a poor peasant from the village of Bol'shaya Mikhailovka. He was a seaman. At the beginning of the revolution, he was one of the first and most active partisans in the southern Ukraine. As early as April, 1918, he headed an insurrectionary detachment which fought against the Austro-German troops. In the struggle against the Hetman's authority and the Austro-Germans, he demonstrated remarkable energy and courage. Among the insurgents and throughout the southern Ukrainian region, his popularity was almost equal to that of Nestor Makhno. He occupied important positions in the Makhnovist insurrectionary army; he was commander of a cavalry unit, head of the army staff, and finally chief of staff of a special unit of insurrectionary soldiers. He was killed in June, 1921, in the government of Poltava, during a battle against the Red Cavalry.

Isidor Lyutyi was a Gulyai-Polye peasant who had finished primary school. He was a painter by profession. He was an anarchist, and one of the first and most active of the revolutionary insurgents. He was a member of the army staff and one of Makhno's closest aides. He was killed in a battle against the Denikinists near Uman in September, 1919.

Foma Kozhin was a peasant who did not belong to any party. He commanded the machine-gun regiment in the Makhnovist army and later became commander of a special detachment. He played an important role in the defeat of Denikin in the fall of 1919, and in the defeat of Wrangel in 1920. He was wounded several times in these battles. In August 1921 he was seriously wounded in a battle against the Red Army. His fate is unkonwn.

Ivan and Aleksandr Lepetchenko were Gulyai-Polye peasants and anarchists. They were among the first insurgents against the Hetman Skoropadsky. They worked actively at the front and in the interior of the insurrectionary region. Aleksandr Lepetchenko was shot by the Bolsheviks in the spring of 1920 in Gulyai-Polye as an eminent Makhnovist. Ivan Lepetchenko retained his post in the Makhnovist army until the very end.

Seregin was a peasant, and an anarchist after 1917. He took part in the insurrection from the beginning, and was head of the supply section of the insurrectionary army.

Grigory and Savva Makhno were brothers of Nestor Makhno.

Grigory Makhno took part in the struggle against the counter-revolution at the Tsaritsyn front, occupying the post of chief of staff of the 37th brigade of the Red Army in 1918 and the beginning of 1919. Joining the insurrectionary army in the spring of 1919, he served as aide to the chief of staff. He was killed near Uman in a battle against the Denikinists in September, 1919, at the same time as Isidor Lyutyi.

Savva Makhno was the oldest of the Makhno brothers. He took part in the insurrection from the time of the Austro-German occupation. At the beginning of 1920 he was seized by the Bolsheviks in Gulyai-Polye, not in the course of a battle, but in his own home, and shot, mainly because he was the brother of Nestor Makhno. He left a large family.

* * *

Lacking sufficient documentation, we are not able to furnish more or less complete biographical information about the long list of active Makhnovists who played important roles in the movement, as for example: *Garkusha,* commander of a special regiment of Makhnovist insurgents, killed in 1920; *Kolyada,* member of the army staff; *Dermendzhi,* liaison officer; *Pravda,* chief of transport; *Bondarets,* who commanded all the cavalry, and was killed in 1920;

Chubenko, head of the demolition command;[2] *Brova*, commander of a special detachment; *Domashenko*, staff commander; *Zabud'ko*, commander of a special detachment; *Tykhenko*, head of the supply section; *Buryma*, head of the demolition command;[2] *Chumak*, treasurer of the army; *Krat*, administrator of the economic section; and many others. All of them emerged from the lowest levels of the working population at the most heroic and revolutionary moment of their lives and served the cause of the movement with all their forces and until their last breath.

[2]During the three years of the insurrectionary movement, various individuals obviously filled the same posts in the Makhnovist army.

238

Chapter 12

The Makhnovshchina and Anarchism.

Anarchism embraces two worlds: the world of philosophy, of ideas, and the world of practice, of activity. The two are intimately linked. The struggling working class stands mainly on the concrete, practical side of anarchism. The essential and fundamental principle of this side is the principle of the revolutionary initiative of workers and their self-liberation. From this naturally flows the further principle of statelessness and self-management of the workers in the new society. But until the present, the history of the proletarian struggle does not contain a massive anarchist movement in its pure, strictly principled form. All of the workers' and peasants' movements which have taken place until today have been movements within the limits of the capitalist regime, and have been more or less tinged with anarchism. This is perfectly natural and understandable. The working classes do not act within a world of wishes, but in the real world where they are daily subjected to the physical and psychological blows of hostile forces. Outside of the world of anarchist ideas, which have not been greatly disseminated, the workers continually feel the influence of all the real conditions of the capitalist regime and of intermediate groups.

The conditions of contemporary life encircle the workers on all sides, surround them, like water surrounds fish in the sea. The workers are not able to escape from these conditions. Consequently it is natural that the struggle which they undertake inevitably carries the stamp of various conditions and characteristics of contemporary society. The struggle can never be born in the finished and perfected anarchist form which would correspond to all the requirements of the ideal. Such a perfect form is possible only in narrow political circles, and even there not in practice, but in plans, in programs. When the popular masses engage in a

239

struggle of large dimensions, they inevitably start by committing errors, they allow contradictions and deviations, and only through the process of this struggle do they direct their efforts in the direction of the ideal for which they are struggling.

It has always been so. And it will always be so. No matter how carefully we have prepared the organizations and foreseen the position of the working class in advance, during times of peace, from the first day of the decisive struggle of the masses, their real activity is very different from what was expected in the plan. In some cases the very fact of widespread mass activity may upset certain expectations. In other cases, the deviations and blows of the masses will require the definition of new positions. And only gradually will the immense movement of the masses engage itself on the well-defined and principled path which leads toward the goal.

This, obviously, does not mean that preliminary organization of the forces and positions of the working class is not necessary. On the contrary, preparatory work of this nature is a necessary condition for the victory of the workers. But in this context we must constantly remember that this is not the end of the task, and that even if it is done, the movement will still need insight at every moment, it will have to know how to orient itself quickly in newly created situations—in a word, it will still need a revolutionary class strategy on which the outcome will largely depend.

The anarchist ideal is large and rich in its diversity. Nevertheless, the role of anarchists in the social struggle of the masses is extremely modest. Their task is to help the masses take the right road in the struggle and in the construction of the new society. If the mass movement has not entered the stage of decisive collision, their duty is to help the masses clarify the significance, the tasks and the goals, of the struggle ahead; their duty is to help the masses make the necessary military preparations and organize their forces. If the movement has already entered the stage of decisive collision, anarchists should join the movement without losing an instant; they should help the masses free themselves from erroneous deviations, support their first creative efforts, assist them intellectually, always striving to help the movement remain on the path which leads toward the essential goals of

240

the workers. This is the basic and, in fact, the only task of anarchists in the first phase of the revolution. The working class, once it has mastered the struggle and begins its social construction, will no longer surrender to anyone the initiative in creative work. The working class will then direct itself by its own thought; it will create its society according to its own plans. Whether or not this will be an anarchist plan, the plan as well as the society based on it will emerge from the depths of emancipated labor, shaped and framed by its thought and its will.

When we examine the Makhnovshchina, we are immediately aware of two basic aspects of this movement: 1) its truly proletarian origins as a popular movement of the lowest strata of society: the movement sprang up from below, and from beginning to end it was the popular masses themselves who supported, developed, and directed it; 2) it deliberately leaned on certain incontestably anarchist principles from the very beginning: (a) the right of workers to full initiative, (b) the right of workers to economic and social self-management, (c) the principle of statelessness in social construction. During the course of its entire development the movement stubbornly and consistently maintained these principles. For their sake the movement lost from 200 to 300 thousand of the best sons of the people, turned down alliances with any and all statist powers, and for three years, in unimaginably difficult conditions and with a heroism rare in human history, it held high the black flag of oppressed humanity, the banner which proclaims the real freedom of the workers, true equality in the new society.

In the Makhnovshchina we have an anarchist movement of the working masses—not completely realized, not entirely crystallized, but striving toward the anarchist ideal and moving along the anarchist path.

But precisely because this movement grew out of the depths of the masses, it did not have the necessary theoretical forces, the powers of generalization indispensable to any widespread social movement. This shortcoming manifested itself in the fact that the movement, in the face of the general situation, did not succeed in developing its ideas and its slogans, or in elaborating its concrete and practical forms. This is why the movement developed slowly and painfully, especially in view of the numerous enemy forces which attacked it from all sides.

One would have thought that the anarchists—who had always talked so much about a revolutionary movement of the masses, who had waited for such a movement for many years the way some people wait for the arrival of the Messiah—would have hastened to join this movement, to merge with it, to give their whole being to it. But in practice this did not take place.

The majority of Russian anarchists who had passed through the theoretical school of anarchism remained in their isolated circles, which were of no use to anyone. They stood aside, asking what kind of a movement this was, why they should relate to it, and without moving they consoled themselves with the thought that the movement did not seem to be purely anarchist.

And yet, their contribution to the movement, especially in the period before Bolshevism blocked its normal development, would have been invaluable. The masses urgently needed militants who could have formulated and developed their ideas, helped them realize these ideas in the grand arena of life, and elaborated the forms and the direction of the movement. The anarchists did not want, or did not know how, to be such militants. As a result, they inflicted a great injury on the movement and on themselves. They injured the movement by failing to devote their organizational and cultural forces to it in time, forcing the movement to develop slowly and painfully with the meager theoretical forces which the poorest of peasants themselves possessed. They injured themselves by remaining outside of living history, thereby condemning themselves to inactivity and sterility.

We are obliged to state that Russian anarchists remained in their circles and *slept through* a mass movement of paramount importance, a movement which is unique in the present revolution for having undertaken to realize the historic tasks of oppressed humanity.

But at the same time, we discover that this deplorable situation is not accidental, but that it has very specific causes, which we will now consider.

The majority of our anarchist theorists have their

242

origins in the intelligentsia. This circumstance is very significant. While standing under the banner of anarchism, many of them are not able to break altogether with the psychological context from which they emerged. They concentrate on anarchist theory more than other comrades; and they gradually come to consider themselves leaders of the anarchist world; they come to believe that the anarchist movement begins with them, and that it depends on their direct participation. But the movement began far away from them, in a distant province and, furthermore, among the lowest sectors of contemporary society. Very few among the isolated anarchist theorists found in themselves the necessary sensitivity and courage to recognize that this movement was in fact the one which anarchism had been anticipating for many years, and they rushed to help it. It would be even more accurate to say that of all the intelligent and educated anarchist theorists, only Voline firmly joined the movement, putting at its service all his abilities, powers and knowledge. All the other anarchist theorists stayed away from the movement. This is not a reflection on the Makhnovshchina or on anarchism, but only on the anarchist individuals and organizations who were so narrow, passive and helpless during the historical social movement of workers and peasants, and who either did not dare or did not want to take part in their own project when it appeared in flesh and blood and called to its camp all those to whom the freedom of labor and the ideas of anarchism were dear.

An even more important aspect of the helplessness and inactivity of the anarchists is the confusion in anarchist theory and the organizational chaos in anarchist ranks.

Although the ideal of anarchism is powerful, positive and self-evident, it contains a number of gaps, obscurities, and digressions into fields that have no relation to the workers' social movement. This creates a foundation for all types of distorted interpretations of the goals of anarchism and its practical program.

Thus many anarchists devote their energies to the question of whether the problem of anarchism is the liberation of classes, of humanity, or of the personality. The question is empty, but it is based on some unclear anarchist positions and provides a broad field for abuses of anarchist thought and anarchist practice.

An even greater field for abuse is created by the unclear anarchist theory of individual freedom. Obviously active people with determined wills and well developed revolutionary instincts understand the anarchist idea of individual freedom as an idea of anarchist relations towards *all other individuals,* as an idea of the continual struggle for the anarchist freedom of the masses. But those who do not know the passion of the revolution, who are most concerned with the manifestations of their "I", understand this idea in their own fashion. Whenever the question of practical anarchist organization or the question of organization with a serious intent is posed, they hang on to the anarchist theory of individual liberty and, using this as a basis, oppose all organization and escape from all responsibility. Each one of them runs to his own garden, does his own thing and preaches his own anarchism. The ideas and actions of anarchists are thus pulverized to the point of derangement.

As a result of all this, we find a large number of practical systems advocated by Russian anarchists. From 1904 to 1907 we saw the practical programs of the *Beznachal'tsi (Without Authority)* and the *Chernoznamentsi (Black Flag),* which preached partial expropriation and un-motivated terror as methods of anarchist struggle. It is easy to see that these programs were nothing more than the arbitrary inclinations of people who were accidentally anarchists, and such programs could be suggested in the context of anarchism only because of an underdeveloped sense of responsibility toward the people and their revolution. Most recently we saw a large number of theories, some of which express sympathy for state authority or the wielding of power over the masses, while others reject all principles of organization and preach the absolute freedom of the per-sonality; yet others are exclusively concerned with the "universal" tasks of anarchism and in practice escape from the urgent needs of the moment.

For dozens of years the Russian anarchists have suffered from the disease of disorganization. This disease destroyed their ability to think concretely and condemned them to historical inactivity at the moment of the revolution. Disorganization is the twin sister of irresponsibility, and together they lead to impoverished ideas and futile practice.

244

Thus when the mass movement, in the form of the Makhnovshchina, rose from the depths of the people, the anarchists showed themselves completely unprepared, spineless and weak.

In our opinion this is temporary. It can be explained by the lack of crystallization and organization among Russian anarchists. They will have to organize themselves, to establish links among all those who strive for anarchism and are genuinely devoted to the working class. The disruptive and arbitrary elements in anarchism will then be eliminated.

Anarchism is not mysticism; it is not a discourse on beauty; it is not a cry of despair. Its greatness is due, above all, to its devotion to the cause of oppressed humanity. It carries within itself the truth, the heroism and the aspirations of the masses, and it is today the only social doctrine which the masses can count on in their struggle. But to justify this confidence, it is not enough for anarchism to be a great idea and for anarchists to be its Platonic spokesmen. Anarchists have to participate continually and directly in the revolutionary movement of the masses. Only then will the movement breathe the fullness of the anarchist ideal. But nothing will come out of nothing. Every achievement requires continual effort and sacrifice. Anarchism needs to find unity of will and unity of action to define its historic role accurately. Anarchism must go to the masses and merge with them.

Although the Makhnovshchina came into being and developed independently, without the influence of anarchist organizations, the fate of the Makhnovshchina and that of anarchism were intimately linked during the Russian revolution. The very essence of the Makhnovshchina glowed with the light of anarchism and unintentionally drew anarchism to itself. The mass of insurgents embraced only anarchism from among all social doctrines. A large number of insurgents called themselves anarchists and did not renounce this name even in the face of death. And at the same time, anarchism gave the Makhnovshchina several outstanding militants who passionately and devotedly gave all their forces and knowledge to this movement. However small the number of these militants, they succeeded in contributing a great deal to the movement, and they linked anarchism to the tragic fate of the Makhnovshchina.

before this in G-P

large-scale, not G-P⊗

This coupling of the destinies of anarchism and the Makhnovshchina began in the middle of 1919. It was consolidated in the Ukraine in the summer of 1920 by the Bolsheviks' simultaneous attack against the Makhnovists and the anarchists, and it was strikingly underlined in October, 1920, at the time of the military and political agreement between the Makhnovists and the Soviet authority, when the Makhnovists demanded, as a first condition of this agreement, that all the Makhnovists and anarchists be released from prison in the Ukraine and in Great Russia, and that they be given the right to freely profess and disseminate their ideas and theories.

We will describe the participation of anarchists in the Makhnovist movement in chronological order.

During the first days of the 1917 revolution, a group of anarchist-communists was organized in Gulyai-Polye; this group carried out significant revolutionary work in the region. Out of this group emerged several remarkable participants and guides of the Makhnovshchina: N. Makhno, S. Karetnik, Marchenko, Kalashnikov, Lyutyi, Grigory Makhno and others. This group retained close links with the Makhnovist movement from its very origin.

Toward the end of 1918 and the beginning of 1919, other anarchist groups were organized in the region of the Makhnovshchina, and tried to relate to it. However, some of these groups, for example in Berdyansk and some other places, did not live up to their name and offered nothing but obstacles to the movement. Fortunately the movement was healthy enough to do without them.

At the beginning of 1919 there were in Gulyai-Polye not only local peasant anarchists like Makhno, Karetnik, Marchenko, Vasilevsky and others, but also anarchists who came from organizations in other cities: Burbyga, Mikhalev-Pavlenko and others. They worked exclusively among the insurrectionary troops at the front or at the rear.

In the spring of 1919 some comrades arrived in Gulyai-Polye with the intention of organizing cultural and educational activity in the region: they created the newspaper *Put' k Svobode*—the principal organ of the Makhnovists—and organized the Gulyai-Polye Anarchist Federation, which worked with the army as well as among the peasants.

At that time, an anarchist group linked to the "Nabat" Confederation was organized in Gulyai-Polye. This group worked closely with the Makhnovists, especially in the field of culture, and published a local newspaper, *Nabat*. Soon this organization merged with the Gulyai-Polye Anarchist Federation.

In May, 36 anarchist workers came to Gulyai-Polye from Ivanovo-Voznesensk. Among them were the fairly well-known anarchists, Chernyakov and Makeev. Some of these people settled in a commune about four miles from Gulyai-Polye, some engaged in cultural work in the region, and the rest joined the army.

It was also in May, 1919, that the Confederation of Anarchist Organizations of the Ukraine, "Nabat," the most active and effective of all the anarchist organizations in Russia, began to see that the pulse of the revolutionary life of the masses was beating in the liberated insurrectionary region. "Nabat" decided to direct its forces toward this region. At the beginning of June, 1919, they sent to Gulyai-Polye several militants, including Voline, Mrachnyi and Iosif Emigrant. They were going to transfer the central organs of the Confederation to Gulyai-Polye immediately after the congress of workers and peasants called for June 15 by the Revolutionary Military Council. But the simultaneous attacks on the region by the Bolsheviks and the Denikinists kept this plan from being carried out. Mrachnyi was the only one who reached Gulyai-Polye, but in view of the general retreat he was obliged to return after one or two days. Voline and others were not able to leave Ekaterinoslav, and it was only in August, 1919, that they were able to join the retreating Makhnovist army near Odessa.

Thus the anarchists came to the movement very late, after its normal development had already been interrupted, after it had been thrown out of the context of social construction and forced by the pressure of circumstances into primarily military activity.

From the end of 1918 to June 1919 the conditions for positive work in the region had been extremely favorable: the front was about 200 miles away, near Taganrog, and the enormous population scattered throughout eight to ten districts was left to itself.

247

Later the anarchists could only work in conditions of military activity, under continual fire from all sides, and were obliged to move daily from place to place. The anarchists who joined the army did everything they could do in these conditions of constant warfare. Some of them, like Makeev and Kogan, took part in military activity; most of them did cultural work among the insurgents and in the villages which the Makhnovist army traversed. But this was not creative and constructive work among the masses in the fullest meaning of those words. Conditions of constant warfare limited this activity largely to superficial propaganda. It was impossible to dream of creative, positive work. Only in a few rare cases, for example after the occupation of Aleksandrovsk, Berdyansk, Melitopol' and other cities and districts, could the anarchists and Makhnovists lay the foundations for more extensive and profound activity. But another wave of war appeared from one side or the other, removing all traces of their work, and once again they were reduced to superficial agitation and propaganda among the insurgents and the peasants. The time was hostile to large-scale creative work among the masses.

On the basis of this period, some individuals who did not take part in the movement or who participated very briefly, drew the erroneous conclusion that the Makhnovshchina was excessively military, that it devoted too much attention to military aspects and not enough attention to positive work among the masses. But in actual fact, the military period in its history did not in any way grow out of the Makhnovshchina, but rather out of the conditions which surrounded it after the middle of 1919.

The Bolshevik statists were perfectly aware of the significance of the Makhnovist movement and of the position of anarchism in Russia. They knew perfectly well that, at present, anarchism in Russia, lacking any contact with a mass movement as important as the Makhnovshchina, did not have a base and could neither threaten nor endanger them. And conversely, by their calculations, anarchism was the only conception on which the Makhnovshchina could depend in its relentless struggle against Bolshevism. This is why they spared no effort to keep the two apart. And, in justice to them, it should be pointed out that they stubbornly carried this out: they declared the Makhnovshchina to be outside of all human law. And as prudent men of affairs, they acted, in Russia and especially abroad, as if the outlawing of the Makhnovshchina was self-explanatory to everyone, as if this could not possibly give rise to any doubts, and that only those who are blind or who are completely unfamiliar with Russia would fail to recognize their measures as just and reasonable.

The Bolsheviks did not officially outlaw the anarchist idea, but they gave the name "Makhnovist" to any revolutionary gesture, any sincere act in which anarchists engaged —and with perfect innocence, as if this was as clear as the light of day to everyone, they threw anarchists in jail, shot them, beheaded them. In the last analysis, the Makhnovshchina and anarchism, because they did not cringe before the Bolsheviks, were treated in the same way.

Conclusion

The history just narrated does not nearly give an exhaustive picture of the movement in its entirety. We have merely traced—very briefly—the story of a single, though central, current of this movement, the current that arose in the Gulyai-Polye region. This current was only a part of a much greater whole. As a social movement of Ukrainian workers, the Makhnovshchina was much more extensive than the picture we were able to draw of it. Its spirit and its slogans echoed throughout the Ukraine. There was social and psychological agitation among the peasants and the workers of almost every government of the Ukraine; everywhere the working masses made attempts to realize their independence in the sense which the Makhnovshchina gave to it; everywhere people heard calls to social revolution and attempted to engage in revolutionary struggle and massive revolutionary creative activity. And if we could have followed the movement in all its ramifications throughout the whole Ukraine, if we could have traced the history of each of the currents and then linked them together and illuminated them in the light of the whole, we could have obtained a great tableau of several million people in revolt, struggling under the flag of the Makhnovshchina for the fundamental ideas of the revolution—freedom and equality. But it is unfortunately impossible to carry out such a work in the conditions of contemporary Bolshevik life, even if one is willing to tolerate all sorts of hardships.

Even the present work, which deals with only one current of the movement, has been drastically condensed. Due to the absence of a large amount of documentary and factual material, this work is unintentionally abridged, both in form and in content.

We firmly hope that a more complete history of the Makhnovist movement will be written one day.

In addition to the flaws we have just mentioned, the

251

present work may also suffer from the fact that the negative aspects of the movement were not sufficiently examined.

No social movement of historical importance, no matter how lofty its aspirations, can avoid errors, serious shortcomings, negative aspects. These were obviously present in the Makhnovshchina. But we must always remember that the Makhnovshchina did not have the opportunity to carry out social experiments, and consequently could not err in this field. The Makhnovshchina is only a powerful *movement* of the masses, their selfless *effort* to overcome the reaction and save the cause of the revolution. Consequently, it is in this field that we must look for the shortcomings of the movement.

The basic shortcoming of the movement resides in the fact that during its last two years it concentrated mainly on military activities. This was not an organic flaw of the movement itself, but rather its misfortune—it was imposed on the movement by the situation in the Ukraine.

Three years of uninterrupted civil wars made the southern Ukraine a permanent battlefield. Numerous armies of various parties traversed it in every direction, wreaking material, social and moral destruction on the peasants. This exhausted the peasants. It destroyed their first experiments in the field of workers' self-management. Their spirit of social creativity was crushed. These conditions tore the Makhnovshchina away from its healthy foundation, away from socially creative work among the masses, and forced it to concentrate on war—revolutionary war, it is true, but war nevertheless.

Even today the enemies of freedom are devoting all their forces to the task of preventing the insurrection from leaving the arduous path of military operations. This is the great tragedy of the Makhnovshchina. It suffered from this for more than two years, and judging by the state of things in Russia, this tragedy will continue.

These facts themselves provide an answer to those anarchists who, on the basis of third- or fourth-hand accounts—distorted at that—reproach the Makhnovshchina for its martial character, and for this reason stand aloof from it. The military character was *imposed* on the movement. Furthermore, all the authorities who appeared in the

Ukraine, and mainly the Communists, made extraordinary efforts to drive the Makhnovshchina into a blind alley with only one outlet: banditism. The Soviet government's entire strategy in its struggle against the Makhnovshchina during the past three years was devised for this purpose. Can these Bolshevik machinations be considered flaws of the Makhnovshchina? Obviously not. When speaking about the military character of the movement, we should not begin with the fact that the Makhnovists devoted a great deal of time to artillery and cavalry combats; we should rather ask how the Makhnovists *began,* what *goals* they pursued, and what *means* they had to realize them.

We know that they began by chasing the Hetman's authorities out of the country, and by proclaiming that all the land and all industry belong to the working people. Their goal was the construction of a free life based on the complete social and economic independence of the working classes. Their means were social revolution and free workers' councils.

As *active* revolutionaries they obviously did not limit themselves to chasing out the Hetman and proclaiming their rights. To destroy the bourgeoisie thoroughly, to secure their rights and revolutionary gains, they organized armed self-defense, thus demonstrating their profound understanding of their role in the social revolution. *The positive program of the revolution can be successfully realized only on condition that the workers destroy the military power of the bourgeois state at the right time.*

Due to the fact that, as an active and offensive force, the movement was not general but was limited to a few governments, it was encircled by hostile forces: statist-Petliurists, statist Bolsheviks, and Denikin's enormous armed forces, all of which assaulted it from all sides with colossal military force. The movement obviously had to undergo great changes in its strategy, in its ways and means of action, and was forced to devote a large part of its forces to the military side of the struggle for freedom. But as we said, this was not its fault, but its misfortune.

The conditions of warfare which constantly surrounded the Makhnovists engendered among them many characteristics which were due to their exceptional situation:

strict discipline in the army and extreme severity toward their enemies. In spite of these characteristics, the Makhnovists remained first of all revolutionaries. When they occupied Ekaterinoslav in October, 1919, the Makhnovists did not in any way disturb the soldiers of Denikin's or of other armies who were being treated in the hospitals of the city, whether they were plain soldiers or officers. And these same Makhnovists shot their own commanders, Bogdanov and Lashkevich, for infractions of discipline and revolutionary honor.[1]

In Chapter 8 we mentioned certain errors and short-comings of the movement. Other faults and defects of the movement are so trivial and unimportant that there is no reason to dwell on them.[2]

[1] *Bogdanov* was chief of staff of the 2nd insurrectionary brigade. He was shot in October, 1919, in Aleksandrovsk, for having imposed an indemnity on the bourgeoisie of the region in the name of the army, but for his own interests.

Lashkevich was the well-known commander of the famous 13th regiment of the insurrectionary army. He was shot in the summer of 1920, after a decision made by a general assembly of insurgents, for having spent army funds for his own pleasure, and, in possession of these funds, having refused to help certain insurgent workers who were in a critical situation.

[2] We might note in passing that the faults and defects which the governmental press attributed to the movement: plundering, violence against the peaceful population, anti-Semitism, are all fantastic lies. To reduce all these lies to nothing, it is enough to point to the exceptionally joyful welcome given to the Makhnovists by all the villagers of the Ukraine and of Great Russia whenever the Makhnovist army passed through. An additional proof is provided by the Bolsheviks' own documents. In all their references to the struggle against the Makhnovshchina (in secret documents, not in those intended for publication), the agents of the Soviet power always emphasized that the struggle against the Makhnovshchina is particularly difficult because of the aid which the peasants everywhere give to the Makhnovist army, while these same peasants place numerous obstacles in the way of the Red Army.

254

* * *

The question is—what next?

During the past year and a half, the struggle of the Makhnovists against the Communist power had an exclusively military character. Neither organizational nor educational work among the peasants and workers was possible. There was no room for free socialist construction. What is the point of continuing such a struggle? What hopes could sustain it?

It is obvious that at the present moment, when a cult of militarism has been implanted throughout the Russian State, when the popular masses of the Ukraine and of Great Russia are completely subjugated, when the entire country is infected by an epidemic of denunciations and unjust trials, the situation of the Makhnovshchina is critical, and any further struggle seems hopeless. But this seems to be so only if the question is considered from a narrow, statist point of view.

We are living in a revolutionary epoch full of massive revolutionary movements of workers and peasants, movements which alternate with reactionary attempts of various authorities to become masters of the movements and to establish their dictatorship. The mass movement which took place in February-March, 1917, gave way to the government of the Duma. The agrarian-industrial mass movement of the summer of 1917 called to life, as a counterweight to itself, the bourgeois-socialist coalition government. And on the crest of the powerful October movement of workers and peasants surfaced the Communist government.

The fact that the Communist power has succeeded in maintaining itself for a long period in revolutionary Russia has made many people think that this system is the product of the Russian revolution and its natural form. But this is profoundly untrue. The Russian revolution and the Communist authority are two antipodes, two opposites. Throughout the Russian revolution, the Communist power has only been the shrewdest, the most flexible and at the same time the most tenacious form of reaction. It struggled against the Russian revolution from the day it began. In this struggle the working masses of Russia have already lost the main achieve-

255

ments of their revolution: freedom of organization, of speech, of the press, the inviolability of life, etc. This struggle spread throughout the expanse of Russia, affecting every village and every factory; its highest point was the revolutionary insurrection in the Ukraine; it re-appeared in several governments in Great Russia, and in February-March, 1921, it reverberated again in the uprising of Kronstadt.

Today Russia is undergoing a phase of acute reaction. It is impossible to predict if the revolutionary movement of workers and peasants will be victorious, or if the reaction will succeed in maintaining itself and consolidating its power. But one thing is clear: the revolutionary epoch which began in Russia is by no means over; enormous revolutionary energy is stored up in the workers and peasants; they still have gunpowder in their powder-flasks, and they may yet engage in massive revolutionary actions in the near future.

Three circumstances might give rise to the resumption of revolutionary activity. First of all, it could arise from the direct struggle of the masses against the Bolshevik reaction. Secondly, it could be caused by the attack of a foreign bourgeoisie against the Russian revolution. And thirdly, it could be stimulated if a power overturned during the course of the revolution attempted to change its course. At first sight it would seem that the latter two circumstances—counter-revolution from without and from within—would not add anything new to the existing Communist counter-revolution. But this is not the case. As new forces they could detonate the masses, who might then break through the reactionary Communist shell which envelops them, and continue the further development of the revolution.

The Makhnovshchina lives from these revolutionary forces of the masses temporarily suppressed by the counter-revolution. It is through them that the Makhnovshchina realized brilliant revolutionary achievements for which the Soviet authority falsely takes credit. It was the Makhnovshchina that buried the Hetman's government, that demolished Petliura's enterprise, that defended the revolution against Denikin, and that contributed significantly to the final defeat of Wrangel.

It might seem paradoxical, but it is nevertheless unquestionable, that the Communist authority implanted and consolidated its power in Russia because of the extraordinary struggle of the Makhnovists against the numerous counter-revolutions.

And in the future, whenever the revolutionary flame is kindled in the masses, the Makhnovshchina will be on the field of revolutionary struggle.

At the present moment it is forced to devote all its efforts to the task of surviving through this period of acute reaction. This is a revolutionary tactic, a strategic maneuver on its part, and it might have to be continued for several years. The next five or ten years will decide the fate of the Makhnovshchina and of the entire Russian revolution.

The Russian revolution can only be saved by its liberation from the chains of statism and by the creation of a social regime founded on the principles of social self-direction of the peasants and workers. And when a thrust in this direction appears among the working masses, the Makhnovshchina will be the center of their general revolutionary unification. It will be the standard and the rallying point for all who are brave, daring, and firmly devoted to the workers. It is then that the Makhnovshchina's devotion to the masses, its experience and its military genius, will serve to protect the truly proletarian social revolution. This is why it continues to carry on the seemingly hopeless struggle against the Communist dictatorship. This is why it continues to disturb the peace and quiet of the Communists.

* * *

Yet another question arises.

The Makhnovist movement is primarily a movement of the poorest sectors of the Ukrainian peasantry. The triumph of the Makhnovshchina will mean the triumph of these poor peasants. But will this mean the triumph of the *idea* of the Makhnovshchina, the triumph of the social revolution?

The day after the triumph of such a revolution the peasants will have to provide foodstuffs to support the urban workers. Assuming that industrial activity in the cities is disorganized and is hardly geared to the needs of the countryside, the workers will not be able to pay the peasants with the products of their own labor. Consequently, in the beginning the peasants will voluntarily and without remuneration have to undertake to support the urban proletariat. Will they be capable of such generosity, of such a revolutionary act? The Communists consistently depict the peasants as a reactionary force imbued with narrow proprietary instincts. Will they be dominated by this proprietary instinct, this spirit of avarice? Will they turn their backs on the cities and abandon them without providing the needed assistance?

We are convinced that this will not happen.

The Makhnovshchina understands the social revolution in its true sense. It understands that the victory and consolidation of the revolution, the development of the wellbeing which can flow from it, cannot be realized without a close alliance between the working classes of the cities and those of the countryside. The peasants understand that without urban workers and powerful industrial enterprises they will be deprived of most of the benefits which the social revolution makes possible. Furthermore, they consider the urban workers to be their brothers, members of the same family of workers.

There can be no doubt that, at the moment of the victory of the social revolution, the peasants will give their entire support to the workers. This will be voluntary and truly revolutionary support given directly to the urban proletariat. In the present-day situation, the bread taken by force from the peasants nourishes mainly the enormous governmental machine. The peasants see and understand perfectly that this expensive bureaucratic machine is not in any way needed by them or by the workers, and that in relation to the workers it plays the same role as that of a prison administration toward the inmates. This is why the peasants do not have the slightest desire to give their bread voluntarily to the State. This is why they are so hostile in their relations with the contemporary tax collectors—the commissars and the various supply organs of the State.

But the peasants always try to enter into *direct* relations with the urban workers. This question was raised more than once at peasant congresses, and the peasants always resolved it in a revolutionary and positive manner. At the time of the social revolution, when the masses of urban proletarians become truly independent and relate directly to the peasants through their own organizations, the peasants will furnish the indispensable foodstuffs and raw materials, knowing that in the near future the workers will place the entire gigantic power of industry at the service of the needs of the workers of the city and the countryside.

* * *

The Makhnovshchina sheds light on only one corner of contemporary Russia. There is no doubt that, with the passage of time, people will come who will expose this Russia from every corner, subjecting all its aspects to the light of truth. And then the role of Bolshevism in the Russian revolution will be clear to everyone.

Already today, in the domain which we examined, we can see its true face. The history of the Makhnovist movement, during which the popular masses tried for years to realize an independence which is better than any known to us, making enormous sacrifices for its sake, definitively unmasks Bolshevism and completely demolishes the legend about its pretended revolutionary and proletarian character.

Throughout the Russian revolution, whenever workers tried to act on their own, the Bolsheviks crushed them. Their reactionary spirit did not even hesitate when it became clear to all, including the Bolsheviks, that the Russian revolution was being killed by their murderous dictatorship. They did not for an instant abandon the insane and morbid desire to forcibly hold the entire revolution within the vise of their program.

It was still altogether possible to rescue the Russian revolution in 1919 and 1920. This is still possible today. What can save it is the revolutionary spirit of the masses, the self-activity of the workers' and peasants' organizations, their independence in thought and action. The revolution would recover its confidence and its will; it would again arouse the great enthusiasm of the masses, stimulating them to heroic struggles and great deeds, curing all the wounds of the social and economic organism.

Statists lie when they claim that the masses are capable only of destroying the old, that they are great and heroic only when they engage in destruction, and that in creative work they are inert and vulgar.

In the realm of creative activity, in the realm of daily work, the masses are capable of great deeds and of heroism. But they must feel a solid foundation under their feet; they must feel truly free; they must know that the work they do is their own; they must see in every social measure which is adopted the manifestation of their will, their hopes and their aspirations. In short, the masses must direct themselves in the largest meaning of those words.

But the Bolsheviks habitually seek only the support and obedience of the masses, and never their revolutionary spirit.

It is a historically established fact that, from 1918 on, Ukrainian peasants and workers were continually engaged in revolutionary uprisings, against Skoropadsky, the Austro-Germans, Petliura, Denikin, etc. These uprisings played an enormous role in the destiny of the entire Russian revolution: they created and sustained *a situation of permanent revolution in the country* which decisively turned the attention of the workers toward the solution of the essential problems of the revolution.

This situation of permament revolution in the country was not broken by the counter-revolution of the bourgeoisie or of the Tsarist generals, but by that of the Communist power. In the name of the dictatorship of their Party, the Communists militarily crushed all the attempts of workers to realize their own self-direction—the basic goal of the Russian revolution—and thus crushed the revolutionary ferment in the country.

Their morbid faith in their own dictatorship led the Bolsheviks to become so callous, so ossified and rigid, that the needs and the sufferings of the revolution became totally foreign to them; they preferred to see the revolution dead rather than make any concessions to it. Their role in the entire Russian revolution was fatal. They killed the revolutionary initiative and the self-activity of the masses and shattered the greatest revolutionary possibilities that the workers had ever had in all history. And for this the proletarians of the whole world will forever nail them to the pillory.

However, one should not make the mistake of thinking that only the Bolsheviks are responsible for the defeat of the Russian revolution. Bolshevism merely put into practice what had been elaborated by decades of socialist science. Its entire program of action is based on the theories of scientific socialism. We can see how hypocritically this same scientific socialism treats the workers in other European States, shackling them to the bourgeois dictatorship.

When the world's working class looks for those who are responsible for the shameful and extraordinarily difficult situation of Russian peasants and workers under the socialist dictatorship, it will have to blame *socialism in its entirety,* and condemn it.

The bloody tragedy of the Russian peasants and workers cannot pass without leaving traces. The practice of socialism in Russia has demonstrated better than anything else that the working classes have no friends, but only enemies who seek to take away the fruits of their labor. Socialism has amply demonstrated that it belongs among these enemies. From year to year, this idea is being implanted more firmly in the consciousness of the masses of the people.

Proletarians of the world, look into the depths of your own beings, seek out the truth and realize it yourselves: you will find it nowhere else.

Such is the watchword of the Russian revolution.

* * *

At the time of their third assault on the insurrectionary region, the Soviet power did everything possible to deal the death blow to the Makhnovshchina. Due to their numerous troops freed from military operations in the Crimea and to their superiority in armaments, they succeeded in defeating the insurrectionary army in the summer of 1921, and in forcing the central core of this army, headed by

Nestor Makhno, to retreat to Roumanian territory. After this the Red Army occupied the entire insurrectionary region, and the revolutionary masses were violently subjected to the dictatorship of Bolshevism.

* * *

The Makhnovshchina is now in a new situation, and it faces a new stage in the struggle for the social revolution.

What sort of struggle will this be?

Life itself will determine its character and its forms. But one thing is certain: until the last day the movement will remain true to oppressed humanity; until the last day it will struggle and be prepared to die for the great ideals of labor—freedom and equality.

The Makhnovshchina is steadfast and immortal.

Wherever the working masses do not let themselves be subjugated, wherever they cultivate the love of independence, wherever they concentrate their class will, they will always create *their own* historical social movement, they will act *on their own*. This is the essence of the Makhnovshchina.

January-June, 1921.
Russia.

End.

APPENDIX

Appendix

Some Makhnovist Proclamations.

The following proclamations of the Makhnovist movement, from the archive of the Italian anarchist Ugo Fedeli, are in the custody of the Internationaal Instituut voor Sociale Geschiedenis (in Amsterdam). It is not known how the proclamations came into Fedeli's possession. They were all written in Russian. Paper out of an account book was used for one, wrapping paper from a candy factory for another, indicating that they were printed in difficult circumstances. [The translation is by Ann Allen.]

* * *

DECLARATION OF THE
REVOLUTIONARY INSURGENT ARMY
OF THE UKRAINE (MAKHNOVIST)

To all the peasants and workers of the Ukraine.
To be sent by telegraph, telephone or post to all villages, rural districts, and governments of the Ukraine. To be read at peasant gatherings, in factories and in workshops.

Fellow workers! The Revolutionary Insurgent Army of the Ukraine (Makhnovist) was called into existence as a protest against the oppression of the workers and peasants by the bourgeois-landlord authority on the one hand and the Bolshevik-Communist dictatorship on the other.

Setting for itself one goal—the battle for total liberation of the working people of the Ukraine from the oppression of various authorities and the creation of a TRUE SOVIET SOCIALIST ORDER, the insurgent Makhnovist army fought stubbornly on several fronts for the achievement of these goals and at the present time is bringing to a victorious conclusion the struggle against the Denikinist army, liberating region after region, in which every coercive power and every coercive organization is in the process of being removed.

265

Many peasants and workers are asking: What will happen now? What is to be done? How shall we treat the decrees of the exiled authorities, etc.

All of these questions will be answered finally and in detail at the All-Ukrainian worker-peasant Congress, which must convene immediately, as soon as there is an opportunity for the workers and peasants to come together. This congress will map out and decide all the urgent questions of peasant-worker life.

In view of the fact that the congress will be convened at an indefinite time, the insurgent Makhnovist army finds it necessary to put up the following announcement concerning worker-peasant life:

1. All decrees of the Denikin (volunteer) authority are abolished. Those decrees of the Communist authority which conflict with the interests of the peasants and workers are also repealed.

Note: Which decrees of the Communist authority are harmful to the working people must be decided by the working people themselves—the peasants in assemblies, the workers in their factories and workshops.

2. The lands of the service gentry, of the monasteries, of the princes and other enemies of the toiling masses, with all their live stock and goods, are passed on to the use of those peasants who support themselves solely through their own labor. This transfer will be carried out in an orderly fashion determined in common at peasant assemblies, which must remember in this matter not only each of their own personal interests, but also bear in mind the common interest of all the oppressed, working peasantry.

3. Factories, workshops, mines and other tools and means of production become the property of the working class as a whole, which will run all enterprises themselves, through their trade unions, getting production under way and striving to tie together all industry in the country in a single, unitary organization.

4. It is being proposed that all peasant and worker organizations start the construction of free worker-peasant soviets. Only laborers who are contributing work necessary to the social economy should participate in the soviets. Representatives of political organizations have no place in worker-peasant soviets, since their participation in a workers' soviet will transform the latter into deputies of the party and can lead to the downfall of the soviet system.

5. The existence of the *Cheka,* of party committees and similar compulsory authoritative and disciplinary institutions is intolerable in the midst of free peasants and workers.

6. Freedom of speech, press, assembly, unions and the like are inalienable rights of every worker and any restriction on them is a counter-revolutionary act.

7. State militia, policemen and armies are abolished. Instead of them the people will organize their own self-defense. Self-defense can be organized only by workers and peasants.

8. The worker-peasant soviets, the self-defense groups of workers and peasants and also every peasant and worker must not permit any counter-revolutionary manifestation whatsoever by the bourgeoisie and officers. Nor should they tolerate the appearance of banditry. Everyone convicted of counter-revolution or banditry will be shot on the spot.

9. Soviet and Ukrainian money must be accepted equally with other monies. Those guilty of violation of this are subject to revolutionary punishment.

10. The exchange of work products and goods will remain free; for the time being this activity will not be taken over by the worker-peasant organizations. But at the same time, it is proposed that the exchange of work products take place chiefly BETWEEN WORKING PEOPLE.

11. All individuals deliberately obstructing the distribution of this declaration will be considered counter-revolutionary.

Revolutionary Military Soviet and Command Staff of the Revolutionary Insurgent Army of the Ukraine (Makhnovist)

January 7, 1920.

* * *

COMRADE PEASANTS!

For many years the working peasantry of the Ukraine has been struggling with its ancient enemies and oppressors. Thousands of the best Sons of the Revolution have fallen in the battle for the complete liberation of the Working People from every oppression. Through the heroic efforts of the peasant Insurgent Army of the Ukraine, the hangman Denikin was dealt a fatal blow. The insurgent Peasants, with their leader—Batko Makhno—at their head, remaining for long months in the home front of the white guard, surrounded ten times by a strong enemy, exhausted by the worst disease—typhus, which took from action a hundred of our best fighters daily, frequently lacking amunition, together attacked the enemy with bare hands and under their powerful blow the best Denikinist forces—the detachments of generals Shkuro and Mamontov—fled. Through incredible efforts and the blood of the best fighters the insurgent peasants smashed the Denikinist front and opened the gates for their nothern brothers—for Peasants and Workers; comrades of the red army came to take the place of the Denikinist hordes in the Ukraine—workers and peasants of the North. Before the Working Peasantry of the Ukraine a question now arose, apart from the common Task—struggle with the white guard—the Building of a Truly Soviet System, under which the Soviets, elected by the Working People, would be servants of the People, implementors of those laws, of those orders, which the Working People themselves will write at the All-Ukrainian Working Congress. But the leadership of the Communist Party, which has made out of the Red Army a blind, obedient tool for the defense of the commissarocracy, smearing with filth and vile slanders the best of the insurgent leaders, decided "to root out the splinter"—to do away with the Revolutionary insurgency, which is preventing the Lord Commissars from wielding power over the Working People of the Ukraine. The Commissarocrats wish to see in the Working People only "human materiel" as Trotsky called them at the congress, only cannon fodder to be hurled against anyone, but to whom it is on no account possible to give any rights whatsoever. Working activity and order will be established without the help of the Communists.

Comrade Peasants! The Insurgent Army of the Ukraine (Makhnovist) came from your midst. Your sons, brothers, and fathers filled up our ranks. The Insurgent Army is Your army, Your blood, Your flesh. Making tens of thousands of sacrifices the Insurgent Army fought for the right of the working people themselves to build their own order, to dispose of their own wealth themselves, and not for the transfer of everything to the hands of the Commissars. The Insurgent Army fought and is fighting for the true soviets, and not for the *Cheka* and the Commissarocracy. In the time of the hangman Hetman, the Germans and the Denikinists, the insurrection stood up staunchly against the oppressors in defense of the Working People. And now the Insurgent Army considers its sacred task to be the defense of the interests of the Working Peasantry against the attempts of the Lord Commissars to harness to their collar the working peasantry of the Ukraine. The Insurgent Army well knows and remembers the last commissar—"liberator". The Autocrat Trotsky ordered the Insurgent Army of the Ukraine, which was created by the peasants themselves, to disarm, for he well knows that while the peasants have their own army, defending their interests, he will never succeed in forcing the Ukrainian working people to dance to his tune. The Insurgent Army, not wishing to spill fraternal blood, avoiding clashes with Red Army people, but subject only to the will of the Working People, will stand guard over the interests of the working people and lay down arms only by command of the free working All-Ukrainian Congress, in which the working people themselves will express their will. The Insurgent Army, the sword in the hands of the working people, calls You, comrade peasants, to convene quickly your working-men's congress and to take into your own hands both the long-range building of your own fortune and your own working peoples' wealth; true, the power-loving commissars will without a doubt take every measure to ban the free working congress; therefore, it is in the interests of the working people themselves not to allow the commissars to suppress their working congress; that is why the congress must be secret and in a secret place.

Comrade Peasants, Prepare for your Congress!
Hasten to Work for Your Cause!
The Enemy Does Not Sleep
And You Must Not Sleep,
In This is the Guarantee of Victory!

Long live the Regional Free Working Congress! Down With the Commissarocracy! Long Live the Peasant Insurgent Army!

*Staff of the Insurgent Army
of the Ukraine (Makhnovist)*

February 8, 1920.

***

A WORD
TO THE PEASANTS AND WORKERS
OF THE UKRAINE

Brother peasants and workers! For more than three years you have been engaged in a struggle with capitalism and thanks to Your efforts, Your steadfastness and energy, You have brought this struggle nearly to a close. The enemies of the revolution have been exhausted by Your blows and You, anticipating victory, got ready to celebrate. You believed that Your unceasing, often unequal, struggle with the enemies of the revolution, would give You a chance to put into practice the free soviet system for which we all were striving. But, brothers, You see who celebrates in Your place. The un-invited rulers are celebrating, the Communist hangmen, who came here in readiness and along open roads which had been cleared with Your blood, the blood of your sons and brothers who make up the revolutionary insurrection. They seized the wealth of the country. Not You, but they, are in charge. You, the peasants and workers, are a support for them in name only; without You they could not call themselves a worker-peasant government, could not be national murderers and hangmen, could not arbitrarily, in the name of party supremacy, tyrannize the people. The name of the people gives them this right in everything. And it is only for this that they need You, peasants and workers.

In every other instance You are nothing to them and they certainly do not take Your opinion into consideration. They enslave, draft, command and rule You. They are de-stroying You. And You, oppressed, patiently bear all the horrors of execution, violence and tyranny committed by the Communist hangmen and which can be eliminated only by Your revolutionary justice, only by Your joint protest—a revolutionary uprising. To this You are called by Your brothers, peasants and workers who, like You, are dying from the bullets of the Red murderers who confiscate cattle, grain and other products by force and send [them] to Russia. They—Your close brothers—, bidding farewell to their own lives, to the whole bright future for which we all strive, urge You to save the revolution, freedom and independence.

Remember, brother peasants and workers, that if you do not personally experience total freedom and independence now, You will henceforth be incapable of settling your own fate, you will not forge your own happiness, You will not be masters of the wealth of Your country or the fruits of Your labor.

All this the uninvited rulers—the Communist-Bolshevik newcomers—will do for You. In order to deliver themselves from these uninvited masters and rulers, all the peasantry and all their finest energies must be devoted to the work of convening secret, rural and regional peasant congresses, at which must be arranged and settled the burning questions of the moment, which are raised by the irresponsibility and dictatorship of these bandits. In the interests of the country, in the interests of the working people of the Ukraine, let us not permit the country to be totally devastated by these uninvited masters and rulers. There must be no place in the Ukraine for them or their hireling-Red murderers, tyrannizers of the people. All the peasants, losing not one day, must organize themselves through their regional congresses. Let us organize in each village and hamlet regional fighting units; let us create a leading battle organ.

Once and for all refuse any help to the Communist hangmen and their base hirelings, refuse both fodder and grain and bread. Workers in their turn, both in the cities and in villages, must refrain from joining the Communist Party, the *Chekas,* or the food requisitioning detachments; must renounce all participation in Communist institutions. The people of the Ukraine must tell the whole world by word and deed: away with murderers and hangmen both white and red! We are moving towards universal good, light and truth, and your violence will not be tolerated.

Long live the international Worker-Peasant Social Revolution!

Death to all white guards and commissars. Death to all hangmen!

Long live the free soviet system!

Staff of the Revolutionary Insurgent Army
of the Ukraine (Makhnovist)

[March-April, 1920]

* * *

271

* * *

WHO ARE THE MAKHNOVISTS
AND WHAT ARE THEY FIGHTING FOR?

1.   The Makhnovists are peasants and workers who rose as early as 1918 against the coercion of the German-Magyar, Austrian and Hetman bourgeois authority in the Ukraine. The Makhnovists are those working people who raised the battle standard against the Denikinists and any kind of oppression, violence and lies, wherever they originated. The Makhnovists are the very workers by whose labor the bourgeoisie in general and now the Soviet bourgeoisie in particular rules and grows rich and fat.

2. WHY DO WE CALL OURSELVES MAKHNOVISTS?

Because, first, in the terrible days of reaction in the Ukraine, we saw in our ranks an unfailing friend and leader, MAKHNO, whose voice of protest against any kind of coercion of the working people rang out in all the Ukraine, calling for a battle against all oppressors, pillagers and political charlatans who betray us; and who [Makhno] is now marching together with us in our common ranks unwaveringly toward the final goal: liberation of the working people from any kind of oppression.

3. WHAT DO WE SEE AS THE BASIS OF LIBERATION?

The overthrow of the monarchist, coalition, republican and social-democratic Communist-Bolshevik Party governments. In their place must be substituted the free and completely independent soviet system of working people without authorities and their arbitrary laws. The soviet system is not the power of the social-democratic Communist-Bolsheviks who now call themselves a soviet power; rather it is the supreme form of non-authoritarian, anti-state socialism, which expresses itself in the organization of a free, happy and independent system of social life for the working people; in which each worker taken separately, and society as a whole, will be able to build without assistance his own happiness and well-being according to the principles of solidarity, friendship and equality.

4. HOW DO THE MAKHNOVISTS UNDERSTAND THE SOVIET SYSTEM?

The working people themselves must freely choose their own soviets, which will carry out the will and desires of the working people themselves, that is to say, ADMINISTRATIVE, not ruling, soviets.

The land, the factories, the workshops, the mines, the railroads and the other wealth of the people must belong to the working people themselves, to those who work in them, that is to say, they must be socialized.

5. WHAT ROAD LEADS TO THE ACHIEVEMENT OF THE MAKHNOVIST GOALS?

An implacable revolution and consistent struggle against all lies, arbitrariness and coercion, wherever they come from, a struggle to the death, a struggle for free speech, for the righteous cause, a struggle with weapons in hand. Only through the abolition of all rulers, through the destruction of the whole foundation of their lies, in state affairs as well as in political and economic affairs. And only through the destruction of the state by means of a social revolution can the genuine Worker-Peasant soviet system be realized and can we arrive at SOCIALISM.

Cultural-Educational Section
of the Insurgent Army (Makhnovist).

April 27, 1920.

* * *

COMRADES IN THE RED ARMY
ON THE FRONT LINE
AND IN THE HOME GUARD!

The people of the Ukraine, oppressed by Your commanders and commissars, and sometimes even directly by You under the leadership of these Commanders and Commissars, protest against such coercion: they waited for You as the liberators of the working masses from the yoke of the Denikinist gang of hangmen; but after Your arrival in the

Ukraine the groans, weeping and wails of the suffering people grew still louder. Executions everywhere, the burning of peasants' huts and even villages, everywhere pillage and violence.

The people have been exhausted and have no more strength to endure such arbitrariness; giving advance notice, they are asking You: will you stop in the face of these nightmares and realize whom, *under the leadership of Your commanders and commissars,* You are shooting? Who are you packing into the prisons and cellars? Is it not Your brothers, fathers and children? Of course it is. You do this oblivious to how the officers and generals of the old regime, profiting by their freedom and Your blindness, recline in soft easy chairs and order You to mock the poor people. And You, comrades, without a moment's hesitation, blindly carry out these orders. Is it possible you do not notice that they are setting you on the poor people, calling them counter-revolutionary because they protest the dictatorship of Trotsky's masters and his gang of communist accomplices who are smothering the revolution in the name of party power? Is it possible you do not see that the Ukrainian peasant cannot tolerate his yoke and, in spite of executions, is standing up for himself, destroying every obstacle and hurrying to lead the project of liberation to a conclusion? And he believes that among You, who are in the Red Army, the majority are his brothers, peasants the same as he, who are oppressed the same as he, and who, in the final reckoning, will take up his protest and join with him against the common enemy: the Denikinist gangs of the right as well as the commissarocracy of the left which clothes itself in the name of the people.

Comrades, see for yourselves, they are creating *Chekas* and punitive detachments in Belorussia and particularly in the Ukraine. And who is helping them? You, Red Army men, and only You. Is it possible that your hearts do not bleed upon hearing the groans and cries of Your brothers, fathers, mothers and children? Is it possible that those illusory political freedoms have deceived you to such an extent that you are too weak to overcome the authority of the commissars and join with the peasants and workers in freeing themselves and all the people from oppression and violence? Is it possible You do not notice in Your ranks those who, owing to Your blood and lives, have risen over You, have taken power for themselves and thus really disgracefully tyrannize the people? Is it possible your hearts are not wrung when, under the command of these tyrants, You go to the villages and hamlets to punish the working people who are protesting the domination of your leaders? We believe that You will come to your senses and catch up, that Your shame is in silence. You will raise a protest against the violence and oppression of the poor people. You will not permit Your commissars and commanders to burn the villages and hamlets and to shoot the peasants who rose for their rights. Let the peasants arrange their lives themselves, as they wish, and You continue to crush the Denikinist gangs, and along with them the commissar-rulers. Do not leave the front; continue the battle against those who wear the gold shoulder straps; do away with your commissars on the spot.

The revolutionary peasants and workers are wiping out the loafers in their ranks in the rear, those who are burdening and enslaving them. The revolutionary peasants and workers will not forget You and the day will come when they will all, as one, close ranks with You, and woe to all parasites and their helpers, all those who weigh upon them from without as well as those who arbitrarily rule over them in the rear.

Remember comrades, the people have recognized the deceit of the government being maintained by You. The people will rise against it and no army will withstand the masses who have consciously risen, who are fighting for total liberation. Join with them; they invite you as their own brothers. Remember that among those who have risen are Your brother-peasants and workers and upon meeting them do not perpetrate a slaughter. Let the commissars and commanders face the rebels themselves.

Let them stain themselves with the blood of the peasants and workers; all the guilt is on them and they will pay dearly for it.

Down with the gold-shoulder-strap gang! Down with their godfathers the commissarocrats! Down with man-made laws and the power of man over man!

Long live the unification of all the working people of the Red Army and the rebellious peasants and workers! Death to all who wear the gold shoulder straps! Death to all commissars and hangmen!

Long live the Social Revolution!

Long live the genuine, free soviet system!

Staff of the Insurgent Army
of the Ukraine (Makhnovist).

May 9, 1920.

* * *

DOWN WITH FRATRICIDE!

Brothers in the Red Army! The stooges of Nicholas kept you in the dark and ordered you to fratricidal war with the Japanese and then with the Germans and with many other peoples for the sake of increasing their own wealth; to your lot fell death at the front and complete ruin at home.

But the storm cloud and the fog, through which You could see nothing, lifted; the sun began to shine; You understood and were finished with fratricidal war. But it was the calm before a new storm. Now once again you are being sent to fight, against us, "insurgent Makhnovists," in the name, supposedly, of a "worker-peasant" authority, which is once again dispensing chains and slavery to You and riches and joys to this horde of a million bureaucratic parasites, created with Your blood. Is it possible that in the course of three years of fratricidal war you have still to this day failed to understand this? Is it possible that even now You will shed your blood for the newly made bourgeoisie and for all the half-baked commissars who send You to war like cattle?

Is it possible that you still, to this day, have failed to understand that we, the "insurgent Makhnovists," are fighting for TOTAL ECONOMIC AND POLITICAL EMANCIPATION OF THE WORKING PEOPLE, for a free life without any of these authoritarian commissars, *chekists,* etc.?

Let day break in Your camp and show You the path which leads to the abolition of fratricidal wars between working peoples. By this path you will reach us and in our ranks you will continue to fight for a better future, for a free life. Before each encounter with us, in order to avoid shedding brotherly blood, send us a delegate for negotiations; but if this does not work and the commissars force You to fight after all, throw down the rifles and come to our brotherly embrace!

Down with fratricidal war among the working people!

Long live peace and the brotherly union of the working peoples of all countries and nationalities!

Insurgent Makhnovists

[May, 1920]

276

* * *

TO ALL WORKERS
OF THE PLOUGH AND THE HAMMER!

Brothers! A new and mortal danger is approaching all working people. All the dark forces that served the bloody Nicholas have united with the help of the Polish landlords, the French instructors and the traitors of the Petliurist movement in the Ukraine in order to establish an autocracy over us, to burden us with landlords, capitalists, *Zemstvo* leaders, policemen and other hangmen of the peasants and workers.

Comrades! The commissars and bosses of the Communist-Bolsheviks are good fighters only against the poor and oppressed. Their punitive detachments and *Chekas* can splendidly shoot peasants and workers and burn down villages and hamlets. But against the true enemies of the revolution, before the Denikinists and other gangs, they flee shamefully, like miserable cowards.

You, comrades, have not yet forgotten how last year the gold shoulder straps came close to entering Moscow and if it were not for the insurgents, the three-colored flag of the autocracy would long since have waved over Revolutionary Russia.

So also now, comrades! The Red Army, which is being sold out every step of the way by its own generals and cowardly commissars, is fleeing the front in panic and surrendering region after region to the Polish landlords. Zhitomir, Kiev and Zhmerinka have long been occupied by the Poles; the white guard front is approaching Poltava and Kherson. And, in the Crimea, the Denikinists have been waiting for the last three months for an opportune moment to once again occupy our own territory.

Brothers! Is it possible you will quietly await the approach of the whites and, crossing your arms, hand over yourselves, your wives and children, to be torn apart by the generals and landlords?

No, this must not happen.

All, as one, in arms and in the ranks of the insurgents.

Together with us, the Insurgent Makhnovists, rise against all tyrants. In every hamlet set up detachments and join with us. Together we are driving out the commissars and the *Chekas* and together with the comrade Red Army men we will build an iron battle front against Denikin, Petliura and the Polish landlords.

Comrades! Time does not wait; put your detachments together immediately.

For the cause!

Death and destruction to all tyrants and landlords!

Let us begin the last and final battle for a genuine, free soviet system where there will be neither landlords nor masters!

To arms, Brothers!

Cultural-Educational Section
of the Revolutionary Insurgents
of the Ukraine (Makhnovist)

May, 1920.

* * *

TO THE YOUNG PEOPLE

Why, comrades, are you sitting at home? Why are you not in our ranks?

Or are you waiting for the arrival of the commissars with punitive detachments to draft you by force? Don't fool yourselves that they won't find you, that you will hide, escape. The Bolshevik authority has already shown that it will stop at nothing: they will arrest your family and relatives, they will take hostages, if necessary, they will fire upon the entire village with artillery—and in some way or another, you and your comrades, who are presently still at liberty, will sooner or later be drafted by the government.

And then they will send you, with weapons in hand, to kill your brother peasants and workers—the revolutionary insurgent Makhnovists.

We, Makhnovist insurgents, are not sitting at home, although each one of us also has a family and relatives and loved ones from whom we do not wish to be separated. But we are revolutionaries. It is not possible for us to look on indifferently as the working people are once again thrown

278

into slavery, as new despots lord it over us, unchecked, under the mask of the socialist-communists, under the banner of worker-peasant authority. Three years of revolution have clearly shown that every authority is counter-revolutionary, without exception, whether it be the authority of Bloody Nicholas or of the Bolshevik-Communists. We Makhnovists raise the banner of revolt for a total socialist revolution, against every authority, against every oppressor; we are fighting for the free soviets of the working people.

Follow us, comrades! Let the faint-hearted self-seeker and coward remain at home near someone's skirts—we do not need sissies. But you, honest peasants and workers, your place is with us, among the revolutionary insurgent Makhnovists. We will take no one by force. But remember: the Bolshevik government, through its own brutal violence to the Makhnovists, compels us also to merciless battle.

And so, decide, comrades! Drafted by the commissars, you will be sent against us, and we will be compelled to treat you as hostile and an enemy of the revolution. With us or against us—choose!

Insurgent Makhnovists
June, 1920.

* * *

A WORD FROM THE MAKHNOVISTS
TO THE LABORING COSSACKS
OF THE DON AND THE KUBAN

Comrade laboring Cossacks! For two years you languished under the oppression of the Tsarist general Denikin. For two years your deadly enemies, the *pomeshchiks* and barons, forced you to defend the interests of the rich, the oppressors of the working people. For two successive years you were forced to knuckle under, and by your own sweat and blood the rich made themselves richer, feasted and led depraved lives. For two years in the region of the Don and the Kuban the tears and blood of the workers of the plow and hammer flowed. For two successive years, laboring cossacks, the revolution was stifled in your land.

But through your efforts, comrades, the yoke of Denikin and his commanders was thrown off and in the Don and the Kuban the revolution triumphed once again.

However, comrades, before you had time to recover from the nightmarish experience of Denikin, a new oppressor appeared in your land. The Communist-Bolshevik Party, seizing power, sent their own commissars and *chekas* to your villages; they ridicule you, laboring cossacks, as much as the Tsarist thugs did.

As in the time of Denikin, punitive detachments of the Bolshevik authority take away your bread and cattle and pick up your sons; and if you try to protest the violence perpetrated upon you, they flog you, imprison you, and even shoot you.

Is this the reason, comrade laboring cossacks, that you rose against Denikin, to take on a new yoke now in the form of the Communist-Bolsheviks? Is this what you shed your blood for, to permit the commissars and lovers of power to rule over you now, to suppress and coerce you?

Listen well, brothers, to what we, the revolutionary peasant-Makhnovists, tell you. We were also oppressed after the revolution by a whole series of authorities and parties. First the Austrian and German authority, along with the Hetman, tried to rule over us, then the adventurist Petliura, then the Communist-Bolsheviks, and also General Denikin. But we very quickly discouraged them in order to continue our own project and, as you probably heard, as early as the summer of 1918, under the leadership of the Gulyai-Polye peasants and other working people, and of the anarchist revolutionary Nestor Makhno, whom the Tsarist authority imprisoned for over ten years for his love of the working people, we rose and drove off the Austro-German bands, and after that, for the last two years we have continued to fight against all oppressors of the working people. We are now engaged in a merciless battle against the agents and commissars of the Bolshevik authority, killing them and driving these tyrants from our regions.

The ranks of our revolutionary insurgent detachments are growing daily. All the oppressed and aggrieved are joining our ranks and the time is near when all the working people in our region will rise and expel the authority of the Bolshevik political charlatans, just as they expelled Denikin.

However, once the Bolshevik tyrants are expelled, we have no intention of giving anyone whatsoever authority over us because we Makhnovists realize that the working people are no longer a flock of sheep to be ordered about by anyone. We consider the working people capable of building, on their own and without parties, commissars or generals, their own FREE SOVIET SYSTEM, in which those who are elected to the Soviet will not, as now, command and order us, but on the contrary, will be only the executors of the decisions made in our workers' gatherings and conferences. We will strive for this, so that all the wealth of the country, that is, the land, the mines, the factories, the workshops, the railroads, and so on, will belong neither to individuals nor to the government, but solely to those who work with them. We will not lay down our arms until we have wiped out once and for all every political and economic oppression and until genuine equality and brotherhood is established in the land.

This, comrades, is what we are fighting for and what we are asking you, the laboring cossacks of the Don and Kuban, to fight for.

In our insurgent army there were quite a few cossacks of the Don and Kuban; they formed two cavalry regiments which bravely and selflessly fought together with us against the Denikinists. Now we are calling you, the laboring cossacks, to our insurgent ranks for the joint struggle against the tyrants and Red hangmen, Trotsky and Lenin. The slaves have obeyed and suffered long enough the yoke of those who call themselves the worker-peasant authority. To arms and into the ranks of the revolutionary insurgents and then we will quickly put an end to the plans of those who wanted to oppress and burden us.

Comrades, do not believe the rumor that says we are bandits and a small group. It is a lie spread by the commissars solely to confuse the worker-peasant folk; the working people know that the Makhnovists are honest laborers who, not wanting to carry a burden, rose in order to liberate themselves once and for all from every oppression. Do not believe the Bolshevik papers, which write nearly every day that Batko Makhno is dead and we Makhnovists smashed. It is not true. Batko Makhno lives and together with us daily defeats regiments and punitive detachments of the commissar authority and causes a mortal panic in the Red oppressors.

Rise, laboring cossacks, against the oppression and coercion of the commissars. Do not tolerate them in your villages. Do not pay taxes to them. Do not give them bread. Do not give your sons to be soldiers. Organize your own insurgent detachments. Kill the oppressors. Unite with us. We will give you every possible assistance.

The slaves have endured enough! It is enough that we have been mocked in every possible manner!

Long live the rising for a genuine worker-peasant soviet system!

Long live the free Don and Kuban!

Long live the brotherly union of the working people of all countries and nationalities!

Long live the socialist revolution!

Council of the
Revolutionary Insurgents
of the Ukraine (Makhnovist)

June, 1920.

* * *

COMRADES IN THE RED ARMY!

Your commanders and commissars are frightening and convincing you that we Makhnovists are murdering captured Red Army men.

Comrades! This infamous lie has been concocted by your leaders only so that you, like slaves, would defend the interests of the commissars, so that you would not let yourselves be taken prisoner by us Makhnovists and so you would not learn the truth about our worker-peasant Makhnovist movement.

We, comrades, have risen against the oppression of all tyrants. For three years our blood has been flowing on all fronts. We drove out the Austro-German tyrants, smashed the Denikinist hangmen, fought against Petliura; now we are fighting the domination of the commissar authority, the dictatorship of the Bolshevik-Communist Party: it has laid its iron hand on the entire life of the working people; the peasants and workers of the Ukraine are groaning under its yoke. We will also mercilessly exterminate the Polish landlords who come to stifle our revolution and to deprive us of its achievements.

We are fighting against all authority and oppression, no matter what its origin. Our deadly, implacable enemies are the landlords and capitalists of all nationalities, the Denikin-ist generals and officers, the Polish landlords and Bolshevik commissars. We are punishing and killing them all mercilessly as enemies of the revolution of the working people.

But we consider you, comrades in the Red Army, our blood brothers, together with whom we would like to carry on the struggle for genuine liberation, for the true soviet system without the pressure of parties or authorities.

Captured Red Army men are immediately set free wherever they choose, or we invite them into our ranks if they consent to this.

We have already freed thousands of Red Army men captured in numerous battles and many of the prisoners are now selflessly fighting in our ranks.

So do not believe, comrade Red Army men, your commanders' cock and bull stories that the Makhnovists are murdering Red Army men. It's an infamous lie.

When they send you to fight against the Makhnovists, do not steep your hands, comrades of the Red Army, in fraternal blood. When the fight begins, kill your leaders yourselves and, without using your weapons, come over to us. We will greet you as our own brothers and together we will create a free and just life for the workers and peasants and will struggle against all tyrants and oppressors of the working people.

Long live the Brotherly union of the Revolutionary Insurgent Makhnovists with the Peasant and Worker Red Army Men!

Insurgent Makhnovists

June, 1920.

* * *

PAUSE! READ! CONSIDER!

Comrade in the Red Army! You were sent by your commissars and commanders to capture the insurgent Makhnovists. Following orders from your chiefs, you will destroy peaceful villages, search, arrest and kill people you don't know but whom they have pointed out to you as

283

enemies of the people. They tell you that the Makhnovists are bandits and counter-revolutionaries.

They tell you; they order you; they do not ask you; they send you; and, like obedient slaves of your leaders, you go to capture and kill. Whom? For what? Why?

Think about it, comrade Red Army Man! Think about it you toiling peasant and worker, taken by force into the cabal of the new masters, who claim the stirring title of worker-peasant authority.

We, the revolutionary insurgent Makhnovists, are also peasants and workers like our brothers in the Red Army. We rose against oppression; we are fighting for a better and brighter life. Our frank ideal is the achievement of a non-authoritarian laborers' society without parasites and without commissar-bureaucrats. Our immediate goal is the establishment of the free soviet order, without the authority of the Bolsheviks, without pressure from any party whatsoever. For this the government of the Bolshevik-Communists sends punitive expeditions upon us. They hurry to make peace with Denikin, with the Polish landlords, and other white guard scum, in order to crush more easily the popular movement of revolutionary insurgents, who are rising for the oppressed against the yoke of any authority.

The threats of the white-red high command do not scare us.

WE WILL ANSWER VIOLENCE WITH VIOLENCE.

When necessary, we, a small handful, will put to flight the legions of the bureaucratic Red Army. For we are freedom-loving revolutionary insurgents and the cause we defend is a just cause.

Comrade! Think about it, who are you with and who are you against?

Don't be a slave—be a man.

Insurgent Makhnovists

[June, 1920.]